MW01120546

Muslim Youth in the Diaspora

In a world where the term Islam is ever-increasingly an inaccurate and insensitive synonym for terrorism, it is not surprising that many Muslim youth in the West struggle for a viable sense of identity.

This book takes up the hotly-debated issue of Muslim youth identity in Western countries from the standpoint of popular culture. It proposes that in the context of Islamophobia and pervasive moral panic, young Muslims frame their identity in relation to external conditions that only see 'good' and 'bad' Muslims, on both sides of the ideological fence between Islam and the West. Indeed, by attempting to break down the 'good' versus 'bad' Muslim dichotomy that largely derives from Western media reports, as well as political commentary, *Muslim Youth in the Diaspora: Challenging Extremism through Popular Culture* will enlighten the reader. It illuminates the way in which diasporic Muslim youth engage with, and are affected by, the radical Islamist meta-narrative. It examines their popular culture and online activity, their gendered sense of self, and much more.

This original book will be of interest to students and scholars interested in the fields of sociology, cultural studies and social anthropology. It offers a particular focus on Islam for research in youth studies, youth culture, political radicalisation and religious identity. It will also be relevant to the sector of youth and social work, where practitioners seek to build cultural bridges with a new generation.

Pam Nilan is Professor of Sociology at the University of Newcastle, Australia.

Youth, Young Adulthood and Society

Series editor: Andy Furlong, University of Glasgow, UK | Andy.Furlong@glasgow.ac.uk

The **Youth, Young Adulthood and Society** series brings together social scientists from many disciplines to present research monographs and collections, seeking to further research into youth in our changing societies around the world today. The books in this series advance the field of youth studies by presenting original, exciting research, with strongly theoretically- and empirically-grounded analysis.

Muslim Youth in the Diaspora

Challenging Extremism through
Popular Culture

Pam Nilan

Routledge
Taylor & Francis Group
LONDON AND NEW YORK

First published 2017
by Routledge
2 Park Square, Milton Park, Abingdon, Oxon OX14 4RN

and by Routledge
711 Third Avenue, New York, NY 10017

Routledge is an imprint of the Taylor & Francis Group, an informa business

British Library Cataloguing in Publication Data
A catalogue record for this book is available from the British Library

Library of Congress Cataloging in Publication Data
A catalog record for this title has been requested

ISBN: 978-1-138-12102-7 (hbk)
ISBN: 978-1-315-65133-0 (ebk)

Typeset in Times New Roman
by Taylor & Francis Books

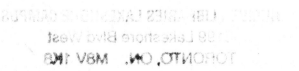

MIX
Paper from
responsible sources
FSC
www.fsc.org   FSC® C013604

Printed and bound by CPI Group (UK) Ltd, Croydon, CR0 4YY

Contents

Preface

This book began at the moment an acquaintance asked me, in a casual way, why young Muslims conduct terrorism. She asked the question because she knew I had been researching youth in Muslim-majority Indonesia since 1995. I replied that I did not know. In the same week, the Australian government announced a new top-down program for the de-radicalisation of Muslim youth. During that same period, my nephew, Muslim-born in Australia, was living near me, and a constant reminder of the challenges faced each day in a suspicious country. I pondered these political and personal conditions. I thought I might write a book about the casually-posed question above that would help me find the answer.

I knew that in principle I was in a reasonably good position to write a book about Muslim youth in the diaspora. I am quite well acquainted with the everyday practice of Islam from living at close quarters with Senegalese people in Paris in my twenties, and from many years of ethnographic research immersion in Indonesia. I have a track record of research publications on youth, gender and popular culture in four countries. I have been involved in an extensive government-funded study of the obstacles facing Muslim job-seekers in Australia. So I was troubled that, as a university professor in the right kind of field, I could not give an academically well-informed answer to the casual question above.

I embarked enthusiastically on the quest for understanding by starting on a book proposal. I quickly forgave myself for not knowing the answer to the question above. A review of the relevant literature showed that other academics were also searching in vain for a straightforward answer; a reason why a young Muslim from a Western country would get involved in Islamist terrorist groups or actions. Some researchers had tested or interviewed young Islamists or convicted jihadis, or returnees from combat, but were unable to find any common factors that did not also apply to a great number of other young Muslims who had not taken up that position. In brief, a simple cause was not evident despite exhaustive research. However, one fact was immediately clear, and I knew it by heart anyway. The vast majority of young Muslims in the diaspora are not attracted at all by the position of Islamist jihad.

Like young people everywhere they are trying to make good lives for themselves, they are looking for life partners, and they are having fun.

So rather than attempt the seemingly impossible task of writing a book about why a very small number of young Muslims in Western countries become terrorists, I chose a more lateral journey of authorship. To make a new contribution to the debate, I turned away from the myriad book titles that claim to give answers on the *why* of Muslim youth radicalism, to the *how* of challenging that position. In other words, I would not look at apparent blind acceptance of the *big story* of Islamist jihad by a tiny few. Rather, I would focus on the everyday activities of the many. I set out to write a book about how young Muslims of all kinds in the diaspora generate counter-narratives to the *big story*, to the narrative of radical Islamism that can inform terrorist events. I decided that I would take the approach of looking at popular culture, with much attention to the digital world. I wanted to acknowledge that Muslim youth themselves are doing this, independent of sometimes awkward and ill-matched attempts at radicalisation prevention from above. The result was this book. I still do not have a precise answer to the important question above, but perhaps it will never be answered in plain terms. On the other hand, through writing this book I know a great deal more about how, and therefore perhaps why, so many Muslim youth *do not* become involved in radical Islamism and go on to conduct jihad. My hope is that readers will also benefit from this understanding.

Pam Nilan
Newcastle, Australia, 2016

Chapter 1

Introduction

Muslim youth in the diaspora

Introduction

This book takes up the hotly-debated issue of Muslim youth identity in Western countries. It does so from the standpoint of popular culture. Given the pervasive moral panic about Islam in those nations, young Muslims frame up their sense of self, their identity, in relation to external conditions which ascribe a distinction between 'good' and 'bad' Muslims, on both sides of an apparent ideological fence between Islam and the West.

The core proposals of the book are as follows:

- First, not only do the prevailing conditions of Islamophobia shape the positioning of a Muslim youth identity in the diaspora, so too does the *meta-narrative of radical Islamism.*
- Second, the radical meta-narrative does not just come to them from Muslim sources, but from Western media reports and opinions, as well as political commentary, further driving the 'good' versus 'bad' Muslim dichotomy in relation to their subjectivity.
- Third, the process by which diasporic Muslim youth engage the meta-narrative is evident. It is – explicitly and implicitly – addressed, endorsed, contested, ridiculed, transformed and transcended in the 'serious play' of Muslim youth culture even as they simultaneously address and contest the intolerance they encounter every day.
- Fourth, the popular culture of Muslim youth in the diaspora is not only characterised by distinctions of piety, but is implicitly organised in forms of *neo-theo-tribalism* that articulate different relationships to the radical Islamist meta-narrative.

Throughout the Muslim world,[1] varying political positions are taken for and against radicalism. This seems inevitable. 'Part urban myth, part grim reality, the Islamic terrorist reconfigures the frame' (Back et al. 2009: 6). It affects ordinary Muslim lives, especially since 9/11. On the other hand, it is possible to sensationalise this impact. All over the world, young Muslims are just getting on their lives and enjoying youth culture. This is why Nasir (2016: 2) states firmly that young Muslims today 'ought to be analyzed through the dialectics of popular culture and Islamic piety'.

Certainly Muslim youth of both sexes in the diaspora experience intolerance and prejudice to varying degrees, depending largely on their appearance, status, language and affiliations (Sirin and Fine 2007; Wise and Ali 2008; Poynting and Mason 2008; Kabir 2008, 2010, 2012; Mishra and Shirazi 2010; Allen 2010; Peek 2011; Sohrabi and Farquharson 2012; Zempi and Chakraborti 2014; Hervik 2015; Lynch 2015; Read 2015). Moreover, it is likely they will find diminished career opportunities, even with a good education (Read 2004; Hassan 2010; Tindongan 2011; Ryan 2011; Nilan 2012a; Lovat et al. 2013; Jakubowicz et al. 2014). Bhatti (2011: 82) argues that in the climate of fear and suspicion in Western countries, 'young Muslims are disproportionately affected'. Muslim youth today may feel defensive. They are under scrutiny because of their religion. They must negotiate their religious identity and religious practice in a context that includes explicit or subtle themes of misunderstanding, fear, and marginalisation (Abo-Zena et al. 2009: 6–7). Yet above all, they are youth living out their lives in late modernity, and share much in common with all other young people living in a '24/7' world. Like the rest, Muslim youth greatly desire appropriate 'recognition' from the society as they move towards adulthood. Yet they must struggle hard to achieve it in conditions of Islamophobia. Where there is any form of conflict, then as Honneth (1996: 1) points out, this is likely to be fuelled by the individualised 'struggle for recognition' that characterises de-traditionalised, modular lives in late modernity.

Youth in late modern Western society

The idea of young Muslims as particularly susceptible to radicalisation refers to some core beliefs about youth as a social category. As many have pointed out, there is a moral panic about youth *per se* that swings between fear *of* them – regarding young people as a threat, and fear *for* them – seeing youth as immature children in need of protection (Krinsky 2008). There is also considerable confusion about who they are in demographic terms, with age boundaries varying, for example, from 12–30 (in advertising) to 15–24 (United Nations). There is also an unproductive blurring of the categories of youth and children. This brings us to the question of who youth are and how they are imagined.

In one sense, there is no such thing as youth. Until relatively recently in human history there were only children (pre-puberty) and adults (post-puberty). In fact, 'youth' as a modern category of person was more or less invented during the Industrial Revolution in Europe, at the same time as the steam engine (Musgrove 1964: 33). Similarly, the 'teenager' was invented amid the youth moral panic of the 1950s (Gilbert 2014). By the late twentieth century, the stage of youth for both sexes had become characterised by distinct patterns of leisure, consumption, social bonding and courting, in the West at least, and in many other countries. During this extended period of 'youth', young people are understood to make the transition to adulthood. Reaching adulthood is signified by 'completing schooling, beginning full-time work, financial independence, getting married, and becoming a parent' (Aronson 2008: 60; see also Furlong and Cartmel 2007).

It is acknowledged that young people today are caught up in the kind of late modern individualising processes described by Giddens (1991), Beck (1992) and Beck and Beck-Gernsheim (2002). Giddens (1991: 81) calls this 'de-traditionalisation', the weakening of traditional foundations of identity derived from family, kin, class and locality. Thus young people come to understand themselves more cogently than before through the self-image they create in education, occupation, lifestyle and consumption. These are the individualising processes we cannot ignore in the lives of youth in Western countries, including Muslim youth.[2] The labour market is fragmented and precarious (Furlong and Cartmel 2004; Woodman 2012). Education and training periods are extended, and without firm job guarantees. Much is made of intimate partner 'choice' and the pressure to create a successful self that can be presented to a variety of social and economic markets (Brannen and Nilsen 2007; Nayak and Kehily 2008). Yet at the same time, class, gender and ethnic factors – as well as religion – can alter transition experiences and outcomes for youth (Aronson 2008: 79), in both developed and developing countries (Nayak 2003).

In the neo-liberal state that prevails in Western countries, much is expected of young people in terms of the choices they make (Nayak and Kehily 2008). The emphasis is on the individual, not the family or community as it was in the past (see Giddens 1991; Beck 1992; Beck and Beck-Gernsheim 2002). So each young person – from any kind of background – is under pressure to consciously tailor-make his or her own life trajectory towards successful adulthood (Furlong and Cartmel 2007; Harris 2004; Kelly 2006). Individuals are subject to enhanced uncertainties as possible life options increase, since 'we have no choice but to choose' (Giddens 1991: 81). Young people grow up in a 'risk' society which did not exist for their parents' generation (Beck 1992; Furlong and Cartmel 2007; Threadgold and Nilan 2009). Achieving a legitimate social identity has therefore become more complex and confusing. In such conditions, the 'self' becomes something to be consciously worked on by the young person to create a successful biography. A successful life trajectory is achieved by making the 'right' individual choices when young (Brannen and Nilsen 2007: 157). This choosing process expresses the need for the young person to find 'ontological security' (Giddens 1991: 44) – a symbolic place of safety and certainty. In late modernity, the self is reflexively understood in terms of a person's 'biography' (Giddens 1991: 53). Thus all young people now live their lives more reflexively; actively planning or projecting themselves imaginatively as individuals into a positive adult existence (Threadgold and Nilan 2009).

Muslim youth in late modernity

Parlaying these insights into the situation of Muslim youth in the diaspora, they too are implicitly anticipated by the neo-liberal state to make individual choices that constitute a life trajectory towards successful adulthood. However, they must negotiate not one but two sets of norms, even beyond their ethnic affiliations (Drissel 2011). In human capital terms they are products of Western societies that reward economic achievement and educational attainment. Yet to succeed in these fields they must actively recast themselves as 'good' Muslims, given that the moral panic casts them as potential radicalised 'outsiders' and 'dangerous foreigners' (Lynch 2015; see also Kundani 2014). Spalek and Lambert (2008) report that in European studies, Muslim youth often describe themselves as victims of prejudice in the workplace. Moreover, in regard to their families, some choices entailed by contemporary education and work may take them beyond traditional expectations of a virtuous life. McGrath and McGarry (2014: 929) argue that we need to recognise the 'complex intersections between religious-cultural ways of life and the dominant discourses of secular-liberal Western-European society' for young Muslims (see also Jacobsen 2010). Youth labour markets in Western countries are already characterised by precariousness (Woodman 2012), and for Muslim youth they are even more insecure (Nilan 2012a). In the process of transition to adulthood, Muslim youth must struggle harder than most others to find a position of 'ontological security' (Giddens 1991: 44) – one that offers safety and certainty. For example, Song (2012) found that British Muslim students who joined Islamic Student Associations did so to *include themselves* – so they officially belonged. Thus formal membership mainstreamed their Muslim identity, endowing some ontological certainty.

Relevant to the general discussion of youth above, it is not clear that Giddens' detraditionalisation thesis can be applied unproblematically to young people in Western countries from non-Anglo backgrounds (Nilan 2011), nor to youth from religious backgrounds. For example, as a counter-discourse to the individualisation trend, the transcendent discourse of Islam provides a collective sense of *ummah*, endowing a sense of 'belonging' to a worldwide constituency of believers. Yet there are two further shaping discourses that encourage the manifestation of Muslim youth collectivities in the face of individualisation and detraditionalisation. The first is the radical Islamist meta-narrative. The second is popular culture.

Even though the radical Islamist meta-narrative is endorsed by only a tiny minority, it has an extraordinarily galvanising exclusion–inclusion effect. Muslim youth are under pressure to show how they stand on radical Islamist precepts and practices. Media and political rhetoric on the non-Muslim side demands they position themselves against radicalism, and in support of the mainstream status quo. Families and the local Muslim community would like them to show themselves as good Muslims, manifested in pious, conservative behaviour directed towards prosperity – as a counter-discourse to radicalism. While these two sets of pressures might appear to have more or less the same goal, public expressions and professions of Muslim piety by youth in the diaspora tend to provoke a negative reaction in fearful and racist members of the non-Muslim majority (Ahmed 2003). So there are some troubling contradictions evident which complicate the making of a successful self.

The second shaping discourse is found in youth culture, both offline and online (see Robards and Bennett 2011). There is a pleasurably attractive youth culture world of fashion, music, gaming, product consumption and socialising which is highly compelling for Muslim youth (Herding 2013), just as it is for other young people in Western countries. However, within the foundation of Islam, this compelling world of youth culture should be negotiated piously, demanding the exercise of reflexivity (Giddens 1991; Threadgold and Nilan 2009) in choosing and filtering popular consumption and practices. Specific participatory communities of practice emerge (see Jenkins 2006). Thus Muslim youth engagement with popular culture pertains to the *reflexive co-production of salient identities* that fuels potential for mobilisation, whether political or cultural. Through the pleasurable constitution of a distinctively Muslim popular culture, young people are engaged in creative acts of reclamation (Willis 1990), of their faith and of their youthful independence and dynamism.

Their popular culture choices demonstrate a particular kind of 'distinction' (Bourdieu 1984), one that is not only about class, but about claiming a moral order of orthopraxy which bestows blessings. *Halal* consumption practices in popular culture constitute for the young Muslim a 'sense of one's place' (see Bourdieu 1984: 468) – in the *ummah*. They are guided – by judicious advertising – towards the practices or goods which 'befit' their position (Bourdieu 1984: 469) – in a moral order. This is 'serious play' (Bloustien 2007: 447) which produces theological identity groupings. Throughout the book I refer to these groupings as *neo-theo-tribalism*.

The concept of neo-theo-tribalism builds on earlier youth culture theorising of neo-tribalism (Maffesoli 1996; Malbon 1998; Bennett 1999a, 2000; Sweetman 2004). For example, Bennett has argued strongly that the rather static term 'subculture' is inadequate to describe the cultural relationship between youth, music and style. In his view the term 'neo-tribal' much better captures the 'unstable and shifting cultural affiliations that characterise late modern consumer-based identities' (Bennett 1999a: 605). These dynamic cultural affiliations are linked to specific lifestyles – supported by selective consumption choices. Following Bennett, my contention is that the combination of shaping discourses described above drives a theologically informed neo-tribalism in the popular culture of Muslim youth. I describe this phenomenon as *neo-theo-tribalism* because its youth culture affiliations and lifestyle distinctions are arranged along a continuum of religiosity, from the near-secular to the overtly pious. Selective choice of popular culture products and restricted forms of ludic engagement signal Muslim theo-tribal belonging, but this is far from fixed and unchanging. It is within these different Islamic youth culture neo-tribes that diverse counter-narratives to the radical Islamist meta-narrative are expressed.

My use of the adjective *ludic* points to the spontaneous and undirected playfulness of young people as digital experts. In the current literature one scholar has declared that the twenty-first century is 'the ludic century' (Zimmerman 2014: 19). For example, digital networks are not catalogues of information but flexible and organic spaces, organised as modular, customisable, participatory resources to play with; a series of games enjoyed with others. Applied here, the term ludic points away from rational choice and ideological structures to the creative use of popular culture identified by Paul Willis in 1990.

The radical Islamist meta-narrative is detailed in the next chapter, and the interpretive discussion proceeds from there. The assumption is that young Muslims from all kinds of ethnic backgrounds in Western countries are under pressure to reflexively position themselves both individually and collectively in relation to that teleological epic. The meta-narrative itself constitutes them as actual or potential social actors in a compelling story of Armageddon and Utopia on a grand scale. Yet as the chapters demonstrate, it also serves as a discursive resource through which diasporic Muslim youth generate counter-narratives (Andrews 2004) as a kind of 'counter-jihad' (Wright 2012: 41). For example, in 2014 a British charity organised a #notinmyname campaign which gave millions of Muslim youth worldwide the opportunity to denounce violent actions of IS in their own words and images through social media. Through such tools they could actively shape new subject positions and identities that transcribed different directions through popular culture. This is a form of embedded critique. Butler (2004) argues that critique is an ethical mode of self-making that questions the limits of epistemology. This rather abstract idea is given an everyday reference point by the following account:

> There are particular people, particular Muslims that call themselves Muslims but ain't doing what is the way of life in Islam. What they're doing is wrong. In our religion Allah said that taking the life of an innocent person is not right [...] They're the wrong Muslims.
>
> (Ali, m, 16, British Bangladeshi, quoted in Franceschelli and O'Brien 2015: 702)

Here Ali criticises followers of the radical Islamist meta-narrative. He thinks they are 'wrong' in their choices. His view is shared by the great majority of Muslims in the diaspora. Yet the meta-narrative is hard to escape because it comes from many sides. At this point the concept of narrative needs to be explained.

Narrative

The word narrative is derived from the Latin word *gnarus*, which derives from the Indo-European root form *gnu* – 'to know'. A told or written narrative gives knowledge to people in either a factual or fictional genre. First, the narrative setting evokes association with an already known or mythic time or place. Second, good and bad characters 'play' out dynamic action. Third, actions take place and plot consequences ensue. Characters react and further consequential actions ensue. Tension builds through plot sequences. There is a resolution of tension when the problem faced by the character(s) is solved. Relief occurs after the climax of the story. A denouement follows in which tensions are resolved and a new status quo prevails. Effective narrative must engage the self as a reader/viewer/listener/consumer by providing compelling characters and plot (Dégh 1995).

All narratives provide a 'semiotic representation of a series of events, meaningfully connected in a temporal and causal way' (Onega and Landa 1996: 6) through the plot. In ontological terms, the story is the 'fundamental instrument of thought' (Turner 1998: 5); a time-honoured strategy for dealing with the human experience. Rushkoff (2013: 13) argues that experiencing the world in narratives constructs a context for how people feel. It is 'comforting and orienting'. A relevant story helps people imagine they are on the way to 'some better place'. Bruner (1990) maintains that an important way people come to understand their world is through the 'narrative mode', which deals with human wants, needs and goals through the structure of plot. Thus a 'big' narrative has the potential to mobilise people (Polleta 2006). All cultures and societies have their own 'big' stories that represent issues of morality, the self and 'the meaning of life' (Braddock 2012: 115). Through them, people can look at how human actors have striven for provision and order over time, and how they have succeeded or failed. In that sense, epic narratives are inspirational.

Narrative analysis has increased in social science fields since the late 1970s. For example, Valentine and Sporton (2009) show how we constitute our social identities through narrative (see also Somers 1994; Dubnick et al. 2009). Yet despite rich promise, there has been relatively little direct application of the 'narrative turn' to the engagement of Muslim youth (or not) with Islamist extremism. Al Raffie (2012: 13) acknowledges that looking at narratives in this field is still 'relatively novel'. Yet as Joosse et al. (2015: 2) point out, narratives make visible the ontological conditions of social life. They can assist in the imposition of subjectivities onto 'real' events, or help neutralise morally suspect behaviour so that 'one person's terrorist is another person's freedom fighter – depending on one's *story*' (my emphasis). Certainly the early poststructuralist work of Davies (1989) and Weedon (1987) supported the idea that intersubjective reality is discursively constructed from the major stories that tell us who we are. This is because the 'big' narratives that circulate in society and culture 'systematically *form* the objects of which they speak' (Foucault 1972: 49, my emphasis). A meta-narrative offers legitimation through the anticipated completion of a (yet to be realised) master idea (see Lyotard 1993). So when originary, heroic narratives are consistently retold over time, they become deeply ingrained in the culture and rise to the level of 'master narratives' (Halverson et al. 2011), or meta-narratives. In a 'big' story – a meta-narrative – there is discursive positioning by the narrator(s), and the receivers of the story are simultaneously invited to position themselves.

Relevant to my argument here, Roy (2007) claims that the influence of the Islamist 'narrative' in the West can create isolation from cultures of Muslim ethnic origin. In the radical Islamist meta-narrative, the anticipated endpoint is the 'final battle', followed by an exclusively Muslim utopia. Beski-Chafiq et al. (2010: 28) find that among young radical Muslims in France there is a 'fantasy vision' of the *ummah* which will one day rule the world. The exclusionary nature of this story strengthens boundaries between Muslims and non-Muslims and feeds Islamophobia. The example indicates that the radical Islamist meta-narrative is highly influential – on everyone. For radicals it offers a distinctive ontology of redemption through extreme transformation – of the self and of the world. For others – Muslim and non-Muslim – it represents a dire threat to be managed and contained. In Muslim youth culture, it also constitutes a resource to be treated creatively and transformed (Leuprecht et al. 2010) into counter-narrative.

In simple terms, a counter-narrative is a narrative that goes against another narrative (Andrews 2004). Either explicitly or implicitly, it embodies an argument that disputes the original authoritative set of beliefs or claims. Yet counter-narratives are not held by people as tangible resources that can be produced on cue. Rather, they are co-produced by interlocutors in lived moments of engagement with the very meta-narrative that they challenge (Bamberg 2004), either directly or indirectly. A counter-narrative may be a large-scale, collectively-authored set of propositions, or a small story that emerges from someone's everyday life and the choices they make. Yet in both cases the counter-narrative advances an identity claim against the ascribed identity implied by the meta-narrative in question.

Subjectivity and discursive positioning

This book depicts some aspects of what popular culture looks like for Muslim youth in Western countries. It does so by documenting and analysing counter-narratives developed through engagement in Muslim youth culture, broadly defined as neo-theo-tribalism. The focus is not on causes of Muslim youth radicalisation. In fact, that would be a futile exercise. It must be emphasised again that no amount of empirical investigation to date has yet been able to identify a typical profile of who will be drawn to violent Islamist radicalism (Roy 2007; Sageman 2014; McCauley and Moskalenko 2014). It is likely this will never be achieved because there are just too many unknown factors.

Much of the concern with Islam in the West today is either implicitly or explicitly driven by perceptions of Muslims as inherently 'dangerous' (McAlveen 2011); as driving a 'clash of civilisations' (Huntington 1993; Barber 1996). The resulting fear and anxiety has produced a kind of xenophobia or 'Islamophobia' (El-Affendi 2009, see also Fekete 2009). Discourses of fear about Islamist attacks aggregate and amplify apparent 'truths' about the Muslim other:

> Fear operates as an affective economy of truth. Fear slides between signs and sticks to some bodies and not others. For example the judgement that someone 'could be' a terrorist draws on past and affective associations that stick various signs (such as Muslim, fundamentalist, terrorist) together.
>
> (Ahmed 2003: 377)

At the time of writing in 2016, previous human rights lawyer Sadiq Khan had been elected Mayor of London, despite a bitter campaign from the Conservative side that sought to link him – as a Muslim – to Islamist extremism (Booth 2016).[3] The example demonstrates the essentialising of a homogenised 'Muslim' identity, which is to be deplored in this context. Yet in this book I do employ the term 'Muslim youth' as an apparently singular category, even while acknowledging the manifold cultural, religious, socio-economic and gender differences between young Muslims in Western countries. In my case, this shorthand represents the kind of 'strategic essentialisms' (Spivak 1987: 205) sometimes deployed for positive political ends. While the subject position of Muslim youth might be an essentialising category in itself, it is also a useful heuristic for considering what the radical Islamist meta-narrative signifies for young individuals and groups who ascriptively occupy that subject position.

The concept of subject position, or *discursive positioning* is based on the poststructuralist work of Davies (1989) and Weedon (1987), and also Davies and Harré (1990). For them, intersubjective reality is 'discursively constructed'. It is made and remade as people talk about and express things using the 'discourses' to which they have access, and which guide their choices. Thus both Western and radical Islamist discourses about Islam form Muslim youth as particular kinds of subjects. The theoretical basis for the concept of subject position also draws on Judith Butler's useful insight that the positioning of resistance is articulated from within existing discourses. 'There is only the taking up of the tools where they lie' (Butler 1990: 145). This insight supports the Foucauldian proposition that any discursive statement; 'circulates, is used, disappears, allows or prevents the realization of desire, serves or resists various interests, participates in challenge and struggle, and becomes a theme of appropriation and rivalry' (Foucault 1972: 105). So, in the retelling and countertelling of a particular authoritative story – a master or meta-narrative – what is told positions the 'other' and, at the same time, positions the teller, re-teller or counter-teller themselves. These acts of positioning involve classification and distinction of the self and others (see Bourdieu 1984: 6).

The notion of discursive positioning by the active, reflexive youth subject assumes a connection between the discourses of the dominant cultural story-line, and the social construction of a particular Muslim self. Positioning takes place in the conditions of a strong moral panic about youth and Islam in the diaspora. The premise is that young people, both individually and collectively, draw on dominant narratives as well as competing narratives in their expressions of national identity (Wodak and DeCillia 2007) and Muslim identity. This points once again to *the reflexive co-production of salient identities*, so that a viable subject position works across the cross-cutting discursive worlds of Muslim youth.

I also make some use of the term *affect*. Wetherell (2012) offers a useful account of affect in relation to discourse. In her view, the notion of affect conceptually illuminates emotion and embodiment. It can be used to talk about how people are moved, and what attracts them, as well as their 'pains and pleasures, feelings and memories'. More cogently, the concept of affect can help us understand how social formations can be so compelling (Wetherell 2012: 2). The constitution of subjectivity within a strong narrative of Islam creates marked emotional intensity – affect. Yet affect also pertains to the workings of desire in forms of 'minoritarian becoming' (Deleuze and Guattari 1987). 'Becoming-minoritarian' is a vector of change prompted affectively by symbolic or actual confinement to restricted social space (Deleuze and Guattari 1987: 106); such as that which prevails in a climate of fear of the Muslim 'Other'. Affect may therefore be considered central to the production of conservative and contesting subjects within diasporic Islam.

The final theoretical source here is Paul Willis' *Common Culture* (1990). Willis proposes that significant points of coherence, identity, and even resistance for young people lie in 'common culture', not political entities. From the cultural resources on offer, important 'symbols and practices are selected, reselected, highlighted and recomposed to resonate further appropriated and particularized meanings' (Willis 1990: 211). In his view, young people thereby create their own meanings for existing ideas and symbols as *creative acts of reclamation*. Willis' early work resonates in principle with findings of the much later study by Herding (2013) on the strategic emergence of a selective new 'Muslim cool' in the youth culture of Western Europe.

The moral panic about Muslim youth

As mentioned above, Muslims in the diaspora are affected by prevailing fear and suspicion of Islam (Pratt and Woodlock 2016). Although intolerance certainly existed previously, since 9/11 we have witnessed intensified fear and anxiety about Islam in Western countries (Moosavi 2015). Outbreaks of militant violence are linked semantically to adherents of the Muslim faith

(Fasenfest 2015). They are believed to threaten dearly-held ontological values and national security. The post-9/11 fear response was evident in the US and throughout the diaspora, and it remains so. For example, an Australian study found that over two-thirds of non-Muslim respondents believed Islam posed a threat. Yet relatively few were able to articulate it specifically. The researchers identified 'a strong level of unsupported (and unsubstantiated) fear of Islam' (Dunn et al. 2007: 571); in other words, a moral panic. A moral panic occurs when a group of people is defined as a threat to societal values and interests (Cohen 1972). It requires a 'melodramatic narrative' where victims are 'empathized with, where villains are denounced and where sanctions against them by sovereign heroes are legitimized' (Wright 2015: 2). As Werbner (2004: 461) points out, in a moral panic, 'underlying social contradictions converge on apparently concrete causes'. As the moral panic escalates, the sense of threat reaches a point of crisis in which ordinary people begin to fear 'the breakdown of social life itself, the coming of chaos, the onset of anarchy' (Hall et al. 1978: 322–323). In this context of fear and suspicion, Werbner (2004: 463) draws our attention to the 'terrible vulnerability of Muslim diaspora communities in the West, susceptible to being essentialized as fanatical and irrational, a potential fifth column in a clash of civilizations'. They are 'racialized to the point of being perceived as contrary to democratic values' just by virtue of following Islam as a religious faith (Tindongan 2011: 83). In short, the events of 9/11 and afterwards have changed the way Muslim people identify themselves and are identified by others.

Central to a moral panic is the way in which the villain of the prevailing melodramatic narrative (the 'folk devil' – Cohen 1972) is constructed through 'stylization and stereotyping, distortion, prediction, symbolization and sensitization' (Wright 2015: 6), connoting distance and separation from the exoticised Other (for example Said 1978). The gap generated by a moral panic is strengthened by the circulation of rumour, gossip and innuendo in the conventional media and on social media. In the case of Muslim youth this inflects the moral panic along two axes. If the vertical axis is young *vs* old, then the horizontal axis is Muslim *vs* secular/Christian. Each risk dimension intensifies the other so that an old person is deemed less of a risk to the community than a young person, while a secular or Christian person is deemed less of a risk than a Muslim person. When it comes to a young Muslim, there is therefore a double load of risk perception. So where the recent fear about Muslims in Western countries overlaps with time-honoured generational suspicion of youth *per se* (see Cohen 1972), the result is a strong moral panic about Muslim youth in the diaspora.

Young Muslims are deemed highly susceptible (Broadbent 2013; Lynch 2015) to the so-called 'death cult' of radical Islamist extremism (Martin Jones and Smith 2014: 18). Poynting et al. describe the young Muslim (male) 'other' as constructing the pre-eminent 'folk demon' (2004: 2). As Islamist-claimed suicide attacks and jihadi events on Western soil continued in the years after

9/11, so did the moral panic about diasporic Muslim youth (Lynch 2015; Mandaville 2002; Werbner 2004; Poynting and Noble 2006; Bayat and Herrera 2010; Beski-Chafiq et al. 2010; Doosje et al. 2013; Mac an Ghaill and Haywood 2014). The search is on to establish causal factors and diagnostic profiles for young Muslims who might be susceptible to terrorist discourse. However, as pointed out above, research efforts have not succeeded in developing any kind of predictive profile (see Lynch 2015; McCauley and Moskalenko 2014; Beski-Chafiq et al. 2010; Sageman 2008; Roy 2007; Werbner 2004). This is discussed in a later chapter.

We need to look closely at expressive discourses around the highly mediated meta-narrative of Islamist extremism (see Roy 2008), as well the counter-narratives directly produced by Muslim youth themselves. Such an examination will yield productive insights into how (not why) only a tiny number end up supporting jihad, while the vast majority never go there. For example, some young Muslims in the diaspora may be drawn to Islamic millennial websites due to their promise of 'fantastical empowerment in the face of perceived, almost cosmic disempowerment' (Werbner 2004: 470). Such sites not only attract poor, marginal youth, but those who feel they have the capacity to make prosperous lives – but are prevented from doing so. Werbner's explanation not only resonates with Willis' (1990) claims about the 'common culture' aspect of youth identity, but acknowledges both the 'push' factor of local conditions and the 'pull' factor of the millennial version of the meta-narrative. Yet it is clear from Werbner's work that while many young people actively participate in Muslim millennial sites, hardly any ever take action. As she observes, they post about the need to forestall any action until the *Mahdi* appears to give them guidance.

In summary, the meta-narrative of Islamist radicalism is variously engaged by diasporic Muslim youth in the everyday practice of popular culture. The book identifies stories, tangents and positions that bridge from everyday conditions of intolerance, sometimes towards, but far more often away from, that radical meta-narrative. In expressions of Muslim youth culture, the stark utopian epic may be embroidered, simplified, made more complex, contested, refuted, scorned, ridiculed, lauded, personalised and reframed. The moral panic in the diaspora is also treated to critical appraisal and reversal in Muslim youth culture. The forms of popular culture chosen for analysis in this book are: internet sites of various kinds, social media, video/computer games, and music. This by no means exhausts the list of neo-theo-tribal popular culture forms. However, selective decisions had to be made to limit the size of the book.

Gender

It is clear that young Muslim women are active in engaging with the radical meta-narrative as well as in the generation of counter-narratives. This is not just a masculine domain of involvement. Gender is a 'variable cultural accomplishment' (Butler 1990: 142), and that also holds true for the distinct discourses of gender that characterise Islam. So for example, a few young female Islamists have become notoriously militant and set out to inspire others like them. Yet at the same time, discourses of femininity and masculinity within Islam strongly distinguish between what is expected of female and male youth (Nayak and Kehily 2008), like gender distinction everywhere. 'The Islamic mode of piety or moral conduct is gender-defined in the sense that the ideals of being pious and how to be a Good Muslim are defined differently for women and men' (Bendixsen 2013: 217). There is strong emphasis on gender segregation.

In the West there is a common public perception that Islam is an oppressive religion that denies women basic human rights, encourages men to violence and condemns GLBTIQ people. In response, many Muslims argue that Islam promotes peace and tolerance. They claim that Islam is not an oppressive religion towards women, despite human rights abuses against women in certain Muslim countries, and in certain strands of the faith. Rather they contend that Islam promotes gender equality and supports the full participation of women in all aspects of community life. According to those arguments, the problem lies in specific cultural interpretations of the Koran and the *sunna*. As for encouraging male violence, it is pointed out that the Koran is little different from the Bible in that regard. Certainly, Islamic teachings are used selectively in nations and cultures with a history of endemic conflict to encourage male militarism. Yet even so, as an Abrahamic religion there is much in the sacred texts of Islam that enshrines gendered expectations of conduct.

Like most world religions, it certainly appears that Islam officially forbids and punishes same-sex sexual relationships, and that GLBTIQ persons are not recognised (Habib 2009). However, Kugle (2010), among other scholars, points to the debate within Islam about the matter, since there is certainly not just one theological position, any more than in Christianity. Even so the situation for young GLBTIQ Muslims in the diaspora is difficult, to say the least. Although they can find support in the secular world, they may be openly condemned and shunned by their own communities. Kugle (2013: 1–2) maintains that gay, lesbian and transgender Muslims can reconcile their sexual orientation and gender identity with Islam. However, that reconciliation requires active struggle to do so. This struggle is most effectively conducted in connection with like-minded individuals within the faith who have built solid support groups.

Discourses of Muslim femininity

It has been argued that 'being a Muslim youth is always a gendered formation' (Bendixsen 2013: 217). Girls before marriage are seen to need protection and are often closely supervised. They are often married quite early, with little time for youth pursuits (Herding 2013: 29). In short, for Muslim girls there is a 'complex pattern of normative values and practices' in terms of choices about female dress, mobility in public spaces, and interactions with the opposite sex (Hamzeh 2011: 485). They are frequently viewed as personifying the moral integrity and honour of the family (Sanghera and Thapar-Björkert 2012). Ghaffar-Kucher (2015: 213) found the responsibility of constituting what was an 'authentic Muslim' among Pakistani-American youth was carried by girls much more than boys. Male family members exercised a controlling gaze over their young female relatives. For example, surveillance of teenage girls was often conducted by their 'brothers – older and younger'. Young men in the same study made sharp distinctions between 'good' Muslim girls and 'shameless' girls (Ghaffar-Kucher 2015: 213). This echoes the finding of Mac an Ghaill and Haywood (2014) on the judgmental gender attitudes of young Muslim men from the same ethnic background in the UK. Notably, in the study by Ghaffar-Kucher (2015: 214), 'girls were especially critical of other girls'; accusing them of shameless behaviour.

Islam specifies the importance of both men and women remaining virgins until marriage (Musso et al. 2002). Yet as Eid (2007) points out, maintaining virginity is seen as a female obligation. Engaging in premarital sex would mean a transgression and they would no longer be considered marriageable. One study found that for Arab-British UK girls:

> Remaining a virgin becomes a means of preserving their Arab culture, especially in view of what they perceived as the 'sexually lax' British society in which they live (...) their 'Arabness' would be endangered, destabilising their sense of self.
>
> (Amer et al. 2015: 14)

Thus the perception of a 'good', virtuous Muslim girl contrasts with the perceived 'bad' non-Muslim girl who is not bound by this obligation, and also with the 'bad' Muslim girl who is perceived to disregard this restriction. Naber (2006), in her study on Arab Americans, refers to this as the battle between the 'Arab virgin' and the 'American(ized) whore'. Purity matters theologically for young Muslim women. In some ethnic Muslim cultures, ritual purity is signalled significantly through restrictions on women's bodies. Sanctions are placed on young women who transgress these expectations. In summary, 'young Muslim women are subject to a far greater degree of regulation' (McGrath and McGarry 2014: 960) compared to young men. For example, the behaviour of young Irish Muslim women was shown to be controlled and regulated by family and community elders in a different, more intensive way, compared to male relatives and age peers. Yet the girls did negotiate certain freedoms for themselves. 'Compliance with particular rules of parental respect could provide bargaining power', especially in regard to accessing educational and shopping opportunities (McGrath and McGarry 2014: 956). This compliance was demonstrated, for example, by covering their heads in public, which gained them greater autonomy.

The headscarf and modernity

The issue of the headscarf/veil (*hijab*)[4] features heavily in the existing Western literature on young Muslim women in the diaspora (Ryan 2011). Yet perhaps there is too much emphasis. It may be of more concern to non-Muslims than to Muslim women themselves. Wearing the headscarf does not just have one meaning (Williams and Vashi 2007; Ryan 2011; Parker and Nilan 2013). While the *hijab* may demonstrate chosen female piety and modesty for some, it can also connote enforced conformity, empowerment (Watt 2011), fashion or even radicalisation in other cases (Tarlo 2010; Scott 2007). Yet Muslim women in the West who wear the headscarf are frequently stigmatised and even expected to hold extreme Islamist views (Ryan 2011), even though this is usually far from the truth. On the other hand, they sometimes receive sympathy because they are oppressed by their religion. In this regard young Muslim women in the West struggle against 'stereotypes related to misogynist religious traditions' (Lynch 2015: 173). In France, where there are some bans on veiling, Butler (2008) shows how the French state actively discriminates against Muslim culture through these forms of exclusion focused on women.

In the public domain, Muslim women in the diaspora are pulled by two different categorical distinctions. Those who cover their heads and wear traditional coverings might be regarded as 'good' Muslims within their own communities, but the non-Muslim public gaze will not view them that way (Tarlo 2010). Conversely, Muslim women who do not wear the headscarf may attract negative comments from their own communities and from other Muslim women, even though they 'pass' in the broader community and are seen there as 'good' Muslims because they have symbolically integrated. Even Muslim women who combine 'a headscarf with trousers and high heels', might attract negative comments from some in their community (Ryan 2011: 1056). Overall, the status of Muslim women in Western countries as 'good' Muslims is continuously contested.

The discursive regime of the pure female self in the regulatory practices of Islam emphasises the strict moral behaviour of teenage girls and young women – in particular – across a number of domains (Nilan 2012b). Ritual purity may be signalled significantly through restrictions on women's bodies, for example, through early marriage, *purdah*,[5] *hijab*, limited career choice and night curfews (Werbner 2004: 458). At the same time, for young Muslim women in both Muslim-majority and Western countries, issues of autonomy and freedom do not necessarily include the wholesale repudiation of tradition, nor the withering of religious belief, nor the waning of trust in marriage and extended family support (Nilan 2008). In many cases their life decisions are shaped by family negotiations that encode traditional and ethnic discourses as well as the strong ethos of moral propriety and gender separation in Islam.

Overall, young Muslim women in Western countries – with and without the headscarf – make both implicit and explicit claims to engagement with late modern discourses of autonomy (McGrath and McGarry 2014; Sanghera and Thapar-Björkert 2012; Hamzeh 2011; Parker and Nilan 2013; Speckhard 2008; Killian 2007; Scott 2007; Naber 2006). Certainly the technological affordances of the internet and new media mean that the majority of Muslim girls worldwide today have broader social access beyond immediate family and friends (Sanchez 2014). This allows a much more extensive engagement with age peers and with debates around the Islamist meta-narrative, as well as with popular culture (see Harris 2008). Moreover, in some ethnic cultures, Muslim women in the West are more active in the public and civic sphere than they were in their countries of origin (Read 2015). Furthermore, in the past decades there has been growing accommodation of some Western norms of courting in the diaspora. For example, in a British study of girls with an Arab background it was found that 'many participants were open to dating, albeit for the purpose of marriage' (Amer et al. 2015: 15).

In brief, to understand Islamic female forms of moral subjectivity and embodied spiritual interiority, we should move beyond the Western observer's dichotomy of resistance/subordination by which Muslim women are so often judged. For example, Mahmood (2005) views Muslim women choosing to wear the headscarf as an agentic act of piety. It is also possible to read the headscarf in the diaspora as a form of 'bodily hexis' (Bourdieu 1998: 93); the way in which the knowledge and dispositions through which we conduct our everyday lives have not just a reflexive form in ideas and concepts, but also operate as a tacit form of cultural capital, constituted through the body. Making theologically sound personal consumption choices and visibly identifying as a Muslim may contribute to feelings of security and self-respect for young women in Western countries. For instance, foregrounding a global Muslim identity above others allowed young women in the US to remain faithful in principle to their religious community while simultaneously challenging racialised-gendered discourse (Naber 2006). Killian (2007: 305) identifies a shift to 'an Islam of the heart' for young Muslim women; a privatisation of religion yet also a public declaration of Muslim identity, such as strategically donning the *hijab* to make a political point (Scott 2007). As this implies, while there are restrictions on independence for some young Muslim women, many others make their own choices in education, dress, leisure and marriage.

Discourses of Muslim masculinity

While a great deal has been written about the construction of women and their role in Islam, much less has been written about the construction of Muslim masculinities (Ouzgane 2003; Nilan et al. 2009). For example, while young men from Muslim ethnic backgrounds generally enjoy more freedom, they too may have different experiences in youth according to the norms of their ethnic culture, level of household piety, and socio-economic status (see

Nilan et al. 2009). This may involve pressure on some to accept an arranged marriage. Moreover, demand for frequent prayers, frequent presence at the mosque, high percentage of donated income and donning traditional dress on occasions may be experienced by some as limiting their autonomy. Conversely, others may move freely about in the social and economic world more or less like their non-Muslim age peers. There has long been a cultural expectation that young Muslim men will have a much greater public profile and spend more time in unregulated spaces than young women. It is young men who are feared most in the Western moral panic (Murthy 2013), even though young women wearing the headscarf are most often abused (Ryan 2011; Zempi and Chakraborti 2014).

In short, young Muslim men do not escape gender stereotyping. For example, in the UK since 9/11 and the London bombings, they have been portrayed as ripe for radicalisation (Lynch 2015). Murthy (2013: 162) points out that:

> Fuelled by the ongoing Anglo-American 'War on Terror', Muslims, especially young Muslim males, continue to be othered/marginalized at best and demonized/violently attacked at worst. It is important to distinguish between fundamentalist 'Islamist masculinities' and modernist 'plural Muslim masculinities'.
>
> (Gerami 2005: 451–452)

Yet this distinction is often not made. For instance, after 9/11, the Muslim 'enemy within' was imagined as a racialised (male) 'folk devil', in countries like Britain and in Australia (Tufail and Poynting 2013: 46). Public scrutiny focused on appearance (Tarlo 2010). For example, in the city of Manchester, it was reported that 'men wearing beards or *shalwar kamiz*,[6] or going to the mosque or in the street during a Muslim festival, felt singled out because of these identifying features' (Tufail and Poynting 2013: 48; see also Bhatti 2011: 88). It is a common public perception that Muslim men are patriarchal and sexually violent. Associated with 'deviance and violence, young Muslim men suffer due to the triple pathology of race, gender and generation' (Hopkins 2006: 338). Much media attention has been paid to 'forced marriages and so-called "honour crime"', constituting the effective criminalisation of young Muslim men' (Tufail and Poynting 2013: 48).

Mac an Ghaill and Haywood (2014) studied shifting constructions of Muslim identity for young men from South Asian backgrounds in Birmingham (UK). The informants contextualised their *represented* Muslim masculine identity as both potential terrorists and highly vulnerable to terrorist recruitment – in the eyes of the British public. However, their *lived* identities as young men of Muslim faith were quite different. They were much less concerned with the political 'signifiers' of their religion such as *ummah, hijab, kaffir* and jihad (Mac an Ghaill and Haywood 2014: 110) and much more concerned with managing their everyday socio-economic resources and their close relationships. Hopkins' earlier study of Muslim young men in Scotland drew similar conclusions. His informants positioned themselves 'in a superior position to young Muslim women, and this is tied in with gendered, classed and racialized expectations' (Hopkins 2006: 345), particularly the breadwinner role through waged labour. Overall, the male Pakistani-Scottish youth used Islamic discourses 'to support, justify and bolster their masculine identities and performances' (Hopkins 2006: 346), and this was shaped by their location within a small Muslim minority dominated by ideals of white hegemonic masculinity. Notably, the main source of generational tension for Hopkins' informants was not religion as such, but clashes with their fathers and the issue of having a girlfriend. They tended to conceal girlfriends from their families. In Hopkins' view this shows how much 'young men's behaviour and conduct is monitored by the local community through discourses of appropriate gendered and religious identities' (2006: 348), even though they were permitted more freedom than their sisters.

Aslam (2012) studied how young men in Pakistan understand themselves post-9/11. Using Judith Butler's (1990) idea of gender performativity and Connell's (2005) concept of multiple masculinities, she explored how the young men negotiated their masculine gender in conditions of hegemony and marginality, with particular attention to their entrenched notions of 'honour'. It has been argued that everyday frustration reflected in aggressive or emasculated masculinities might sometimes feed into support for jihad when other avenues of masculine performativity fail (Aslam 2012: 272). This is the view favoured by Western media, that male Muslim youth are 'ripe for radicalisation' (Lynch 2015: 173). Yet Sageman (2008) finds Muslim youth radicalisation to be constituted primarily in masculine sociality. He suggests that those most likely to become Muslim radicals are primarily young men chasing thrills, fantasies of glory, and sense of belonging (Sageman 2004). This is often referred to as Sageman's 'bunch of guys' theory of radicalisation. The emphasis is on masculine sociality and bravado rather than theology. Finally, Kenway et al.'s (2006) notion of 'melancholic masculinity' may help us understand feelings of failure, hopelessness and anger experienced by some young Muslim men in the diaspora. Enduring intergenerational intolerance and restricted labour market opportunities (Furlong and Cartmel 2004) and needing to demonstrate loyalty to their religion and culture, they may come to favour an oppositional identity expressed in radical Islamist discourse. Yet there is no causality here. They might or they might not make the turn.

Islam: the big picture

In demographic terms Islam is the world's second largest religious group,[7] comprising over one-fifth of the world population. Islam is dominant in the Middle East and North Africa (MENA). There are 49 Muslim-majority countries, with Indonesia the largest. These countries are very diverse. While Saudi Arabia and Brunei are two of the richest countries in the world, Chad and Somalia are two of the poorest. The largest concentrations of European Muslims live in Eastern and Central Europe where they have lived for centuries. In contrast, Muslim populations in Western countries come from relatively recent migrations and are concentrated in major cities. It is the latter I refer to as constituting the 'diaspora'. According to Clifford (1994: 304), diasporas 'connect multiple communities of a dispersed population'. So it can be argued that there is a Muslim diaspora among immigrants of Islamic faith. Muslims living in Western countries often have a sense of belonging to the worldwide *ummah* (population of the faithful). Diasporic imaginaries such as the global *ummah* 'offer a way of imposing an imaginary coherence on the experience of dispersal and fragmentation' (Hall 1990: 224).

In 2010 Islam represented approximately 6 per cent of religions in Western Europe, with France showing the highest concentration. Elsewhere, Islam was around 2 per cent of religions in Australia and almost 3 per cent of religions in Canada (Pew Research Centre 2011). Despite these low proportions, a recent survey (IPSOS Mori) found that the public in Western countries greatly overestimated the Muslim percentage of the population. For example, the average estimate in France was 31 per cent compared to the actual figure of under 8 per cent of Muslims in the population. Australians estimated 18 per cent (it is actually less than 2 per cent), Americans thought it was 15 per cent (it is actually less than 1 per cent) and on average Britons guessed 21 per cent even though it is only 5 per cent (Kuruvilla 2014). These overestimations speak directly to the moral panic (Khan 2013).

In the Middle East and North Africa (MENA), a high fertility rate in the context of poverty and high religiosity is further complicated by endemic civil conflicts which disrupt basic infrastructure and prevent economic sustainability (Hett and Groth 2011). The populations of most Arab countries, for example, are mostly young, with a majority under the age of 25 (Mirkin 2013). Yet one in three young people is without a job (Urdal 2012). Conservative estimates suggest that 12 million jobs need to be added by 2025 to absorb this young workforce, while others estimate the provision of 5 million jobs per year until 2020 (Harb 2014). Thus the challenge for many Muslim nations is not just addressing high fertility rates, but meeting the needs of very high numbers of young people, who are also those most likely to leave. When they migrate, this means a brain drain and flight of skills from poorer countries.

The prosperity of Western countries attracts Muslim migrants from poorer countries. Western countries need migrants – given their falling birth rates – to ensure that the workforce maintains the required size and quality. In receiving countries, the key enabler for integration is language, closely followed by education. Apart from refugee intake, Australia, Canada and the US attract a greater proportion of skilled Muslim migrants than do Western

European countries and the UK, which have complex relationships with previous colonies (Hett and Groth 2011). In 2010, the median age of Muslims throughout Europe was 32, eight years younger than the median for all Europeans (Pew Research Centre 2011). A similar trend appears in other receiving countries. This is primarily due to the process of demographic transition.

When Muslim people migrate to Western countries they are not always welcomed with open arms. Indeed, they may find widespread suspicion, fear and intolerance, even after several generations (for example, Schmidt 2004; Dunn et al. 2007; Sirin and Fine 2007; Noble and Poynting 2008; Kabir 2008, 2010, 2012; Allen 2010; Hassan 2010; Steuter and Wills 2010; Hage 2011; Lovat et al. 2013; Ryan 2011; Sirseloudi 2012; Moosavi 2015; McGrath and McGarry 2014; Zempi and Chakraborti 2014; Fasenfest 2015; Lynch 2015). Tindongan (2011: 75) claims that 'Muslim immigrant communities in all their varieties of origin and practice have been Othered by the West, and held hostage to Orientalist misunderstandings and exoticized impressions perpetuated by Western governments, media, religions, and hysteria'. In France, Butler (2008) finds there is a prevalent understanding of Islam as backward; a deplorable anachronism within the secular state. Thus, 'the hysterical reaction becomes phantasmatic (...) The so-called war against terror is constantly invoked to spread fear and anxiety, such that a hard and fast line is drawn between the upright French citizen and the dangerous immigrant' (McRobbie 2011: 102). By mid-July 2016, multiple Islamist terrorist attacks had left more than 230 people dead in France, precipitating a permanent state of maximum security alert (Fouquet 2016). Under that declaration, police have extensive powers for raid and arrest without judicial oversight. For example, following the November 2015 Paris attacks, police searched 4,000 houses, opened more than 500 criminal cases and placed 382 people under house arrest. Yet only five court proceedings directly linked to terrorism resulted from the thousands of raids (Al Jazeera 2016). Intelligence sources find great difficulty in identifying potential small group and 'lone wolf' attacks.

One significant effect from situations such as that in France is to strengthen the distinction between 'good' Muslims and 'bad' Muslims (Beydoun 2016; Mamdani 2002). They heighten the demand for reassurances of normality from Muslim people in the diaspora. The discourse of reassurance is exemplified in books like *What's Right with Islam is What's Right with America* (Rauf 2005) which maintain that liberty, equality, fraternity, and social justice are foundational in Islam.

At the same time, experiences of racial and religious exclusion and discrimination against Muslim ethnic communities in Western countries have been accompanied by a revitalisation of Islam (Modood 2005), especially among young people. A strong allegiance to Islam offers a sense of global belonging and solidarity. Modood (2005) points out that these very circumstances have proved productive for Islamist groups to appeal to the grievances of disaffected Muslim youth in the diaspora. In reference to the radical meta-narrative, for Muslim youth in the diaspora there may be a longing for the utopian caliphate because of the dysphoria between their Muslim selves and the intolerant non-Muslim society around them. Meer (2010) points out that the rise of a specifically Muslim consciousness among the relevant ethnic diasporas has implicitly problematised the politics of multiculturalism from one side, while widespread Islamophobia has problematised it from the other side.

Muslim youth making their own reflexive identities

Having set the scene, it seems clear that as diasporic Muslim youth 'make' their own identities in a highly reflexive way, they negotiate different forms of cultural belonging. First, they want to make a successful biography according to the norms of the society where they live: completing education, getting a job, buying nice things, marrying well, and creating a prosperous family in their own home. Second, they would like to demonstrate belonging to their families and communities. 'Islamic faith places a high level of adherence to the structure of parental respect' (McGrath and McGarry 2014: 929). So they respond to their parents' wishes in matters such as obligatory prayers, Friday mosque attendance for boys, dress codes for girls, and long-term marriage and career plans for both sexes. Third, at a personal level, belonging may be signified by a strong identification with Islam *beyond ethnic traditions*. This allegiance can provide a young person with a feeling of collective solidarity. Finally, as young people immersed in global popular culture, they can show they belong to the youthful tribe of Muslim 'cool' – a neo-theo-tribal configuration – by selective consumption and inclusive online engagement.

Working to achieve a legitimate cultural and moral identity for Muslim youth in Western countries is a highly reflexive exercise amid the moral panic. Young people today make choices in an increasingly reflexive way due to current and future uncertainties (Threadgold and Nilan 2009). Yet they do not enjoy a completely free set of choices. As Karl Marx said, while each person does make their own life to some extent, 'they do not make it as they please; they do not make it under self-selected circumstances, but under circumstances existing already, given and transmitted from the past' (Marx 1978/1852: 595). The circumstances 'existing already' for diasporic young Muslims includes their location as the stigmatised Other (Said 1978) in a non-Muslim society. Their reflexivity around a Muslim identity is also shaped by the teleological meta-narrative of radical Islamism.

Conclusion

Having set the scene for the book, this first chapter concludes by describing the methodology that generated the data used throughout. I employed a digital ethnographic approach that was primarily observational. Virtual ethnography (Hine 2000) is also sometimes termed cyber-ethnography (Ward 1999), netnography or digital ethnography (Kozinets 2010; boyd 2009). It may be defined as 'participant-observational research based in online fieldwork', examining communities that exist primarily online. Thus the procedures for data collection 'set it apart from the conduct of face-to-face ethnography' (Kozinets 2010: 60). This approach allowed the collection of relevant material from most of the Western countries that comprise the Muslim diaspora, thus overcoming the usual restrictions on face-to-face local research, which does not access the vivid online world of global connection with which young people routinely engage as they make and reinvent youth culture. The first method was to gather and analyse texts, images and blog comments from websites and social media favoured by Muslim youth in the diaspora. The second method was to access existing studies and reports on Muslim youth in the diaspora that directly report what the young people themselves have to say about their everyday cultural lives and practices. The third method was to follow sequences of media reporting and public blogging about specific terrorist events, or about creative products such as games and music. I was delighted at the volume and richness of the material collected through digital ethnography. This allowed a deep interpretation of selected examples. The other benefit was broad coverage of countries in the Western diaspora which permitted a wider set of discursive analyses compared to a single country focus. The following chapter sets the scene by describing and explaining the radical Islamist meta-narrative.

Notes

1 'Muslim world' refers to a discursive entity, not a geographic region.
2 Muslim youth identity is not understood in this book as essentialist, static nor unchanging. As a multi-layered, contested and negotiated (Bhatti 2011) sense of self it is better understood in the plural. However, the singular is used for the sake of brevity.
3 In the aftermath he said he was proud that Londoners had chosen hope over fear.
4 The word *hijab* means generally covering up the body, but the term is mainly used for headscarves worn by Muslim women. The headscarf most common in the West leaves the face clear. The *niqab* is a face veil that leaves the area around the eyes clear and is worn with a headscarf. The *burkha* is a one-piece veil that covers the face and body, with a mesh screen to see through. The *chador* is a full-body cloak that leaves the face clear.
5 *Purdah* is the term for strict female seclusion.
6 A long, loose, long-sleeved collarless shirt or tunic, with loose-fitting pants.
7 The Christian faith is the largest.

Chapter 2

The meta-narrative of Islamist extremism

Introduction

This chapter begins the task of looking at how the radical Islamist meta-narrative is variously considered and inflected by young Muslims in the diaspora. It sets the scene by looking at the meta-narrative and its implications. Al Raffie (2012: 13) says we must grasp the 'constituent narratives' of radical Islamism if we want to understand the 'reasons behind its resonance with certain individuals'. Similarly, McCauley and Moskalenko (2014) urge us to understand the Islamist meta-narrative to comprehend jihad. Zackie (2013) concurs, stating that it is necessary to investigate what young Muslims themselves have to say about the 'story' of Islamist extremism, on either side. It is therefore logical that the meta-narrative of radicalism should be explained before we proceed further.

This author does not unequivocally accept the death of grand narratives predicted at the end of the twentieth century (for example Lyotard 1993). There is too much in recent literature on the rise of radical Islamism that points to a distinctive guiding narrative on an epic scale. Certainly some notable studies of Muslim youth radicalisation have acknowledged the importance of 'narrative' analysis (Roy 2008; Halverson et al. 2011; Al-Raffie 2012; Samuel 2012; Bernardi et al. 2012; Ryan 2014; Vergani 2014; Joosse et al. 2015). However, none has specifically explored how Muslim youth might position themselves subjectively, either within the meta-narrative in accordance with the offered subject position, or rather differently – and not at all through engagement with popular culture.

At this point we need a quick overview of Islam as a world faith. Islam as a religion can then be epistemologically separated from the radical meta-narrative of Islamism (Ghaffar-Kucher 2015). The two must be considered separately. Basically, the faith in Islam held by millions is very different to the fanatical pursuit of extreme Islamism.

Islam

The vast majority of Muslims in the world today lead orderly lives based on the tenets of Islam, just as those of the Christian faith and other religions live their everyday lives based on key tenets of faith that regulate and order their personal conduct. The word *Islam* means submission to God's will. A monotheistic faith, Islam is a comprehensive religion that regulates both matters of faith (*ibadat*) and social relations (*muamalat*). The five pillars of Islam are: *shahadah* (truthful profession of belief in one God, Allah, and Prophet Muhammad as his messenger), *hajj* (pilgrimage), *zakat* (almsgiving), *salat* (daily prayer) and *sawm* (fasting during the month of Ramadan). The moral categories of human behaviour are *haram* (forbidden) and *halal* (permissible). *Al-Quran* (the Koran) is the sacred text. The *hadith* texts are claimed to contain the words and deeds of the Prophet Muhammad (Drissel 2011: 148). The texts constitute the *sunna*, guides for leading the life of a Muslim and avoiding sin (*zina*). *Sharia* is the 'path' of Islamic canonical law based on the *sunna*. [1] The community of Muslim believers is the *ummah*. Like Christianity and Judaisim, the other Abrahamic faiths, Islam is a proselytising religion (Werbner 2004). Islamic orthopraxy is vitally important. For example, the actions of five-time daily prayer hold much significance. 'Mosque participants identified the act of prayer as the key site for purposefully molding their intentions, emotions and desires in accord with orthodox standards of Islamic piety' (Mahmood 2005: 828). Mahmood's study also points to disciplinary acts of filtered selection, a form of distinction through which pious Muslims avoid seeing, hearing, and speaking about the things that make faith weak. Rather, they focus on those things that make faith strong. This is perhaps one reason why moderate Muslims might be sometimes reluctant to publicly condemn extremism.

Following the death of the Prophet Muhammad in 632 AD, Islam split into two sects; Shia and Sunni (Osman 2014). Sunni and Shia Muslims share the basic tenets of faith outlined above. However, Sunni Muslims believe that a new Muslim leader should be elected from among those most capable. The Shia position is that leadership must stay within the Prophet's own family. Shia followers reject the traditions of the *hadith*, and there some minor differences in praxis. Sunnis are around 85 per cent of Muslims worldwide. In some current conflicts in the Middle East, Sunni Muslims are on one side and Shia Muslims on the other. Another variant of Islam, Sufism, is a movement rather than a sect. Sufism arose as a mystical ascetic movement in the early Middle Ages. Sufi praxis aims for self-control and ritual practices to attain the goal of mystical union with God. Sufi practices include writing and reciting poetry and hymns as well as hypnotic dance – the famous whirling dervishes – all with the aim of experiencing the love and peace of divine union.

Since the middle of the twentieth century, conflicts and attacks linked broadly to Muslim interests in the Middle East and North Africa (MENA) have politicised ordinary Muslims in all parts of the globe, focusing their interest on what constitutes Islam in terms of both personal faith and the public sphere (Zammit 2010). It is common to describe the constitution of Islam in the last three decades as a: 'resurgence, a revival or an awakening. These terms all point to the same reality, i.e. that Islam today plays a much more pronounced role than 40 years ago' (Kühle and Lindekilde 2010: 36). While beliefs and practices vary quite markedly between countries, sects and movements, the revitalisation of Islam has increased the feeling of *ummah*, the sense of belonging to a community of Muslim believers worldwide. Notably though, the vast majority of Muslims worldwide emphatically reject the use of violence and instead emphasise reaching out to 'hearts and minds' (Al Raffie 2012) – in the ongoing battle against 'sinfulness' (Werbner 2004: 455).

For those 'ordinary' people of the faith that Ali (2015) calls 'Mecca Muslims', emphasis in the public sphere is on broad values of Islam such as public modesty, education, public service and accountability. Here Islam 'inspires rather than dictates the good life' (Mandaville 2007a: 105). Moderate Muslims are 'those who live and work "within" societies, seek change from below, resist religious extremism, and consider violence and terrorism to be illegitimate' (Esposito 2007: 26). Such a position is highly compatible with secular democracy, operationalised at the level of secular state governance in the Muslim-majority countries of Indonesia and Turkey.[2]

Islamism

To be an Islamist is different from being what Ali (2015) calls a 'Mecca Muslim' – a moderate. Islamists reject secular law and emphasise the need to impose strict Sharia law. They strive for pan-Islamic political unity and the removal of non-Muslim elements from the Muslim world. Islamism means all aspects of everyday life should be firmly ruled by Islamic law. This means taking one's religion very seriously indeed (Hage 2011). Islamism connotes the desire to impose strictly-interpreted Islamic law on society to create a viable moral order through the political re-ordering of government and governance. In brief, 'Islamism is a response to modernity that has transformed the religion of Islam into political ideology' (Barton 2004: 29). It has been described as 'a closing down of Islam's discursive parameters' (Mandaville 2007a: 106). Wiktorowicz (2005b) notes that the popularity of Islamism rose in Western countries during the first half of the first decade in the new millennium.

Islamist praxis usually follows the *salafi* or *wahhabi* philosophy. *Wahhabi* was an eighteenth-century sect of Sunni Islam that demanded purification of the faith (Wiktorowicz 2005b). The sect was eventually defeated by the caliph of the Ottoman Empire (Cheong and Halverson 2010: 1119). Later, *salafi* thinkers built directly on *wahhabi* precepts, arguing that to achieve a true faith, Muslims must purify the religion by strictly following the Koran and the *sunna* and the consensus of the companions (Calvert 2010; Wiktorowicz 2005a). *Salafi* Islamists hold that a 'true' Islamic society must be reconstituted through a restored caliphate (*khilafah*) – the legendary Islamic multinational theocratic empire.

In principle, an Islamist adherent turns completely away from the secular world. He or she is fully equipped 'to diagnose the prevailing circumstances and behave accordingly, secure in the knowledge their actions fit the requirements' (Mandaville 2007a: 107). Influential hard-line theologian Qutb's argument was that all those who do not exclusively support the *sharia* legal system and do not strictly obey the rules, 'are part of the modern *jahiliyya*[3] and no longer Muslims' (Wiktorowicz 2005a: 79). This is a contentious claim because it categorically excludes moderate Muslims entirely from the faith. Obviously moderate Muslims do not agree. Hefner (2002: 41) emphasises 'the long struggle between moderate Muslims and Islamist hardliners for the hearts and minds of Muslim believers'. This struggle points to a profound schism in contemporary Islam worldwide. Yet despite theological rigidity, not all Islamists support terrorism and endorse militant violence to achieve their goals (Barton 2004). For example, despite hardline thinking, *salafi* Islamism per se does not specifically mandate the use of violence. Rather, a small faction of *salafi* radicals believes that violence can and should be used to establish the caliphate of pure faith through defeating the enemy – the United States, Israel and its allies, both Muslim and non-Muslim (Husain 2007), through the praxis of terrorist jihad.

As for actual numbers, according to Rabasa and Benard (2014), Western European intelligence agencies estimate that less than 1 percent of the Muslim population living within their borders are Islamists at risk of becoming radicals. That means approximately 325,000 Muslims identified as hardline Islamists who are deemed to have some potential for taking radical action, either domestic or overseas. They are identified because they are under some form of surveillance. However, there is nothing to indicate whether they will, or will not, ultimately take such action. A person who is not on the surveillance list may choose to attack. I pick up this argument again in subsequent chapters.

The radical Islamist meta-narrative

In general, Islamists cite some version of the heroic, grand scale meta-narrative described below. In fact Zackie (2013) argues that to really grasp the persuasive process by which Islamist jihadi actions are taken up, we need to distil the key guiding narrative, because it promises 'recognition' (see Honneth 1996) on a grand scale through heroic and self-sacrificing action. For my purposes, Zackie (2013) has created a useful summary of the radical Islamist meta-narrative, one that seems to validate violent jihad. To achieve this summary Zackie carefully studied (in Arabic) the influential extremist manual *Call to Global Islamic Resistance* written by *Al-Qaeda* theoretician Abu

Mus'ab al-Suri (sometimes referred to as '*Mein Kampf*' for jihad [Zammit 2013]), as well as other texts. Zackie's analytical thread in the summary uses terms from Eidelson and Eidelson's (2003) taxonomy of beliefs that propel groups toward conflict.[4] Zackie starts his summary of narrative with the claim of *superiority*, that Muslims are the people chosen by God to rule over the earth. Yet this God-given right has been denied by 'others' through oppression. This is a claim of *injustice*. Moreover, the 'others' threaten Muslims with extinction. This is a claim of *vulnerability* (Zackie 2013: 15). Zackie continues:

> The Crusader-American-Zionist-West wants to occupy and subjugate us and appropriate all our wealth and riches; and our apostate Arab and Islamic governments are their accomplices (*distrust*). The ummah must wake up and join the Jihadist vanguard elite to defend itself and reclaim its God-given right to rule the earth (*mobilization/radicalization*).
>
> (Zackie 2013: 15, my emphasis)

Zackie's summary of the Islamist meta-narrative finishes with a strident call for Muslims not to accept their apparent fate of extinction, but to fulfill the prophecy of greatness by fighting back. This is a claim for *anti-helplessness* (Zackie 2013: 15).

In Zackie's summary, the setting of the Islamist meta-narrative is now, but the mention of 'prophecies' locates the origins of the story in the past. The future is referenced in contrasting ways, firstly by hypothesising the extinction of Islam, and secondly by presenting the utopian vision of Muslims ruling the earth. The characters in this narrative are Muslims (good), the 'Crusader-American-Zionist-West' (bad) and 'apostate Arab and Islamic governments' (bad). The plot episodes move from God's original promise that Muslims rule the earth, to denial of this right by the oppressors. The next plot episode is the consequential action of Muslims rising up together to defeat the oppressors and reclaim their birthright. This is the climax of the story. The denouement is the God-promised status quo of Muslims ruling the earth – with all enemies vanquished. At base, this is a flexible story with a simple plot. It is simultaneously modern and anti-modern, traditional and anti-traditional. It is grounded in an 'eschatological vision that combines the reconstruction of the mundane world according to a sharply articulated transcendental vision' of a pure, unsullied past (Eisenstadt 1995: 263). The implicit logic of the plot is vengeful action and total global victory (Esposito 2002), while the theme of oppression is designed to instil in Muslims a sense of collective identity by framing the narrative as 'us versus them' (Drissel 2011: 161).

Key discourses are: *superiority, injustice, vulnerability, distrust, mobilisation* and *anti-helplessness*. All these discourses invite the affective subject positioning of the receiver of the story. Emotive terms on the negative side are: *deprived, oppressed, extinction, occupy, subjugate* and *appropriate*. Emotive terms on the positive side are: *elite, defend, reclaim, God-given, rule, destined* and *greatness*. There is strong appeal to personal heroism in the story even while it promises totalitarian universalism and rigid globalisation. As Mozaffari (2007) points out, the narrative of radical Islamism more or less matches other totalitarian ideologies such as communism and Nazism, which also emphasised mass mobilisation, collective action and leadership legitimisation. As history tells us, totalitarian regimes can seem appealing because they provide a comforting, single answer to vexing questions of the past, present, and future (Arendt 1951).

As for violent struggle, the narrative begins by implying that all crimes committed against Muslims anywhere in the world, for any reason, are on the same level (see Roy 2008: 19). The second part implies the individual who will 'avenge the sufferings of the community'. The third part implies struggle as a personal compulsory duty. It implies the idea that a 'few outstanding and devoted heroes' will gain salvation through sacrifice and death. The final part of the meta-narrative is the 'fight against the global order' (Roy 2008: 20) which ends in utopia.

Other scholars have also attempted to summarise the radical meta-narrative. Here is another version:

> (1) Islam is under attack by Western crusaders led by the United States; (2) jihadis, whom the West refers to as 'terrorists', are defending against this attack; (3) the actions they take in defence of Islam are proportional, just, and religiously sanctified; and, therefore (4) it is the duty of good Muslims to support these actions.
>
> (McCauley and Moskalenko 2014: 70)

Some tellings of the narrative emphasise caliphate:

> This narrative is comprised of stories that romanticize previous Caliphates and claim they were undermined by Western powers bent on subjugating the Muslims and destroying Islam. The solution to this downward spiral is restoration of the Caliphate, which will throw off the yoke of oppression and realize the divine plan for all Muslims.
>
> (Furlow et al. 2014: 2)

As a teleological epic, the 'big' story – however told – directly encodes the binary world view found in extreme religious rhetoric (Savage and Liht 2009). Here the history of the world is 'a story of conflict between truth, represented by Islam, and falsehood – the infidels, "the *Kufr*"' (Mendelsohn 2012: 606). As a classic tale of struggle and heroism the Islamist meta-narrative produces meaning through defining subjects and establishing their relational positions within a distinctive system of signification where good and evil are in contest, for example:

On the 'us' side of the equation are a vanguard of virtuous Muslims, conscious of the true Islam. The 'them' is an unholy alliance of Crusader-Zionists, with a centuries-long record of scheming to do down Islam, allied with the corrupt and degenerate political leadership of the Muslim world.

(Payne 2009: 111)

All meta-narratives contain the element of 'transformation' (Ryan 2014). In the radical Islamist story the thing to be transformed is nothing less than the moral order of the world, and thus the moral order of the self. The struggle for caliphate looks forward to a major world-altering transformation which will restore the religious utopia of the past (Drissel 2011: 161). Simplification is the key heuristic. The establishment of caliphate implies transcending myriad complex ethnic traditions in the name of one 'pure', homogenising praxis of faith made modern by strategic use of technology. At least one writer has called this synthesis '*sharia* plus electricity' (Cevik 2015: 12).

Dissemination and variation

Critics might argue that there can be no single radical Islamist meta-narrative because there are many versions and multifarious re-tellings by different interpreters with different interests at stake. Quite so. Yet in another sense a singular meta-narrative is distinguishable as a compelling teleological pathway through which more or less the same idealised culmination or resolution is anticipated. Al Raffie (2012: 13) proposes the varying stories of jihad, for instance, form a 'master narrative'. For example, one striking piece of Islamic State (IS) online propaganda features a dynamic map of the world with an IS flag growing and spreading over all global territories (Saltman and Smith 2015: 73). Here, total global domination mirrors the logic and plot of the radical Islamist meta-narrative described by Zackie (2013). In another example, the transnational Islamist group *Hizbut Tahrir* spreads propaganda to the effect that the West is actively working to split the *ummah*, 'in order to weaken the Muslim community and prevent Muslims from realising their religious and political destiny' – the single, all-encompassing caliphate (Mendelsohn 2012). For *Hizbut Tahrir*, moderate Muslims in the diaspora are tools and dupes of Western propaganda. The answer is for Muslims everywhere to recognise the truth of the Islamist meta-narrative (Mendelsohn 2012) and take it on as a personal quest to achieve global caliphate. This mirrors the logic and plot of the radical Islamist meta-narrative described by Zackie (2013).

One reason for variation in the meta-narrative is that there are many different voices of Islamism, just as there are many strands of Islam. The faith facilitates this polyphony. In history, Islam never had a centralised hierarchy of religious leadership authority (Turner 2007), unlike Catholicism for example. It seems that Islam 'officially has no clergy' (McGrath and McGarry 2014:

952). Following the principle of equality in the *ummah*, any man with sufficient theological knowledge can become a self-styled *imam* (Turner 2007: 120). Religious authority originally rested with a small educated elite who were recognised to interpret the *sunna*.[5] However, a breakdown in authority took place from the mid-nineteenth century which gradually eroded traditional knowledge production and dissemination (Mandaville 2007a, 2007b). This shift in religious authority was accelerated by rising literacy rates and mass education in the Muslim world as well as the emergence of new technologies and modes of communication.

Within this legacy of decentralised authority, interpretations of the *sunna* have become more diffuse, disparate, polyvalent and translocalised (Appadurai 1996; Mandaville 2007a). Contemporary Muslims 'are increasingly reshaping religion with their own hands' (Mandaville 2007a: 102) according to their micro-cultural norms. For example, it is obvious that a highly varied range of voices claim to speak for the *ummah* at any one time on any one issue. Similarly, there are highly varied versions of the Islamist endeavour, even though all refer implicitly back to the radical Islamist meta-narrative as described above.

The Islamist meta-narrative and radicalisation

Governments throughout the world are keen to understand militant Islamism and there is an abundance of literature on the topic that refers to the meta-narrative. For example, McCauley and Moskalenko (2014: 70) offer a model shaped like a pyramid where the wide and deep base represents the vast majority of Muslims worldwide who do not accept any of what they call the 'global jihad *narrative*' (my emphasis). A narrower layer of Muslims above the base represents those who sympathise with the first part of the meta-narrative: that the West is waging a war on Islam. An even narrower layer above that represents Muslims who believe that jihadis are acting in defence of Islam and that their actions are morally and religiously justified, but do not take action themselves. Finally, the tiny but sharp apex of the pyramid represents those who fully engage the radical Islamist narrative and make it their personal duty to conduct violent jihad (McCauley and Moskalenko 2014).

In the tumult of competing claims represented within that schematic pyramid, we can see what Toren (1988: 696) refers to as the 'mutability of tradition'. The stark, simple radical Islamist meta-narrative serves as a legitimating anchor point in the numerically small upper levels of the radicalisation pyramid, and a significant point of departure from the lower levels. When Muslims choose to support the Islamist meta-narrative, 'authentification of the present' is established by 'continuity with the past' (Asad 1996: 266) with a guarantee of future reward. The inspirational meta-narrative of radical Islamism is significant for recruitment to jihad because it provides a heroic explanation for everything that has happened, is happening, and will happen.

Young Islamists

Roy (2008) has succinctly described Islamism in the West as a *youth movement* characterised by the *power of a narrative*. The radical Islamist meta-narrative is an eminently heroic narrative of world-shaping (Mamouri 2014). It is also a conduit through which anger can be channelled. Ali and Moss (2010: 2) claim that 'perceived injustices over the sufferings of fellow Muslims in conflict zones can generate feelings of "humiliation-by-proxy"'. This encourages 'radicalized individuals to seek revenge' (Ali and Moss 2010: 14). The meta-narrative gives so-inclined youth 'a clear strategy for changing the world' (Mamouri 2014). They are constructed as agents of a vast transcendental transformation; as courageous fighters for global Muslim justice; as world-savers. Young jihadis believe that as a band of brothers – a 'bunch of guys' as Sageman (2008) calls them – they are on the 'right' side and reward is due. The radical Islamist meta-narrative tells them they are 'God's chosen' and their militant task of killing is 'God-given' (Roy 2008).

The following sections of discussion explain some elements of the radical Islamist meta-narrative that might seem attractive to some young Muslims and Muslim converts if they are seeking not only a strong structure of meaning, identity and order, but revenge, utopia and post-millennial order. Publicised accounts from radical Islamist recruits indicate that violent jihad connotes for them the subject position of hero; a warrior who is not afraid of death.

Jihad

Drissel (2011: 170) identifies a competitive Islamic discourse about jihad. In Arabic the word *jihad* translates simply as 'struggle' or 'striving'. In Islam, jihad can be internal/personal – which is regarded as the greater jihad, or external – the lesser jihad, which refers to armed struggle or *jihad bil-sayf* (jihad by the sword). On the one hand, militants push for an external 'holy war' against infidels, while other Muslims see jihad primarily as a personal strategy for overcoming sin in their lives. Notably, the doctrine of militant jihad itself is not the product of a single authoritative interpretation but the outcome of diverse authorities choosing to interpret sacred texts in specific historical and political contexts (Esposito 2002). In fact the Koran contains many verses urging that innocent civilians should not be killed,[6] and Muslims in general support that position.

Strategic hard-line propaganda attempts to shift mainstream Muslim thinking towards the ideology of jihad as armed struggle (Kepel 2004). This is usually constructed as a holy war in which sacrifices must be made:

> Culturally astute jihadists know well the themes that resonate with the wider Muslim public, and have done an extraordinary job in harnessing three narratives to mobilize for martyrdom: humiliation of Muslims at

the hands of foreigners, impotence of official Muslim governments in the face of hegemonic powers, and redemption through faithful sacrifice.

(Hafez 2007: 95)

Support for holy war is proselytised as *fard ayn*, individual obligation towards fellow Muslims and God. It is justified by carefully chosen verses:

> The Qur'an is taken as guidance very selectively to suit the jihadists' particular strategic and political agenda and to strengthen the accompanying *narrative* set forth by proponents of militant Islamism. Numerous verses and sections of the Qur'an that call for peaceful co-existence and mutual respect, counter-balancing many of the verses used to justify (terrorist) violence, are ignored and excluded.
>
> (Holbrook 2010: 23, my emphasis)

As a general theme, jihadi terrorists proclaim the West is at war with Islam, so violence is justified[7] (Husain 2007; Wiktorowicz 2005a). For example, the militant logic of domestic terrorism goes like this: Islamist violence in the diaspora creates terror, which fosters favourable conditions for Islamophobia and authoritarian measures that will increase recruitment to jihad. Moreover, more Muslims will be politicised by local intolerance and come to support jihad in a variety of ways.

Tilly (2004: 5) argues that the basic logic of terrorism is to create fear. Braddock (2012: 3) concurs, 'terrorism is more than violence for violence's sake; terrorism is meant to be persuasive. It is meant to induce fear'. It is also meant to provoke retaliatory action that then justifies further terrorist action. For my purposes here, terrorism can be defined as:

> A doctrine about the presumed effectiveness of a special form or tactic of fear-generating, coercive political violence and, on the other hand, a conspiratorial practice of calculated, demonstrative, direct violent action without legal or moral restraints, targeting mainly civilians and non-combatants, performed for its propagandistic and psychological effects on various audiences and conflict parties.
>
> (Schmid 2011: 86)

As we can see, the emphasis is on killing civilians and non-combatants. Whether Muslim or not, all these people are defined as the enemy and so attack is justified. The theological rationale relies on a key claim of the radical Islamist meta-narrative – that the enemies are both the 'Crusader-American-Zionist-West' and the 'apostate Arab and Islamic governments' that support them. Following this logic, the people that live harmoniously in those countries, Muslim and non-Muslim, are supporting the enemies of Islam, and are therefore deemed to be infidels or *kaffir*, for the purposes of conducting militant jihad. For example, a guide produced by *Al-Qaeda* some years ago states that only one of the following conditions is necessary to justify attacks on 'non-believers'. Here is a summary:

1   The enemy has wilfully killed Muslim civilians.
2   Civilians have aided the enemy in 'deed, word, or mind'.
3   Combatants and non-combatants cannot be readily distinguished.
4   There is a need to burn enemy-held places where there are civilians.
5   There is a need for heavy weaponry.
6   The enemy is using human shields made up of civilians.
7   The enemy has violated an agreement so civilians must be killed as a lesson.

(Wiktorowicz 2005a: 89)

The conditions above were used to justify killing civilians from all backgrounds in the 9/11 attacks, on the basis that by living peaceably in the United States they were assisting the enemy in kind; an enemy that had previously killed Muslim civilians at various times in history. They were thus 'legitimate targets' (Wiktorowicz 2005a: 88).

According to *Al-Qaeda*, the jihadi martyr who dies in 'justified' attacks on infidels is assured of reward in the afterlife (Wiktorowicz 2005a: 93). Sometimes the martyr's family will receive a compensatory payment from the organisation. As indicated, jihadis routinely kill other Muslims. Joining the conflict in Afghanistan, for example, was constituted by the Taliban as an individual religious obligation of jihad, elevated to the status of the five pillars of Islam in defining what it was to be a Muslim. Anyone who did not join or support was then categorically not a real Muslim. This position mirrors what Roy (2004) calls 'nomadic jihad' against disbelievers and apostates, even if those same people are Muslims too. This requires accepting the idea that such people are not really Muslims but disbelievers, even though they themselves feel they are believers.

Within Islam most people exercise extreme caution on *takfir*, the process of judging whether or not a fellow Muslim is an apostate (disbeliever). In contrast, jihad supporters do not hesitate on *takfir*, drawing a sharp distinction between 'true believers' of Islam – militants like themselves – and false Muslims deemed as infidels because they do not directly engage struggle against the West. Re-categorised as infidels, apostate Muslims must be fought and removed, in order to establish God's rule on earth. In summary, as Wiktorowicz (2005a: 94) concludes, the jihadi position sidesteps theological constraints used in classical Islam to minimise violence and warfare. It employs a highly selective theology of justification. Those drawn to it must not only fully engage this justificatory rhetoric as total believers, but ignore anything that contradicts it, including specific verses from the Koran.

As explained above, terrorist actions on home soil aim to provoke Western powers to send more and more forces to combat in the Middle East, which is where the final victorious battle is scheduled to take place at the climax point of the radical Islamist meta-narrative. As a second outcome, greater involvement of Western military forces on soil claimed as Muslim is calculated to arouse ever more intense feelings of anger and desire for revenge among Muslims worldwide. In summary, home-grown jihadi attacks in the diaspora are designed to spark broad community outrage and strong anti-Muslim feelings, fuelling support for further Western military engagement in MENA countries, and driving angry local Muslims towards support for jihad against their persecutors.

The last decade has seen significant changes in the landscape of jihad militancy in MENA countries. Sunni–Shia struggles have intensified. *Al-Qaeda* as a centralised organisation has declined, while IS (Islamic State) has grown very strong, as have *Al-Shabaab* and *Boko Haram* in North Africa. Many, many, other Islamist jihadi groups have emerged.[8] There is not a unified jihadi movement at all (Crenshaw 2015). The same report notes that the currently most successful jihadi group, IS – also known as *Daesh*, has been utterly ruthless in destroying its perceived opponents even when they have been former allies in a pan-Islamist struggle.

Another significant trend is of more youth from Western countries, some Muslim, some Muslim converts, travelling overseas to fight with Islamist militias. Jihadi recruiters construct their own emotionally charged tales that build on the radical Islamist meta-narrative. These stories are 'rooted in themes of humiliation, collusion, and redemption'. They 'demonize their enemies and heighten the sense of threat facing Muslims' (Hafez 2007: 111). In such propaganda, young jihadis are depicted as 'inspired individuals with heroic motivations seeking opportunities to fulfil their obligation to God, sacrifice for the nation, and avenge a grieving people' (Hafez 2007: 112; see also Hasan 2010). Cheong and Halverson (2010) studied the discursive strategies employed by *Al-Qaeda* to mobilise and direct Muslim youth worldwide. They propose that 'jihadists offer Muslim youth an internally cohesive and preferred identity based on an Islamic revival bound to militant revolutionary action' (2010: 1110; see also Silke 2008). Jihadi identity relies on the radical meta-narrative. Here young recruits can locate themselves as heroes, fighting with a brave band of brothers. The sensational sub-story of violent jihad is an important variant of the radical Islamist meta-narrative for militant groups and for 'lone wolf' terrorist attacks in the diaspora. 'This narrative motivates the individuals; they act alone or with minimal support' (Sanchez 2014: 12). Yet the idea of violent jihad does not sit alone as a goal in itself. Its purpose is to bring about caliphate.

Caliphate

A caliphate (*khilafah*) is the dominion of a caliph, a ruler of Muslims. A caliphate is governed under Islamic law. Prior to reforms enacted by the

Prophet Muhammad in his lifetime, pre-Islamic surrounding areas were composed of warring city-states. Their dysfunctionality was deemed to stem from the state of ignorance of their constituents: *jahiliya*. Islam offered not only a path for people to move beyond personal ignorance, but a system of governance under a caliph that guaranteed good conduct and an orderly public sphere. According to Mamouri (2014) the *salafi* vision of caliphate builds on the writings of Islamist scholars Abul A'la Maududi and Sayyid Qutb. There are three stages in achieving caliphate: *eman* (to believe in pure Islam), *hijra* (to immigrate to an Islamic society) and *jihad* (to fight for establishing caliphate).

The utopian caliphate in the radical Islamist meta-narrative takes its cue from the Ottoman Caliphate (1362–1924) rather than earlier caliphates that followed the death of the Prophet in 632. The Ottoman Caliphate was 'a vast empire from India to the east, spreading across the Middle East, North Africa and into Spain'. Throughout the centuries there was armed struggle by Western Europe against the caliphate. It was eventually abolished by Turkish leader Mustafa Kemal Ataturk in 1924 (Fasenfest 2015). Subsequently, early anti-colonial movements in the Muslim world used the idea of reviving the caliphate to rally followers, as have later Islamist movements such as *Hizbut Tahrir* (Osman 2014: 2; Gross 2012). The re-colonising geopolitics of caliphate form an important discourse of jihad militancy in MENA countries.

In 2014 the leader of Islamic State (IS), Abu Bakr al-Baghdadi, declared caliphate over an area the size of the United Kingdom that included eastern Syria and northwestern Iraq. Banners throughout the war-torn, poverty-ridden occupied area claim it to be *khilafa 'ala minhaj al-nubuwwa* – caliphate in the prophetic tradition; the same model of Islamic governance set out by the Prophet Muhammad over two centuries ago and exemplified in the Ottoman Caliphate during what many Muslims regard as the Golden Age of Islam. For some Islamists the IS announcement of caliphate signified the beginning of the ultimate victory predicted in the Islamist meta-narrative. For Shi'ites, who are excluded by IS, it signified a small, temporary territorial claim. For many Islamists, the utopian ideal of caliphate is much bigger and grander; a reinvention of the glory days of Muslim empire. It is imagined as a beautiful, prosperous, clean and green, utopian realm where moral rule ensures orderly conduct[9] (Furlow et al. 2014).

When IS declared the new caliphate, with IS leader Abu Bakr al-Baghdadi as the new caliph, there was a call for all Sunni Muslims regardless of geographical location to support the new state, and if possible to join them. However, the International Union of Muslim Scholars, which supports the idea of caliphate in general, released a statement declaring the IS claim for caliphate was illegitimate because it was not based on consultation with people's representatives, scholars, officials, and Islamic groups – as required. There was also a flood of arguments from theologians detailing religious, socio-cultural, and political arguments against recognition of the claim. Moreover, while some fellow Islamist militant groups quickly pledged their support, including the Pakistani Taliban, *Ansar Al-Sharia* in Yemen and the Abu Bakar Ba'asyir-led *Jamaat Ansarul Sunnah* in Indonesia,[10] many others contested the declaration, including the Muslim Brotherhood in Egypt and high profile global Islamist group *Hizbut Tahrir* (Osman 2014: 1).[11] At the time of writing, the self-declared IS caliphate in the conflict region appears to be on the brink of collapse, as key strongholds are lost (Silva 2016).

In fact, the putative claim to caliphate by IS is unlikely to dent the romanticised ideal of caliphate in general terms, since utopian visions are routinely pitched against present chaos and perceived anarchy (Werbner 2004), even while factionalism pulls them apart. As Osman (2014: 2) argues, the contemporary ideal of caliphate is 'an imagined construct that never existed in Islamic history'. Turner (2007: 132) maintains that the historical fragmentation and breakdown of traditional Islamic authority gave rise primarily to 'an inflationary expansion of claims to purity and strictness that has a compulsory upward trajectory'. For many Muslims today, this trajectory is realised by emphasis on the accomplishment of personal piety and spiritual self-purification, not on imagined utopia. Utopias – by definition – transcend existing spatial and temporal boundaries, and this transcendence is intensified in virtual reality. In urban late modernity, the space of flows (Castells 1996) dissolves time through disordering any string of events so they seem coterminous. Thus the sacred here and now of religious faith becomes simultaneously something which has always nascently existed and which will be fully delivered in the future. In that sense, reinvented religious movements capture the atemporal sentiment of being-in-the-world, invoking new imaginings of self and society redeemed from the past and projected into the future (Robins 1995). The idea of caliphate is enduring.

Most sociological theorists have been scathing on the topic of utopia. For example, Karl Marx (1985) criticised utopian thinking because it emphasised speculation without concrete analysis of prevailing socio-economic conditions. Karl Mannheim maintained 'a state of mind is utopian when (a) it is incongruous with the immediate situation and (b) when passed onto actions, tends to shatter the order of things' (1936: 341). According to Zygmunt Bauman (1976) a utopia is socially constructed out of desire for transformation, but is ultimately unworkable. Yet the desire to imagine a different world or a different world order arises from a 'gap between the needs and wants generated by a particular society and the satisfactions available to and distributed by it' (Levitas 2010: 210). So 'we should take imagination and the imaginary reconstitution of society more seriously' (Levitas 2010: 41). Applying this advice, it seems the attractive idea behind caliphate is that a deeply religious ontology will be distinctly different to a secular ontology. Religious ontology inheres in transcendent faith rather than logic, rationality and proof. For example, in reciting the Koran and reading it over and over again, the book itself is constituted as the actuality of God through the engagement of the pious follower. In a similar way, the caliphate is imagined as a distinctive polity where religious ontology constitutes everyday reality, so the immanence of God is everywhere. In online propaganda designed to appeal to the imagination of young Muslims in the diaspora, junior jihadis are sometimes referred to as young lions in the Islamist struggle; 'cubs of the caliphate'.

The final battle

The idea of final victory in the meta-narrative is a popular theme for a younger generation of Muslims reared on Hollywood action blockbusters (Werbner 2004). According to IS ideology the site of the newly proclaimed caliphate – greater Syria – *Al-Sham* – will also be the location of the final war before the day of judgement. Their message is that the ultimate battle between good (Muslims) and evil (infidels) will take place here, so true followers of Islam must join them. This will be an 'end-of-days' Armageddon.

According to millennial discourse, the armies who fight the final battle will be led by two mythical figures from centuries-old Islamic prophecies. First is the *Dajjal*, a kind of Antichrist (Werbner 2004: 454) who will lead an army of infidels and deceived Muslims. The second mythical figure, and polar opposite, is the *Mahdi*, the Muslim 'messiah' (Drissel 2011: 145) who will lead true Muslims to victory. Drissel (2011: 163–4) identifies three millennial versions of the *Dajjal*. In the first version the *Dajjal* is an actual person – a wicked yet charismatic man who will rise to power through deception. The second version presents the *Dajjal* as a depraved nation (or group of nations), which is especially malevolent toward the Muslim world. In the third version the *Dajjal* is the Dark Messiah who leads the evil hegemonic global empire against Muslims. There is less ambivalence about the *Mahdi*. He is the 'Prince of the South' who wields his conquering sword of justice at the head of a righteous army and defeats the military might of the *Dajjal*. Some sources propose the newly proclaimed caliph Abu Bakr al-Baghdadi in eastern Syria is the *Mahdi*. Other sources claim he is the *Dajjal*, the great deceiver. In any case, the millennial, apocalyptic version of the Islamist meta-narrative is an attractive story for a new generation of Muslim youth, and for extremist recruiters. This is discussed further in the next chapter. The millennial example shows that simple epic narratives are a principal means through which radical Islamist groups share information with, and attempt to influence, the public (Braddock 2012: 116). The final battle is a vital component of the 'big' story of radical Islam because it represents a heroic union with God at the point of death in war.

The radical Islamist meta-narrative and the US war on terror

In terms of 'big' stories, the radical Islamist meta-narrative has been met and matched on Western soil with a similar military battle discourse: the war on terror. There is a close thematic relationship between the Islamist meta-narrative and the US war on terror that was launched after 9/11. The same can be said for Western European countries. For example, in Denmark the 'totalizing discourse' of the war on terror in post-9/11 news media treated Denmark 'as a unitary actor that opposes itself to "Islam", "Muslim culture", "The Muslim World", and "The Muslim Community"' (Hervik 2015: 67). In the process, Danish citizens from specific ethnic backgrounds were reified as the Muslim 'Other' to be hated and feared. The actual horrifying events of 9/11 could conceivably been viewed as appalling international crimes against humanity. However, the instant response of the US and its Western allies was to narratively frame an epic 'war' that required the mustering of military might.

In fact, the war on terror in any part of the diaspora uses almost exactly the same story as the radical Islamist meta-narrative, but with moral polarities reversed. The two big stories are similar because they are both simply structured plots of oppression, outrage, revenge and final victory. Meta-narrative as a form of melodrama reduces complexity and ambivalence by starkly presenting 'us against them', and 'good against evil' (Anker 2005). As Wright (2015: 9) points out, any melodramatic meta-narrative 'taps into our fascination and facilitates our projection and we are attracted to it for these reasons', whether by loving it or hating it. Thus the polarity of the war on terror mirrors the radical Islamist meta-narrative by placing a Muslim identity on one side and a Western identity on the other side, with black and white moral values reversed. That is, the definition of normality takes place through a simultaneous negation of its opposite (Foucault 2003). Here the enemy is the oriental 'Other' of Islam (see Said 1978, 1997). If we look analytically at the dramatic story encoded in the war on terror, points of similarity with the radical Islamist meta-narrative can be quickly recognised. It not only uses the same story, it basically is the same story turned around.

In the war on terror 'crisis' narrative of threat and suspicion, Americans are scripted as 'innocent', 'good', 'heroic', 'decent' and upholders of 'civilization' (Jackson 2009: 28); defenders of the 'free' world. In war-on-terror rhetoric, the 'beauty' of America is emphasised against the 'evil' of Muslim terrorism (Abu El-Haj 2010). Between the designated good and the evil there will be a 'just war'; one where Western forces will use extraordinary military measures that are normally disallowed, but which are justified in the new 'age of terror' (Jackson 2009: 28–29), because the events of 9/11 were 'acts of war' carried out by Muslim militants. Dubnick et al. (2009: 19) argue that after 9/11, the United States declared the war on terror with no effective 'state of war narrative' such as that has characterised American involvement in other theatres of actual conflict. In that sense, the war on terror represents a revivified version of the Cold War, rather than an actual war. The message was that 'the Muslims' were 'coming for us' (Kundani 2014: 1).

In speeches to US parliament and CIA briefing papers, Islamist terrorist actions were said to constitute a 'new Pearl Harbor' which demanded retaliation. It would be a 'long war' and demand 'a major *collective* effort' from American society (Jackson 2009: 26–27, my emphasis). The 'enemy' was constructed as 'a massive, global terrorist' force that *threatens* not only America, but the whole 'civilised' world and its 'entire way of life'. *Al-Qaeda* was claimed to be assembling thousands of sophisticated, ruthless, fanatical, well-resourced, and determined terrorist killers, 'schooled in the methods of murder' and just waiting to strike again. Muslim terrorist cells were planning to use weapons of mass destruction (WMD) on American cities. These genocidal weapons were supplied by 'rogue regimes' such as Iraq and other countries along the 'axis of evil' (Jackson 2009: 27). The 'enemy within' was made up of terrorist 'sleeper cells' existing side by side with ordinary Americans. Patriotic unity was demanded. The public was urged to exercise surveillance over their fellow (implicitly Muslim) citizens and over immigrants (from Muslim countries).

Thus the war-on-terror narrative holds up a morally reversed mirror to the radical Islamist meta-narrative. First, there is emphasis on the global – either 'taking over the world', or 'defending the world', which are both assertions of *superiority*. Second, each narrative expresses the aim of dominating the 'other' by defending the defined *superior* values of faith/morality in the Islamist version, and freedom/democracy in the Western version. Pleas for the *mobilisation* of Western patriots echo pleas for *mobilising* the *ummah*. The West is depicted as *vulnerable* to Muslim terrorist attack, just as Islam is threatened with extinction (*vulnerability*) by the West in the radical Islamist meta-narrative. Identifying 'rogue regimes' and countries along the 'axis of evil' mirrors the extremist identification of apostate nations which *cannot be trusted* and therefore must be attacked, invaded and harried. The use of extraordinary military means in the war on terror by the US and its allies is justified as a form of *anti-helplessness* because the enemy could attack anywhere and at any time, just as Muslims everywhere are urged to fight back against the West everywhere so as not be positioned as *helpless*. Finally, the war-on-terror narrative stresses the epic scale of the enemy force and the vast parameters of the 'just war'. These are features which echo the glorious 'final battle' of global proportions in the radical Islamist meta-narrative.[12] Other scholars have noted the narrative similarity. For example, 'what is most remarkable about the xenophobic narratives of Islamaphobia (sic) and their counterparts among Muslim radicals and extremists is that they appear to echo and mirror each other' (El-Affendi 2009: 46). A most important effect of moral panics is that they 'stimulate a sense of an imagined community' (Wright 2015: 7), not only among those deemed the victims/heroes in the story, but among those constructed as villains. In this case, it happens on both sides.

Abdul Haleem (2010: 164) feels that 'Muslim extremists and anti-Muslim propagandists hold the same views'. Both negatively stereotype the 'other', and both inaccurately report the Koran. Another study echoes the same point. 'The West is a construct imagined and described as the opposite of

Islamic virtue and justice' (Cheong and Halverson 2010: 1113), just as the Muslim Other is imagined in the war on terror as cruelly alien to core democratic values. Al Raffie (2012: 14) hypothesises that the narrative match has the unfortunate effect of cementing core jihadist messages in everyone's minds – Muslims and non-Muslims alike.

The highly influential war-on-terror narrative is disseminated around the world. It is a 'living discourse' that creates for people in the West a 'grid of intelligibility' through which to interpret events and make decisions (Jackson 2009: 30), just as the radical Islamist meta-narrative attempts to appeal as a grid of intelligibility for Muslims worldwide. Both 'ascribe to the drama that unfolds in the battle between good and evil'. People 'position themselves within the narrative as one of the core characters: as a villain, a victim or a hero' (Wright 2015: 13). Thus Muslim youth in the diaspora are exposed to both the radical Islamist meta-narrative and the semantically reversed war-on-terror narrative at one and the same time. They are positioned as heroic protagonists in the radical Islamist narrative and as the villainous Other in its Western counterpart of the war on terror. Both narratives point in hyperbolic terms to 'what Muslims might be capable of'. Young Muslims living in Western countries constitute their subjectivity and position their identities as 'good' or 'bad' in relation to each big story, which offers them contradictory moral positions. It is not surprising then that they create complex counter-narratives of who they are.

Dealing with radical discourse

One story of a Muslim girl arriving in Australia to confront this post-9/11 dual reality exemplifies how some young people deal with the resulting tensions. She writes:

> My parents, who had once dictated the rules that governed our relatively moderate Muslim upbringing in Pakistan, were suddenly not calling the shots.
> (Anooshe Mushtaq 2015)

Anooshe's family were moderate Muslims in Pakistan, and she grew up surrounded and protected by parental authority. In the new country, that parental authority diminished relative to strong local voices from the religion, and presumably, the surrounding mainstream fear of Muslims. Significantly, since Anooshe had only read the Koran in Arabic, she had never really grasped its content:

> In Pakistan we grow up with the idea that reading the Koran in Arabic has more *sawab* (ie. you will be rewarded) than reading it in English. The only problem was that I never fully understood what I was reading.
> (Anooshe Mushtaq 2015)

In other words she did not have a deep knowledge of her religion so she did not feel she had an informed theological position from which to speak, and neither did her peers. Tradition demanded that they should not question the wisdom of their elders. Challenging the opinions of religious preachers was not allowed at all according to traditional norms, so 'to question their judgment would be to risk gruesome punishments in the afterlife' (Anooshe Mushtaq 2015). In retrospect, she believes this is the reason some of her Muslim peers were susceptible to extremist messages. Those messages seemed to be based on authoritative readings of the Koran by Muslim preachers: 'some imams constantly deliver anti-West sermons. The Muslims who seek advice from these authority figures trust their word' (Anooshe Mushtaq 2015). In her view it was theological ignorance that favoured susceptibility to the extremist anti-Western views of some local preachers. However, Anooshe herself formulated her own challenge by embracing the norms of her new country while remaining Muslim.

Ryan's (2014) study reveals a similar dilemma for young diasporic Muslims who found they did not have a practical knowledge of Islamic teachings. When they became devout they moved beyond recitation in Arabic to actively reading the Koran as a charter for human rights. From this base, they were able to more effectively construct their identities as pious young Muslims against the background of Islamophobia – both individually and collectively. Ryan's analysis of interviews shows how their individual narratives blended discourses of 'freedom' and 'choice' with 'observance of prescriptive Qur'anic instructions'. In short, they constituted themselves as 'modern', theologically-informed Muslims compared to the 'traditional' ethnic cultures of their parents (Ryan 2014: 455). In both cases it seems that deeper theological knowledge persuaded them against sympathy for extremist actions. The study by Bartlett and Miller (2011) confirmed that violent radicals hold simplistic ideas about Islam, while non-violent radicals are much more knowledgeable about sacred texts and theological complexity. The two examples just above, one from Australia and one from the UK, point to the rise of reflexive individualism as young Muslims become responsible for creatively designing their own identities in late modernity. It seems Islam has become an important marker for self-esteem even as multi-faith secular democracy is actively embraced.

Conclusion

This chapter has considered the radical Islamist meta-narrative in relation to young Muslims in the diaspora. It was pointed out that while there are many versions of the radical Islamist meta-narrative in circulation, the basic story remains more or less the same. The key concepts of jihad, caliphate and final battle were examined, on the premise that they have particular appeal for extremist recruits. Finally, the Islamist meta-narrative and the US-driven war on terror were shown to not only follow the same genre of melodramatic military story, but to be basically the same story, with names changed and moral polarities reversed. The effect of this double narrative on young Muslims in the diaspora was considered through some examples, and will be taken up more fully in the next chapter.

Notes

1 *Sharia* guides both religious and secular duties. The matter of how it should be applied in modern states is argued differently by Muslim traditionalists and reformists.
2 The aftermath of the July 2016 attempted military coup in Turkey raises some questions on this matter, however.
3 Ignorance, lack of God-awareness.
4 Zackie uses the term discourse rather than belief.
5 Especially through *sharia* courts and the issuing of *fatwa,* as well as the production of scholarly writing.
6 The author has read the Koran in translation.
7 Some passages in the *hadith* explicitly praise martyrdom in the service of God and urge others to follow. They are often cited in exhortations to undertake terrorist missions.
8 For example, *Abu Nidal* Organisation (ANO), *Abu Sayyaf* Group (ASG), *Al-Aqsa* Martyrs Brigade, *Ansar al-Islam* (AI), Armed Islamic Group (GIA), *Asbat al-Ansar, Gama'a al-Islamiyya* (IG), *Harakat ul-Mujahidin* (HUM), *Jaish-e-Mohammed* (JEM), *Jemaah Islamiya* (JI), *Al-Jihad* (AJ), *Lashkar e-Tayyiba* (LT), *Lashkar i Jhangvi* (LJ), Libyan Islamic Fighting Group (LIFG), *Mujahedin-e Khalq* Organization (MEK), Salafist Group for Call and Combat (GSPC), *Tanzim Qa'idat al-Jihad fi Bilad al-Rafidayn* (QJBR), *Al Shabaab, Ansar al Sharia* (Libya), *Ansar al Sharia* (Tunisia), *Jemaah Islamiyah* (Syria), *Abu Sayyaf* (Syria), *Ansar Bayt Al-Maqdis* (Syria), *Al-Nusra* Front (Syria), *Jaish al-Muhajireen wal-Ansar* (JAMWA), *Harakat Sham al-Islam* (HSI), *Al-Qaeda* in the Islamic Maghrib (AQIM), *Al-Qaeda* in the Arabian Peninsula (AQAP), *Jabhat al-Nusra, Tehrik-e Taliban Pakistan* (TTP), *Jundallah*, Army of Islam (AOI), Indian *Mujahidin* (IM), *Jemaah Anshorut Tawhid* (JAT), *Abdallah Azzam* Brigades (AAB), *Haqqani* Network (HQN) *Ansar al-Dine* (AAD), *Ansar'u al-Mulathamun* Battalion, *Ansar al-Shari'a* in Benghazi, *Ansar al-Shari'a* in Darnah, and so on.
9 Brandon (2008) uses the term 'virtual caliphate' to designate the detailed fantasy space online that offers Muslims a foretaste.
10 By 1 May 2015, the following groups had pledged their allegiance or expressed support for the IS-declared caliphate: *al-I'tisam* of the Koran and Sunnah [Sudan], *Abu Sayyaf* Group [Philippines], *Ansar al-Khilafah* [Philippines], *Ansar al-Tawhid* in India [India], *Bangsamoro* Islamic Freedom Fighters (BIFF) [Philippines], *Bangsmoro* Justice Movement (BJM) [Philippines], *al-Huda* Battalion in Maghreb of Islam [Algeria], Heroes of Islam Brigade in Khorasan [Afghanistan], The Soldiers of the Caliphate in Algeria [Algeria], *Jundullah* [Pakistan], Islamic Movement of Uzbekistan (IMU) [Pakistan], Islamic Youth Shura Council [Libya], *Jaish al-Sahabah* in the Levant [Syria], Faction of *Katibat al-Imam Bukhari* [Syria], *Jamaat Ansar Bait al-Maqdis* [Egypt], *Jund al-Khilafah* in Egypt [Egypt], *Liwa Ahrar al-Sunna* in Baalbek [Lebanon], Islamic State Libya (Darnah) [Libya], Lions of Libya [Libya], *Shura* Council of *Shabab al-Islam Darnah* [Libya], *Mujahideen Indonesia Timor* (MIT) [Indonesia], *Mujahideen Shura* Council in the Environs of Jerusalem (MSCJ) [Egypt], *Tehreek-e-Khilafat* [Pakistan], *Okba Ibn Nafaa* Battalion [Tunisia], *Mujahideen* of Yemen [Yemen], Supporters for the Islamic State in Yemen

[Yemen], *al-Tawheed* Brigade in Khorasan [Afghanistan], Supporters of the Islamic State in the Land of the Two Holy Mosques [Saudi Arabia], *Ansar al-Islam* [Iraq], Leaders of the *Mujahid* in Khorasan (ten former TTP commanders) [Pakistan], *Boko Haram* [Nigeria], *Jund al-Khilafah* in Tunisia [Tunisia], *Jemaah Islamiyah* [Philippines].

11 Pankhurst (2013) maintains that the adoption of the caliphate ideal by both the Muslim Brotherhood and *Al-Qaeda* is half-hearted, and rather incidental to their doctrine and programmes, while *Hizbut Tahrir's* primary quest is the re-establishment of caliphate.

12 Moreover, in pragmatic terms, use of the term 'war', in the title 'war on terror' retrospectively validated Osama bin Laden's 1996 formal declaration of war on the United States.

Chapter 3

Muslim youth radicalisation

Introduction

In the previous chapter we looked briefly at two examples of faithful young Muslims who constructed late modern identities in the diaspora. In doing so they committed themselves to gaining a deep knowledge of the religion, and therefore established a stable, theologically-informed subject position as proponents of peace and harmony. Yet it is clear that some young Muslims in the diaspora are convinced by extremist messages and head in the opposite direction. However, nobody knows precisely why one alienated Muslim youth becomes radicalised while another finds no attraction in extremism. In fact there is 'no single, unifying "terrorist profile" that predicts who will become a violent radical or a terrorist' in Western countries (RAND Europe 2011: 11).[1] Neither is there a viable profile of the characteristics of individuals who become group-based terrorists (McCauley and Moskalenko 2014: 69). So in essence, we still do not know 'what leads a person to turn to political violence' (Sageman 2014: 565). Even so, the search for causes is ongoing.

Becoming radical

As stated previously, becoming an Islamist does not automatically connote that a young person will engage in the conduct of jihadi violence. It is a series of choices. Roy (2007) points out that many never make the choice to proceed to violence. However, many Islamists pledge support for the principle of militant jihad, so it is not the case that Islamism has nothing to do with jihad. Western commentators deploying war-on-terror rhetoric routinely frame intense Muslim religiosity as the precursor to jihadi terrorism, even though the causal evidence is thin. For example, Silber and Bhatt (2007: 16) from the New York Police Department define radicalisation as the development of an 'extreme belief system [Islamism] to the point where it acts as a catalyst for a terrorist act'. In short, radical religious beliefs are activated by some kind of input so that individuals go on to become terrorists (Kundnani 2012; Dalgaard-Nielsen 2010; Kühle and Lindekilde 2010). Efforts to understand why such terrorism occurs, and attempts to prevent it, rely on this logic. A further strong belief is that 'youth are particularly prone to violent radicalisation processes that lead to religiously motivated terrorist acts' (Ramakrishna 2011: 1). The result is a masculine stereotype – *young, Muslim, violent*.

Typical evolutionary models of radicalisation are ladders, pyramids or staircases which start from simply being Muslim. Thus the popular pyramid model, as described in the previous chapter, rises from the largest level at the bottom, consisting of Muslims who are neutrally oriented, to subsequent levels, each with diminishing numbers, until the small apex of terrorism is reached (McCauley and Moskalenko 2014). The evolutionary schema is sustained in Moghaddam's (2005) 'narrowing staircase' model. Halafoff and Wright-Neville (2009) added detail to the pyramid schema so that as individuals rise upwards through the levels they are more and more alienated from their immediate communities (see also Rahimullah et al. 2013). Pantucci (2015) offers the very different analogy of a fruit machine. A jihadist recruiter looking for new militants hits the 'jackpot' when three drivers – ideology, grievance and mobilisation – all come together at the same time in a young Muslim. However, none of this modelling tells us what actually happens in the mysterious gap between Islamic piety and violence. All we know for certain is that 'all terrorists are radicals but not all radicals are terrorists' (Pisoiu 2013: 247).

Terrorist action is not the inevitable outcome of Muslim religious intensification. Bartlett and Miller (2012) productively distinguish between 'non-violent radicalization' and 'violent radicalization'. They found that while violent radicals clearly supported violent jihad in the West, non-violent radicals did not (see also McCauley and Moskalenko 2014). It seems that deeper theological knowledge dissuades young adherents from sympathy for extremist actions. Bartlett and Miller (2011) found that violent radicals hold simplistic ideas about Islam, while non-violent radicals were much more knowledgeable about sacred texts and theological complexity. Similarly, Sageman (2008) and also Roy (2007), maintain that jihadi groups are driven less by deep Islamic doctrine and more by anti-American and anti-Israel military intentions. In short, it seems that the greater the focus on actual knowledge about Islam, the less likely it is that the follower will favour violence. Moreover, the process of becoming radical is non-linear and indeterminate; 'individuals can turn away or be pushed away from further radicalisation at each and every stage' (RAND Europe 2011: 5). While the impact of radical religious authorities such as extremist preachers has certainly had influence in some cases (O'Neill and McGrory 2006), in other cases the process is one of 'self-radicalization' (Kirby 2007: 415) or the horizontal radicalisation of a small group of friends. Diverse factors of choice are clearly at play.

Islamist radicalisation of youth: factors and accounts

The single most common factor is youth (Roy 2008; Sirseloudi 2012). Yet youth is also the common factor in a range of other troubling and criminal phenomena, so that single fact tells us little. It demonstrates correlation, not causality. Moreover, as Sageman (2008: 5) points out, 'millions of second-generation children of immigrants are subjected to prejudice throughout the West, but very few become terrorists'.

Nevertheless, research on possible 'causes' of the radicalisation of Muslim youth has been conducted in a range of academic disciplines. Leaving aside political science accounts that primarily emphasise macro perspectives, the fields of both psychology and sociology have produced accounts as to 'why' individuals become radicalised. Psychological accounts of Muslim radicalisation have, for example, identified individual factors such as 'uncertainty' (Hogg et al. 2013; Hogg and Adelman 2013), 'cognitive dissonance' (Maikovich 2005), and a deficient 'personal construct' (Canter et al. 2014). On the other hand, sociological accounts have most often looked for explanations in deficient structural conditions and marginal social contexts (for example Hassan 2010; Sohrabi and Farquharson 2015). Both disciplines have favoured a biographical approach – focusing on the individual to examine characteristics and background factors that could explain why they became radical.

Accounts from the field of psychology

There is an abundance of psychological studies of Muslim radicalisation and progression to militant action in the diaspora (King and Taylor 2011). The discussion below looks at some selected examples that have something to add to the arguments made in this book. In pop psychology, the oft-expressed belief about Islamist terrorists is that they behave and think the way they do because they are deranged, or at best infantile, narcissistic and unstable, so their acts of violence stem express uncontrolled impotence and frustration. However, testing convicted terrorists for these distinctive psychological traits has not revealed them as common at all (Pisoiu 2013; Sageman 2008). The more cautious finding from Veldhuis and Staun (2009) is that at the micro-individual level, young recruits to extremism showed perception of discrimination against them. This sense of discrimination might be amplified by personality characteristics like authoritarianism and narcissism in some cases.

Islamist radicalisation is more convincingly understood in the field as a quite rare theological-psychological process activated by group dynamics and/or personal trauma (RAND Europe 2011; Doosje et al. 2013). In a study of Muslim youth in the Netherlands it was found that susceptibility to adopting a 'radical belief system' comprised four elements:

> (1) perceiving out-group authorities as illegitimate; (2) perceiving the in-group as superior, (3) perceiving distance towards other people, and (4) feeling alienated and disconnected from society.
>
> (Doosje et al. 2013: 600)

Three indicators of youth engagement were identified: 'high levels of perceived injustice, personal uncertainty, and group threat' (Doosje et al. 2013: 586). Yet these identified indicators are neither causal nor predictive. The same indicators apply in principle to a much larger number of Muslim youth, and to ethnic or otherwise marginalised youth, rather than just the very small minority who take up a radical Islamist position.

Also within the field of social psychology, Rahimullah et al. (2013) identified multiple 'risk factors' for a possible Muslim youth pathway towards violent radicalism in Western countries. Religious risk factors included: the *salafi/wahhabi* movement, radical Muslim figures, justification of Muslim terrorism, perceived scholarly authority, and transitional religious experiences, especially conversion. Personal risk factors were lack of social integration, a feeling of anomie[2] and whether or not the individual suffered from narcissism. Moral disengagement, terror management (death made more salient) and uncertainty reduction were also named. A further risk factor was perception of injustice in Western policies towards Muslim countries. Notably, the social risk factor was not socio-economic disadvantage per se, but the 'perceived disadvantage of fellow Muslims, locally or internationally' (Rahimullah et al. 2013: 24). These last two risk factors would seem to usefully distinguish the possible pathway of radical Islamist youth from that of other discontented or troubled youth.

Veldhuis and Staun (2009) propose three radicalisation levels: macro, micro-social, and micro-individual. At the macro level, factors include international relations, poverty, and globalisation/modernisation. At the microsocial level, issues include social identity, social interaction and group processes. At the micro-individual level there was a sense of relative deprivation. The recruits were theorised to feel a great need for significant recognition (see Honneth 1996). Veldhuis and Staun (2009) list three catalysts for the cognitive progression towards radicalisation: active recruitment, exposure to radical media via the internet (see also Torres Soriano 2012; Weimann 2006), and large-scale trigger events. Notably, these identified catalysts are all exterior to the young person rather than deriving from a pre-existing psychological weakness or a history of deprivation.

Hogg and Adelman (2013) emphasise the uncertainty–identity nexus in their account of why some young people join radical groups. They propose that when beset by self-uncertainty about identity, joining a group with strong boundaries, such as an extreme religious group, bestows a sense of certainty for young people. This seems to support the 'bunch of guys' thesis (Sageman 2008, see below). Joining an Islamist group is then understood as *one way* to solve the 'existential frustration' of youth, the depressing sense that 'one's life is meaningless, directionless, boring, banal, uneventful, anodyne, soulless, aimless, passive, cowardly', by offering excitement, meaning and glory (Cottee and Hayward 2011: 979). Finally, in social psychology studies that overlap with criminology, the similarity between joining a radical group and joining a gang has often been pointed out. For example, Mullins (2009) recognises similarity in Muslim youth radicalisation and pathways into crime, since youthful recruits share similar cognitive progressions towards a 'deviant career' (Becker 1973). Once again this tends to support Sageman's (2008) thesis, which is described at length below.

This brief review of social psychology studies indicates some useful understandings, but also reveals the lack of a definitive causal model for exactly what causes a young Muslim to take up a radical Islamist position. While some productive variables and risk factors have been identified, most hold true for much greater numbers of young Muslims (and young people generally) than just the very few who step onto a radical Islamist path. As Pisoiu argues critically, 'it remains largely unclear how these various types of factors "contribute" to radicalization, apart from being simple independent variables' (2013: 251). We are reminded once again of Roy's (2007) comment that there is no viable way to predict what kind of young Muslim in a Western country might or might not become a violent Islamist radical.

Accounts from the field of sociology

There is a flourishing market in sociological accounts of Muslim radicalisation in the diaspora. The discussion here selects a sample of studies that productively advance our understanding of the phenomenon. Sociological accounts often suggest that Muslim youth radicalisation is an outcome of experiencing Islamophobic prejudice in the prevailing moral panic, in a context sharpened by lack of socio-economic opportunities (for example, Spalek and Lambert 2008; Hassan 2010; Sohrabi and Farquharson 2015; Mandaville 2007a; Poynting and Mason 2007; Noble and Poynting 2008; Back et al. 2009; Hassan 2010; Kundnani 2012; Fasenfest 2015). Many argue strongly that socio-economic disadvantage among Muslims in the West increases the risk of radicalisation (for example Hassan 2010). Yet this is clearly not the whole story, and Islamist recruits in the West do not necessarily hail from poor and marginalised situations (Sageman 2008). In fact quite a few are well educated. Certainly Beski-Chafiq et al. (2010: 12) found that Islamist radicalisation among French youth could not be explained by socioeconomic problems alone. Instead they found a 'search for recognition, an ideal or a connection, particularly in case of resentment against injustice, humiliation or experiences of exclusion'. It seems clear that rather like over-determined accounts from psychology, sociological theorising of primary socio-economic causes is rather weak because there are far, far more poor and disenfranchised Muslim youth in the diaspora than ever turn to extremism. In general, I found that the more nuanced the account, the more useful it was for the arguments presented in this book.

There is a strong sociological claim that young Muslims seek out an Islamist cultural identity because they feel marginalised in the broader non-Muslim society (see Lynch 2015), and in the generational divide of their own ethnic group (Kühle and Lindekilde 2010; Kashyap and Lewis 2013). For example, Schmidt's (2004) extensive study recorded intense Islamic identity formation among young Muslims in three Western countries. Through this collective identity they gained a sense of belonging to a much larger and more heroic Muslim constituency than the local ethnic group. Feelings of marginalisation tend to be far more acute among second generation immigrants than among recent arrivals (Hage 2011). In this 'problem of the generations' (Mannheim 1952) it seems the very question of how to live within the faith is contested. In short, the sense of being Muslim – in the pan-Islamic sense – is understood as more marked for young people in relevant ethnic communities in the West than for their parents' generation (Bayat and Herrera 2010). The feeling of 'belonging' as a Muslim to a cross-ethnic *ummah* has become most pertinent for young people struggling to establish a bicultural identity in conditions of Islamophobia, an experience that Hage (2011) describes as 'shattering':

> While a fragmented subject can always manage to pull themselves together to be operational in the world, the shattered racialised person needs a space immune from the effect of racism in order to 'pick up the pieces' as it were. It is here that Islamic religion has been playing an important role among Muslim youth in the west.
>
> (Hage 2011: 170–171)

In other words, culturally identifying as piously Muslim can provide a kind of 'immune space' in which to pick up the pieces of a self-esteem compromised by racism/Islamophobia. However, there are other ways to create this kind of 'ontological security' (Giddens 1991: 44) and remain within the faith.

Sirseloudi's (2012) research on Islamism among Turkish youth in Germany emphasises generational tensions in the diaspora. When young Muslim Turks leave the familiar world of their families and school, 'they are shown that they are not wanted in this group, the German one, which they want to belong to in order to dissociate from their parents' (Sirseloudi 2012: 816). They are implicitly thrown back to the ethnic group of origin from which they want to separate themselves because the elders are behind the times and condemn them for their adolescent behaviour. In this context, radical Islam seems to offer an attractive solution because it gives 'simple explanations for a complex world' (Sirseloudi 2012: 816). It should be noted that Sirseloudi's account did not identify the factor of socio-economic deprivation.

Taking a different tack, German sociologist Ulrich Beck (2010) identified resurgent religion not only as a contemporary risk but a resource. Piety certainly figures in post-traditional lifestyles (Turner 2011). People look for a 'God of one's own', removed from the constraints of tradition (Beck 2010: 79). This kind of reflexive religiosity meets people's yearning for security and belonging. Resurgent religious faith thus represents 'moral fixity in day-to-day life' (Giddens 1991: 207). In this reinvention, religious traditions of the past are reflexively mined for narratives and strictures which construct a valid-seeming life pathway (Speck 2013). Young people increasingly define themselves through 'individually expressive personal action frames mobilized around personal lifestyle values' (Bennett 2012: 20). Yet since the very concept of identity is born from the crisis of belonging (Bauman 2004: 20) collective identity is vitally important (Castells 1996). Active participation in the movement of global Islam constitutes a strong collective identity (Wiktorowicz 2003) for young Muslims in the diaspora who feel disconnected from civic participation and are confused by 'individualised ethical, consumption and lifestyle choices' (Harris and Roose 2014: 807).

Religious resurgence promises an empowered self characterised by intensity of affect. 'Enjoyment of faith, a pleasure in belief, in being in touch with God are clearly manifested (...) this religiosity is modern, based on the idea that the self is at the centre' (Roy 2004: 31). Such engagement is very much about emotion and pleasure; the joyous sensation of transcendental connection and salvation that is world-shaping and life-changing. For example, a personal, affective engagement with the Islamist meta-narrative is offered by membership of the worldwide radical organisation *Hizbut Tahrir*. Here youth can daringly experience the heroic cutting edge of Islamism without committing to the worrying trajectory of actually conducting militant violence, since this group ostensibly offers support only for the *logic* of violent jihad.

Muslim youth radicalisation is also seen in sociological terms as a social movement. This kind of social movement is a loose configuration (Butler 2015). For example, the Occupy Wall Street movement was not a campaigning youth movement with a concrete goal but was 'meant more as a way of life that spreads through contagion' (Rushkoff 2013: 57). This bears comparison to the social movement-like phenomenon of Muslim youth radicalisation worldwide (Sirseloudi 2012). Sharing common ground with other forms of collective dissent, young Islamist radicals define for themselves what should be the principles of their lives. 'They never refer to traditions or to traditional Islam, they don't mention *fatwa*[s] from established clerics' (Roy 2008: 15). As a social movement they creatively harness the cultural energy of marginalisation across the diverse contexts of the diaspora.

In summary, both psychological and sociological accounts are useful for understanding some of the background conditions, situations and processes that might favour a youthful move towards Islamist radicalism. Yet fully causal explanations have yet to be convincingly identified (Roy 2008; Sageman 2008; Wiktorowicz 2003; Kundnani 2012; McCauley and Moskalenko 2014; RAND Europe 2011; Doosje et al. 2013). It is time to consider some other explanations.

A 'bunch of guys' saving the world

Marc Sageman's 2008 book, *Leaderless Jihad: Terror Networks in the Twenty-first Century*, provides a different kind of argument. As a previous forensic psychiatrist, Sageman effectively challenges popular understandings of the 'typical' young Islamist terrorist. After analysing 500 cases he concludes that the commonly cited factors of socio-economic disadvantage, low education, family problems, religious indoctrination, sexual frustration, prior criminality and psychological abnormality are not significant. He does, however, identify like-minded gender-peer networking as significant.

Bringing together some of the new social movement theorising, Sageman (2008) proposes that pro-jihadi radicalisation develops through collective ties of kinship and friendship. His findings turn our attention to the question of who knows who, rather than who knows what – theologically. Networks of young jihadi sympathisers form and expand on the basis of contacts and connections, both online and offline. A key component of their bonding is that they come to believe themselves to be collectively following the right path. In an earlier book, Sageman (2004) concluded from studying a smaller sample of terrorists that ideology and political grievances did not matter very much during the early stage of involvement. Rather those who would later become terrorists felt isolated and lonely. These same young men would congregate at mosques where they found others like them. They often formed close-knit groups while sharing *halal* food together. Thus the 'bunch of guys' that evolved from shared talk and action came to represent a closed society of peers. From this affiliation, a sense of meaningful identity developed that the 'guys' had not found as individuals.

Sageman identifies a non-linear, loosely bounded, radicalisation process by which the terrorist subject position comes about. First, the individual experiences feelings of moral outrage because of perceived crimes against Muslims both worldwide and at a local level. Second, these feelings of anger and resentment are interpreted as evidence of a war against Muslims and against Islam itself. Finally:

> This ideology appeals to certain people because it *resonates with their own personal experiences* of discrimination, making them feel that they are also victims of the wider war. A few individuals are then *mobilized through networks*, both face to face and now more and more commonly online, to become terrorists.
>
> (Sageman 2008: viii, emphasis in original)

The structural resemblance between this explanation and the radical Islamist meta-narrative must be obvious. As a member of a daring and heroic 'bunch of guys' who believe themselves to be on a world-saving mission, individual young men find a high level of recognition and legitimation.

Sageman's account resonates with a much earlier landmark work on radicalism by Lofland and Stark (1965). The authors propose that new recruits to religious fundamentalism are attracted by the idea of becoming a world-saver. Affiliation with the radical group provides them with a sense of higher purpose. They gain strong new social bonds, and stimulating personal goals. Thus conversion gives a young person a problem-solving identity as a religious seeker with special knowledge who can help change the world. The significant 'world-saving' change prefigured in an Islamist position is the eventual governance of all Muslims by *sharia* law within the structure of a traditional Islamic caliphate (Kepel 2004). For example, the convicted jihadis studied by Ali and Moss (2010: 41) all subscribed to 'utopian thinking'. In pursuit of an idealised caliphate, 'they were willing to accept violence as a necessary measure'. Thus the immanence of the past leans into the decision-making of the present. There is a lost place of perfection and they have strong feelings about why and how it will be restored. In their view 'saving the world' justifies the use of violence.

Making sense of life around the radical Islamist meta-narrative

Young Muslims in the diaspora inevitably experience at least some instances of discrimination; this would be almost impossible to escape. Widespread misunderstandings and misrepresentations of Islam after 9/11 have driven prejudice against, and exclusion of, Muslim youth (Lynch 2015; Peek 2011; Tindongan 2011). 'Muslim Generation Y faces issues such as identity crisis, political backlash, redefining their faith, and the severe need to belong to the mainstream culture' (Javed 2013: 34). Where opportunity, recognition and respect are not forthcoming, other legitimising constituencies (and narratives) may be sought. The main 'big story' on offer is the radical Islamist meta-narrative (Halverson et al. 2011). It may be tempting for some young Muslims to make sense of their lives by giving credence to the story, even if they do not fully endorse it. As pointed out previously, it provides a heroic explanation for everything that has happened, is happening, and will happen. So it may allow local experiences of anti-Muslim discrimination to be depersonalised to some extent. Feelings of resentment can be channelled into heroic meanings at the global level.

There is ample evidence of discontent among second-generation Muslim youth in the diaspora, especially those descended from MENA-sending countries (Read 2015: 47). They are called on to condemn any and all acts of violence committed 'in the name of their religion' (Mandaville 2007a: 112). In other words, Muslim youth in Western countries, like their elders, are under pressure to metaphorically stand up and declare themselves at every moment of their public lives as either 'good' Muslims or 'bad' Muslims (Beydoun 2016; Mamdani 2002). Yet the demand to stand up and be counted as 'good' may present a problem for youthful identities aligned with being 'cool' rather than 'good', where cool may be read as bad.

The construction of a Muslim youth identity in the West is more ambivalently framed than for youth in Muslim-majority countries. The core of that ambivalence comes from the fact that they forge more sharply defined

Muslim identities because of the diaspora context where they stand out, while at the same time 'they are freer to express youthful desires as they face far less social control and moral constraints than in the Islamic mainland' (Bayat and Herrera 2010: 21). Hage (2011) maintains they have a sense of disappointed entitlement. In the diaspora they have to deal with ascribed Muslim youth identities that evince fear and risk (Mac an Ghaill and Haywood 2014). One possible trajectory of reaction is that peer-shared Muslim cultural identity becomes intensified into pure and unassailable piety (Ryan 2014). Another trajectory is to seek out iconoclastic outlets for their youthful energy, such as gangs, music or religious radicalism. In such spaces they can develop a viable (and cool) sense of themselves (Hage 2011). As Sageman (2008) points out, a few Muslim youth at points of vulnerability may then come to believe they should take their place at 'the vanguard of internationalist jihadists who fight the global superpower and the international system' (Roy 2004: 309), a membership claim which echoes the 'world-saver' ethos of radicalisation (Lofland and Stark 1965). In conditions of late modernity, streams and flows of 24/7 information and communication online produce a 'mash up', bringing 'multiple moments into a single whole' (Rushkoff 2013: 155) of epic possibility. In this case the mash up is an imagined continuum of heroic narrative stretching from the golden age of Islam to this very moment. Thus the radical Islamist meta-narrative may offer extremist choices to Muslim youth that 'make sense of the world in the present tense' (Rushkoff 2013: 198).

The consequences of presenting as a Muslim in the diaspora

It is a risk to look or behave like a 'Muslim' in the diaspora. Mullins (2013: 738) lists some categorical criteria for identifying Islamist terrorists: (a) membership of a terrorist organisation, (b) promoting jihad, (c) fundraising, (d) facilitating jihad, (e) domestic training, (f) attempted overseas training and combat, (g) successful overseas training, (h) joining jihadi fighters in foreign conflicts, and (i) planning and conducting attacks. It is clear that few if any Muslim youth in the diaspora fit any of these criteria. However, perception matters. They need only look as though they might match the description.

We know that only a tiny minority is drawn in to what Hasan (2010) calls the 'drama of jihad'. Nevertheless, any signs of subcultural rebellion or deviant behaviour on the part of Muslim youth in the diaspora may be interpreted as evidence of radical leanings (Lynch 2015). It seems that non-Muslim people may 'read' their visual presentation in the frame of the Islamist meta-narrative and its counterpoint, the war on terror, ascribing to them a potential role in the scenario. They are perceived as though they could be part of the dual story. Muslim youth are therefore compelled to exercise surveillance over how they present themselves. In a 2011 study by the author of this book (and colleagues), a young female Muslim jobseeker in Sydney said of her prospective employers:

They would like me without *Al-Hijab* and I was born here. When I go to look for a job they would look at your scarf and they judge you because of that. I would suffer quietly. They probably think I am complicated because I am Muslim.

(Aisha, f, 26, Lebanese second generation)

By 'complicated', she means they think she might object to some everyday practices in the workplace; that she might have unacceptable ideas and would not get on with other workers. Customers or clients would be put off. In short, she would not fit in, despite that fact that she was born in Australia and sounds just like everyone else. Complicated is a polite way of saying 'Other'.

In the same study, a young male Muslim jobseeker said he carefully shaved every day and wore the same clothes as non-Muslim peers so that Sydney employers would not judge him negatively. 'I don't think my accent is too much of a problem. But my appearance, because of the problems going on with the Middle Eastern crisis and other situations, I reckon that affects it a lot' (Hatib, 22, Arab-Iraqi refugee). In response to an interviewer question about employer assumptions about Muslims, another informant mentioned 'trouble-maker, terrorist'. In short, these young Muslim jobseekers in Sydney were working hard to present socially acceptable Muslim selves as they strove to construct a successful career and life trajectory. This was judged to be more of a struggle than if they had been non-Muslim, even given a similar ethnic background (Nilan 2012a).

In short, looking like a Muslim and/or having a Muslim name presents a problem in the diaspora. Sirin and Fine (2007: 151) propose that contemporary Muslim American youth 'live on the intimate fault lines of global conflict'. They are 'teens who carry international crises in their backpacks and in their souls'. It matters very much how they look and what their names are in school, and this can be a source of much anxiety (Tindongan 2011: 79). For example, Ghaffar-Kucher (2015) examined the everyday identity negotiation of working-class Pakistani-American students. The school viewed Islam as oppressive and an obstacle to Muslim pupils' academic and professional futures. However, the families of pupils viewed Islam as the main guide for youth. They wanted their child to be a 'good Muslim'. The resulting clash implies that 'being Muslim and being American is not compatible'. Faced with the dilemma, some Pakistani-American youth took up an Islamist position (Ghaffar-Kucher 2015: 202). They constructed Islam as a 'superior culture' compared to American norms. This served to 'combat the indignity of racism and feelings of not belonging' (Ghaffar-Kucher 2015: 203; see also Zine 2007). However, they did not necessarily endorse violence in the name of Islam. Others do make this choice though, and it is time to look at some of their stories.

Going abroad to conduct jihad

By November 2015, it is estimated that IS had attracted more than 500 British citizens to fight in Syria and Iraq (*The Guardian* 2015), among them the Kuwaiti-born Londoner known as Jihadi John (mid-20s), who appeared in several IS videos beheading Western hostages. British police claim that over half who went to fight have since returned home, where they are now viewed as posing a significant threat. Of those arrested in 2014, 11 per cent were women and 17 per cent were aged under 20 (Holden 2015). For example, Amer Deghayes, now 23, is on the international terrorist watchlist and the only survivor of four young jihadis who travelled together from England to fight in Syria three years ago. 'I'm happy for them that they were killed in the path of Allah', he says of his dead friends (SBS 2015).

Other Western recruits to IS, however, do not maintain their earlier convictions when they reach the battle zone. For example, young Australian Abu Ibrahim told US broadcaster CBS in April that he wanted to leave the IS caliphate after becoming disillusioned by the executions of Western aid workers and journalists. 'A lot of people when they come, they have a lot of enthusiasm about what they've seen online or what they've seen on YouTube. They see it as something a lot grander than what the reality is.' Ibrahim said he joined IS because he wanted to live under strict *sharia* law, but said life under the caliphate was not what he had envisaged. He was negotiating with the Australian government to return, even though he faced a jail term (Bourke and Calligeros 2015). British twin sisters Zahra and Salma Halane, aged 17, were also trying to return home in 2015. Initially radicalised online, they were assisted by IS to follow their brother to Syria, where they married jihadi fighters. However, they quickly became widows when their husbands were killed in battle. They were then disillusioned and homesick. The British Home Secretary at the time, Theresa May, said: 'We look on a case-by-case basis, and people have come back – youngsters who have gone there and suddenly realize what a mistake they've made' (RT 2015). Despite recruitment materials promising a thrilling adventure, the experience fails to deliver on expectations, and may end in death or imprisonment. These examples also indicate the differently gendered pathways of young Western Muslims who sign up for involvement in jihad.

Gender matters

McCauley and Moskalenko (2014: 69) suggest two kinds of people who might sign up to jihadi involvement. First there are 'individuals with a grievance and weapons experience'. Second, there are individuals who 'strongly feel the suffering of others and feel a personal responsibility to reduce or avenge this suffering'. It seems the former might apply more often to young men and the latter more often to young women. As explained earlier, Islamic theology prescribes different conduct for female and male youth (Nayak and Kehily 2008; Bendixsen 2013). Gender distinction is observable in the radicalisation patterns of Muslim youth in the diaspora.

In Canada, Mullins (2013: 744) found that his entire sample of Muslim terrorist cases 'both before and after 9/11, was made up of youth (male)'. They were in the 'same average range (i.e., twenties to early thirties) as found in global, European, Australian and British and American samples of Islamist militants'. In his account, Sageman (2008) characterises Muslim youth radicalisation as a 'bottom-up' process constituted in masculine sociality; his 'bunch of guys' theory of radicalisation. Aslam's (2012) findings echo Sageman's claim that Muslim radicals are primarily young men chasing thrills, fantasies of glory, and a sense of belonging. Similarly, Speckhard (2008: 11) describes the radicalisation of young Muslim men in Western countries in terms of their 'desire for adventure and heroism'. This becomes synthesised with subcultural norms of masculine bravado and crude humour. A stark example of the latter was provided by a militant of British origin, former rapper Abdel-Majed Abdel Bary, who posted a picture of himself in Raqqa in 2014 holding up a severed head. The caption read: 'chillin' with my other homie, or what's left of him' (Buchanan 2014).

Both Sageman's glory-seeking 'bunch of guys' perspective and Aslam's book (2012) on Muslim masculinities and jihadi terrorism echo the pioneering work of Messerschmidt (1993) on 'compensatory' constructions of masculinity. He proposes that violence may affirm a legitimate masculine identity for men who for some reason lack other means of demonstrating status and authority in their immediate social environment. Messerschmidt's thesis has often been used to talk about young men involved in criminal gangs. Thus the cultural logic of male gangs expresses 'an aggressive masculinity expressing values of respect and honor and condoning violence as a means' to an end (Hagedorn 2003). Emphasis on masculine honour also resonates with Bourdieu's (2001) findings on men and conflict in North Africa. To some extent the work of Honneth (1996) on recognition is also salient here. Through the elevated bonding experience of collective violence, young men mutually recognise one another as warriors, and gain recognition from above as heroic foot soldiers engaged in a mythic battle for territory and honour (see Nilan 2016a).

The recruitment of young Muslim women offers a more ambivalently framed version of the hero(ine) position, one that usually infers the supporting role of wife and mother. For example, *Al-Qaeda* offered Muslim women a vision of supporting jihad by 'encouraging their husbands, sons, and brothers to participate in armed struggle, while at the same time helping to maintain the home and raise the next generation of jihadi fighters' (Ducol 2012; see also Haq 2007). The circular logic here is that if mothers are 'willingly sacrificing their sons, then the cause of jihad must be just' (Haq 2007: 1038). Elsewhere the depiction of Muslim women as morally pure victims is a key resource. First, 'the veiled body of the Muslim woman is a signal to the rest of the world of the purity of the revitalized Muslim *ummah*'. Second, 'the violated body of the raped Muslim woman turns into a call to action for young Muslim men' (Haq 2007: 1040).

Yet women have taken more active roles in militant Islamist groups. Some have been directly involved in extremist activities in the UK (Alexander and Ceresero 2013), the US (Ahmed 2010) and Europe (Jacques and Taylor 2013). Al-Tabaa (2013) suggests that Islamist terrorist organisations in MENA countries now actively recruit young Muslim women from Western countries because they more easily evade scrutiny and have a sensational impact when their actions are publicised globally. Zakaria (2015) argues that the narrative of radical Islamism is drawing Muslim women from Western countries to heed the call of extremist groups even though they are well known for their misogynist ideology. She claims that the 'Muslim woman warrior' is an ideal celebrated by jihadists (Zakaria 2015: 119). It seems women can be glorified as martyrs if they die in jihad (Speckhard 2008; Wojtowicz 2013). Yet in principle the female jihadi must conform to the idea that women's roles should be 'complementary'.

It has been argued that young Muslim women from conservative families in Western countries are specifically targeted because they might be frustrated with their constrained and over-protected lives (Speckhard 2008: 12). Certainly through the internet young Muslim women can 'communicate and interact with radicals, zealots, and fundamentalists, without familial knowledge or permission' (Sanchez 2014: 9). Moreover, they can freely and anonymously search for material that facilitates their radicalisation (Ducol 2012). For example, US Muslim convert Colleen LaRose, later known as Jihad Jane, became radicalised after watching media coverage of Palestinians suffering atrocities. She then made online contact with a jihadi group. She joined a plot to assassinate Lars Vilks, the notorious Swedish cartoonist who depicted the Prophet Muhammad's head atop a dog in 2007. In January 2014, 'Jihad Jane' was sentenced to ten years in a US prison for her role even though she had failed to meet up with her contacts in Sweden and quickly returned home (Sanchez 2014: 16).

Female recruits are valued by organisations like IS because they assist the cause, they cost less, and are believed to be easier to persuade. They can more easily pass security checks (Speckhard 2008) because they do not attract as much suspicion. So funds are saved on bribes, fake documents and disguises. Moreover, women's suicide missions are more cost-effective than men's because the amount of death gratuity paid to relatives after death is less for females. Finally, young women can be deceived into suicide martyrdom on the grounds that they broke the Islamic cultural norm of sex outside marriage, even if they were raped (Sanchez 2014: 26). Notably, despite many stories of poor treatment of young female militants by IS and other groups, some young Muslim women from the diaspora are still prepared to sign up (Nacos 2015). This is explored in more depth in Chapter 8.

Recruitment and the new technology

The principle means of disseminating the radical Islamist meta-narrative to the diaspora is through new technology. This is a most important tool for radicalisation. The big story of Islamism is readily available online not just to Muslim youth, but to all youth, and some of them will become converts. In fact, youth are the main target of militant recruiters. Thus *Al-Qaeda* disseminated the big story online to Muslim youth worldwide in the belief that as young people they had greater capacity to apprehend 'true divine guidance from God as *mujahideen* (warriors), in contrast to adults and *ulama* (scholars), whose hearts have been sealed to the true message' (Cheong and Halverson 2010: 1115). In other words, they thought Muslim youth would find the meta-narrative convincing because they were young and searching for answers. This certainly works in some cases. For example, an ex-radical young Muslim man in Indonesia put it simply:

> I was confused as a teenager, I thought there was more [to life] than problems with love (...) I was seeking something bigger than vanity. The IS slogan was live nobly or die a martyr (...) [so I thought] if I carry an AK-47, maybe people will look at me as a brave young man trying to do something.
>
> (Akbar, quoted in Topsfield 2016)

In the diaspora, such young Muslim men are searching for answers in the post-9/11 context of Islamophobia that marks them out stereotypically as a Muslim 'folk devil'. They react by creating their own Muslim sense of self, both individually and collectively, using Islam as the identity marker. This is found among all kinds of young Muslims 'modern or traditional, rich or poor' (Bayat and Herrera 2010: 19). They assemble this identity both offline and online. This does not mean that young people who strongly identify as Muslim are more likely to get involved with IS. It does mean that groups like IS continuously refine their online propaganda material to appeal to the *zeitgeist* of particular young Muslim cohorts in the diaspora as they observe them.

Taking up Sageman's (2008) framework of networked radicalisation, the *moral outrage* necessary for radical thinking can be encouraged through online depiction of alleged crimes committed against Muslims both globally and locally. That moral outrage can be *contextualised* through online depictions of past glories and future utopian visions, as well as heroic testimonials that circulate on social media sites. The big story of radical Islamism then makes sense of all that for youth who are ready to receive it. Some claim that contemporary youth are continuously 'assaulted by the presentism' of 24/7 online input. This is hypothesised to give rise to 'a kind of post-traumatic stress disorder – a disillusionment, and the vague unease of having no direction from above, no plan or story' (Rushkoff 2013: 73). In such conditions, a big world-changing narrative may offer a tempting ontological security, and narrow the filter for online content. 'This is why the return to simplicity offered by the most extreme scenarios is proving so alluring' (Rushkoff 2013: 247). We know that radical Islamist groups can and do reach out using the new technologies to troubled youth from Muslim backgrounds (Klopfenstein 2006; Rogan 2006; Hafez 2007; Torres Soriano 2012; Zackie 2013).

Moreover, youth radicalisation 'does not occur in individual isolation, but rather in the realm of networks that convey symbols, rituals and *narratives* that shape their cognitive frames' (Ahmad 2016: 19, my emphasis). Given the technological affordances of the internet and social media, it is relatively easy for jihadi groups to embed their violent messages in content about Islam. Here they convey the idea that 'supporting violence is in agreement with religion' (Sirseloudi 2012: 818). Using the structural plot framework of the Islamist meta-narrative, extremist groups build a sense of 'subculture around certain phrases and images' that infer belonging. They transmit this sub-cultural categorisation using online media that directly appeal to young people (Cheong and Halverson 2010: 1107), such as Facebook and Twitter. In that way, the radical Islamist meta-narrative is a vital component in the online process of building a neo-tribal youth grouping of potential extremists. However, the Islamist position is not the only possible neo-tribal grouping encouraged in online and new media messages to Muslim youth.

In another direction, the sense of belonging online to a pan-Islamic identity may facilitate expression of strong concern for social justice and human rights, one which results in advocacy formations rather than jihad. It has been observed that revitalised young Muslims devise endlessly creative ways to assert who they are, establish their rights and carve out unique lifestyles (Bayat and Herrera 2010: 11). In doing so they often disturb an older generation who see the world in different terms and who are offended by this ludic engagement. Thus the youthful revivalist Islam described by Kühle and Lindekilde (2010) in Denmark was characterised by a generational dis-association of Islam from particular ethnic cultures, and a commitment to reconstructing the global Muslim community, online. Kashyap and Lewis (2013: 2137) found 'marginally stronger support for *sharia* law among youth' from Muslim backgrounds in the UK compared to their parents' generation. However, although this might be seen as a generational marker of sympathy for an Islamist position, the authors note that contemporary global debate online about a modern Muslim life revolves around questions of *sharia*, so it is not surprising young Muslims are more aware of it.

Moreover, the principle of *sharia* is variously interpreted. For example, one devout young woman wrote about how *sharia* is a positive force in her life:

It is *Shari'ah* that encourages me to cleanse my body and the spiritual diseases of my heart through fasting. It is *Shari'ah* that urges me to not just forgive those who hurt me but to repay injury with compassion. It is the *Shari'ah* I read in the *Qur'an* that demands me to stand against oppression and injustice, even if it is committed by Muslims. It is the *Shari'ah* I read in the sayings of the Prophet Muhammad that inspires me to strive for the rights of all vulnerable people throughout the world, including women and minorities affected by Muslim oppressors.

(Rodrigo 2016)

The message here is clear. For her, *sharia* tells her the proper way to live. The strong implication is *sharia* as chosen and flexibly applied, rather than strictly and narrowly imposed in a top-down, law-like fashion.

Overall, the discussion above indicates that for young Muslims in the contemporary diaspora, technological affordances of online platforms and new media provide ample opportunities for debate and discussion that reference the radical Islamist meta-narrative. The resulting plethora of words and images facilitates the production of highly diverse counter-narratives to the story itself and to Muslim youth identities produced by it. Similarly, Muslim-oriented computer games and popular music genres engage the meta-narrative both performatively and ironically, also generating a range of counter-narratives within which young Muslims worldwide might position themselves. These topics are covered in detail later in the book.

Final thoughts – how does radicalisation happen?

It is time to synthesise the arguments about radicalisation that have been considered in this chapter. As explained earlier, there are no systematically occurring psychological features of individuals who conduct Islamist terrorism or plan it. Moreover, there are no consistently identifiable socio-economic indicators among young radical Muslims in the West. In fact, structural factors that might conceivably push some young Muslim people towards violence are shared by a much larger population of non-Muslim diasporic youth, such as poverty, racial prejudice and lack of opportunities. Media reports often claim that young people attracted to Islamist radicalism tend to be disaffected loners with a chip on their shoulder. However, exactly the same claim is made about young people who join criminal gangs, become school shooters, join skinhead groups, become white supremacists, and so on. Sageman's (2008) analysis is useful because it smoothly joins everyday social practices of male youth in particular to the phenomenon of Islamist radicalisation. Yet for this 'bunch of guys' framework to be more convincing, there must be an appeal to the imagination. Here the Islamist meta-narrative plays a vital affective role. It offers a transcendentally meaningful explanation for everything that happens in their lives and for everything they might do in the future, no matter how dangerous.

An Australian journalist spent a year undercover with Islamist radicals. He posed as a convert to Islam who wanted to fight in Syria. Three hours after first pledging allegiance online he got a response from Australian IS recruiter Neil Prakash[3] through one of the encrypted instant messaging services they use. Prakash asked him to kill some Australian journalists. He demurred. He was then put in contact with a local 'sleeper' radical who introduced him to a small group of men who met in a suburban park.

> When I approached the park, about seven young men were sitting in a circle talking. Their ages ranged from 17 to 30. Some of them had the beginnings of a beard, others had no facial hair. One older man wore a white *thawb*, a traditional Middle Eastern garment (…) It looked like a bunch of friends getting together. Some had brought tea to drink.
>
> (Journalist[4] 2016)

The older man emotively narrated all the key points of the Islamist meta-narrative to his enraptured listeners. The undercover journalist wrote, 'in front of me was a group of young men who were clearly falling through the cracks, feeling they didn't belong'. It was clear to him that many were 'angry or lost in alcohol or drugs'. The older man's words were 'dangerously seductive: they play on the confusion of young men struggling with their sense of identity and life in a society whose politics and media seem increasingly alien and hostile to them'. The young men in the group met on numerous occasions to enthusiastically discuss what they had learned and their plans. The undercover journalist concluded that 'much of their talk was hot air, but the intentions were crystal clear' (Journalist 2016), even though the undercover journalist could not later identify any actual militant action that eventuated from those intentions. This detailed account anchors our understanding, so we can better map out the *how* of Islamist radicalisation for young people in the diaspora.

First, the meta-narrative makes sense of the Islamophobia that is a shaping condition of life for young Muslims in the diaspora. Unsurprisingly, they resent the way they are treated (Bayat and Hererra 2010; Lynch 2015). They have become the new folk devils (Alexander 2004; Moosavi 2015). Where marginalisation of Muslims is pronounced, youthful forms of pan-Muslim belonging are intensified by experiences of exclusion and fear. From this resentful awareness of how their pan-Muslim identities attract discrimination, a radical orientation might develop in which the Islamist meta-narrative becomes a structuring force in who they imagine themselves to be, and what they might be capable of doing. On the other hand the big story of Islamism might not achieve practical salience, but remain as a sense-making reference point for complaining about, and discursively resisting, the discriminatory environment of the diaspora. We know that numerically there are many more young Muslims experiencing marginalisation and exclusion than actively support the radical cause.

Second, the Islamist meta-narrative offers to make sense of any lack of certainty Muslim youth might be feeling about who they are and what their lives mean (Hogg et al. 2013). The young men in the journalist's account above had little if anything to do with established religious leaders or groups in their own communities. They felt they did not belong there either. The Islamist story implies that they feel uncertain in the diaspora and in their local Muslim communities because they have not yet found the one and only path that will save the world and their souls. As explained previously, possible life options have increased in late modernity, so young people face a dizzying array of choices (Giddens 1991), fostering a sometimes uneasy questioning of self-identity. The young person may be attracted to discourses and practices that offer 'ontological security' (Giddens 1991: 44) – a simplified position of certainty. Here the 'self' can find firm narrative ground on which to take a stand. The big story promises 'recognition' (Honneth 1996) through heroic and self-sacrificing action on a world-saving scale.

Third, the Islamist meta-narrative is deliberately packaged to appeal to contemporary youth tastes (Sanchez 2014). Sageman's 'bunch of guys' thesis finds firm ground here. For example, the older man in the journalist's account above offered his listeners a version of themselves as a courageous vanguard of heroes for the cause; a band of righteous avengers. This kind of face-to-face radicalisation is supplemented by the very glossy 'brand' of radical Islamism available online, from slick interviews with celebrity militants to sophisticated online fashion and lifestyle magazines that anticipate the pleasures of a prosperous global caliphate (Al-Tabaa 2013). In short, if a disenfranchised and stigmatised young Muslim in the diaspora is looking for a sensational 'deviant career' (Becker 1973), then IS invites them right into a starring role in a compelling world drama (Halverson et al. 2011). It is clear that social media is a prime conduit for both recruitment and dissemination (Brachman 2006) because it successfully synthesises individual subjectivity with collective identity claims (boyd 2010). In the real-time, media-online-networked, 24/7 barrage of the 'now' – the continual present (Rushkoff 2013) – it may be that the Islamist meta-narrative offers young Muslims in Western countries a useful filtering lattice through which the proliferation of temporal soundbites can be sifted for attribution of meaning. For example, reports of conflict and civil war from the Middle East or local instances of intolerance of Muslim minorities can be productively interpreted and made personal in the light of global Islamist struggle (see Husain 2007). For a tiny few, this may prompt militant action, joining a brave band of brothers and sisters on a world-saving mission of vengeance and triumph.

Finally, the Islamist meta-narrative is vitally important for understanding the process of Muslim youth radicalisation because it continuously disseminates not only the heroic stereotypes by which those of Islamic faith might evaluate themselves, but the stigmatised stereotypes by which others judge, and discriminate against, Muslims. When read through the eyes of non-Muslims, the Islamist meta-narrative connotes 'fanatical, intolerant, militant, fundamentalist, misogynist and alien' social actors who threaten the community (Dunn et al. 2007: 569). In that sense it serves to heighten the Islamophobia that young Muslims experience in the diaspora, and thereby intensifies their feelings of resentment at unjust treatment.

The inference of this chapter is that the mainstream emphasis on combating Muslim youth radicalisation relies on some convenient causal assumptions that leave little room for recognising the agency of Muslim youth who are coming up with highly diverse ideas of their own about who they are and where they fit in the world. The danger of this non-recognition is that it implicitly positions most Muslim youth in the diaspora as 'vulnerable to the wiles of propagandists – that is, unless they are pre-emptively interdicted by powerful counterframes developed by experts in the counterterrorism field' (Joosse et al. 2015: 4), some of whom profit from the design of their interventions. Yet Muslim youth in Western countries have been, and still are, busy expressively developing their own counter-narratives, which receive relatively little recognition. Indeed, as McCauley and Moskalenko (2008: 430) point out, radicalisation is primarily a reactive process. Thus the same structural and discursive mechanisms that might move some diasporic Muslim youth towards radicalisation will move others to react against extremism. For example, the same kind of peer socialising described by Sageman (2008) may encourage some young Muslims to repudiate extremist discourse in favour of a collective human rights orientation that addresses their direct concerns about social justice in the diaspora.

Conclusion

This chapter has considered how some young Muslims in the diaspora might find the radical Islamist meta-narrative compelling. A range of explanations for Muslim youth radicalisation was examined. This included psychological hypotheses of uncertainty and other states. Also included were some examples of the sociological view that second-generation Muslims facing racism, social exclusion and loneliness may find that extremist groups offer a legitimising identity. Yet the reader is reminded that there is still no defining profile for who might become radicalised, despite intense efforts to develop one. Neither are there any systematic psychological deficiencies found for individuals who have partaken in terrorism or planned it. Socio-economic disadvantage, intolerance and marginality affect far greater numbers of Muslim youth than ever come to support jihad. Moreover, analyses of Islamist radicalisation do not lead directly to explanations of why some young Muslims get involved in jihadi terrorism at home and abroad. In fact a regrettably infrequent question is: 'Why do most people with militant extremist beliefs *not* engage in violent action?' (Borum 2011: 56, my emphasis). The next chapter looks specifically at how young Muslims in the diaspora engage with Islam and the radical meta-narrative through interactive websites and social media.

Notes

1 At the time of writing (2016), there are no grounds to moderate that RAND claim.
2 *Anomie* in psychology refers to a sense of hopelessness or emotional alienation from a societal group following social upheaval of some kind.
3 Neil Prakash was reported as killed in a bombing raid, although some in the counter-terrorism community have doubts about his death. It now seems he is alive after all.
4 The published account was anonymised to protect the identity of the journalist.

Chapter 4

Online extremism and digital counter-narratives

Introduction

This chapter considers how Muslim youth engage with Islam through the technological affordances of interactive websites and social media. First, there is some general discussion of new online potentialities. Attention is then turned to Islamist sites; what they are, what kind of radical positions they advance, and who they seek to influence. The construction and dissemination of digital counter-narratives occupies the rest of the analytical discussion in this chapter, with inclusions from the online voices of young Muslims themselves.

Muslim youth websites run the whole gamut of taste and lifestyle distinctions, from fashion to jihad, and from ascetic piety to *halal* dating. Abundant content online and in social media informs Muslim youth in the diaspora about what they should, and should not, be doing. At the same time, 're-styling', a reworking of both aesthetics and identity, takes place online in response to the provocation of the radical Islamist meta-narrative. Muslim discussion sites permit many voices to create theological debate and varied standpoints, offering prime spaces for counter-discourse to be expressed.

Castells (1996) argued over twenty years ago that the network society is a 'space of flows', exemplified by online connectivity. More recently Shifman (2013) drew our attention to the active digital culture of young people everywhere. The 'affordances' – potentials, opportunities – of the internet (Papacharissi 2009) are crucial to the contemporary social practices of youth (boyd 2010; Robards and Bennett 2011). They constitute a 'digital generation' (Buckingham 2013: 1), networked into virtual communities and news/gossip sources through which vast amounts of information flow. They are immersed in digital technologies of connection, creating and sharing as they go. In fact social media connect to a broader regime of 'selfbranding' (Goodwin et al. 2016: 3; see also van Dijck 2013). Here the socially connected digital 'self' gains attention from significant peers who share the same identity frame, the same neo-tribal affiliation. Virtual groupings and affinities develop 'beyond traditional boundaries' (Bunt 2009: 7). Thus internet 'flows' have helped construct transnational communities (Mandaville 2001; Castells 1997) with which young people can align themselves. Online interactions amplify the compelling salience of global youth identities, including all kinds of Muslim identities (see Aly 2012). Notably, the same technological affordances that can facilitate extremist mobilisation can also invite the assembly of virtual communities of young Muslims who take a position contesting that same meta-narrative.

Online Muslim selves

Youthful followers of Islam have easy access to transnational Muslim identities through their extensive use of Facebook, Twitter, Tumblr and so on.[1] Here they can (virtually) assemble in neo-tribes and co-construct narratives of identity and lifestyle (Braddock 2012). All kinds of ideas are expressed on Muslim youth Facebook sites (Drissel 2011), from the worryingly militant to the mundane – 'why does my head ache when I pray?' They achieve consolidation of their own youthful sense of *ummah* through the sharing of tastes, ideas and stories online. They reflexively represent and negotiate the significant identities that constitute their everyday worlds as Muslims and as young people at home in the West. Notably, such websites usually include young Muslims of both sexes, which may be acceptable in moral terms since there is no direct contact. Cross-ethnic transnational groupings subvert conventional understandings of Muslim identity anchored in local ethnic norms. The online groupings of Muslim youth extend well beyond the local context of the diaspora to suggest the neo-theo-tribalism of their global contemporary popular culture.

When it comes to learning about Islam, modern information technology has changed the social conditions by which religious authority is produced (Turner 2007). Particular theological websites often seem to have more appeal for contemporary youth than the local mosque or religious leader. There are literally thousands of Muslim preachers and theologians online, promoting many versions of Islam. As 'iMuslims' – those who constitute their faith primarily in the digital realm – they find 'no conflict between technology and living life Islamically' (Bunt 2009: 19). Yet while the internet consolidates a virtual *ummah* as 'imagined community' (Lim 2012: 138), it also provides decentred opportunities for religious debate and discussion. While versions of the radical Islamist meta-narrative are pitched on numerous websites and social media pages, so too are the counter-narratives that challenge it. For example, Turner (2007: 120) reports that US Muslim youth on some websites 'compete with the established specialists on *fiqh* (Islamic jurisprudence)'. Elsewhere he finds a 'Queer Jihad' website in California – which really is an example of 'counter-jihad' (see Kugle 2013).

In short, websites are now critical for offering multifaceted guidance relevant to Muslims living in secular societies. More than fifteen years ago Mandaville (2001) drew our attention to how the generation of young Muslims living in the West were using the internet to obtain and communicate interpretations of Islam suited to the demands and concerns of their particular circumstances. He called this 'media Islam' or 'soundbite Islam' (Mandaville 2001: 177). It provides the tools for marketing 'Islamic' products to Muslim youth. This is described in detail in the following chapter.

The content of cyber-Islam must have a universal 'hook' with which large numbers of youth can connect. Debate about the radical Islamist meta-narrative is one of these 'hooks'. Most sites invite blog comments where debates about theology, jihad and injustice unfold. These debates operationalise the technological affordance of 'spreadability' (boyd 2014: 3). Another example of this is when social media networks pick up new ideas and stories and disseminate them rhizomatically from person to person. For example, bizarre and horrific jihadi content can be exposed virally to millions of people within the hour. It seems logical that such material should trigger feelings of either support or contestation for different individuals.

Islamist sites that attract youth

The discussion in this section sets out to demonstrate the ways in which the Islamist meta-narrative generates both positions of support and positions of subversion. It begins from the assumption that extremist narratives can influence the beliefs, attitudes, and intentions of young Muslims drawn to websites and social media pages by the quest for identity and knowledge, even though 'very few individuals are radicalized to the point that they engage in terrorism' (Braddock 2012: 167–168).

Sageman (2004) argues it was new technology that actually made global jihad possible. Sympathisers around the world can 'read about the breaking news from Iraq, follow links to attack videos from active jihad campaigns, view motivational imagery of martyr operatives in heaven' and so on (Brachman 2006: 151). This is because the relative freedom of the internet allows any Muslim group or organisation to publish inexpensively. Information is largely uncensored and readily accessible (Sanchez 2014). Blog commentary input and social media networking enhance the twin goals of attracting a loyal audience and creating a sense of community (Rettburg 2013; Drissel 2011). Of course Facebook and Twitter monitor posts for extremist content that urges violence. It seems that Twitter has cancelled more than 125,000 IS-related accounts since the middle of 2015 (Segall 2016). However, if one conduit of Islamist radicalism is ruptured, another interconnected line/trajectory will emerge rhizomatically in the form of a new online site or account. Thus the technological affordances of the internet and new media subvert both the established religio-political institutions of Islam itself and the normalising power of internet regulatory mechanisms.

Jihadist websites make use of all kinds of persuasive rhetoric, images, and symbolism (Bhui and Ibrahim 2013). For example, *Al-Qaeda* in the Arab Peninsula (AQAP) offers slick digital media publications to target middle-class men and women for recruitment (Sanchez 2014: 14). Their online magazines mirror the layout and production quality of *Cosmopolitan* and *GQ*. So *Al-Shamikha* (Majestic Woman) targets female followers, while *Inspire* targets young men (Al-Tabaa 2013). Both can be downloaded in full colour. IS produces *Dabiq*, a glossy jihad propaganda magazine uploaded to anonymous text hosting services and disseminated on social media by supporters. This online publishing is a new montage of logic-morality that attempts to shape Muslim youth identities through the re-imagining of *ummah* in popular culture terms. Thus the radical Islamist 'virtual community' is no longer tied to any nation, a 'condition that corresponds to the mythical umma' of like-minded extremists (Sageman 2004: 161). Yet at the same time irony and dissent are present. It is evident that many more young people search out extremist sites than ever take up a militant position.

Extremist websites

The internet offers 'a virtual library of jihadist material, granting easy access to everything from political, ideological and theological literature, via *fatwa*[s] and *khutba*[s],[2] to videos of assaults and beheadings' (Rogan 2006: 24). Propaganda online incorporates images, sermons, slogans, music and personal stories. It is carefully designed to increase 'feelings of hatred towards the West, kinship between sympathetic Muslims, and strengthen bonds between potential recruits, sympathizers, and radical groups' (Sanchez 2014: 11). Such sites have a wide reach, and as fast as they are taken down, they reappear under another name. Extremist websites are of concern to security analysts. They believe such sites encourage group militancy, and/or 'lone wolf' terrorist attacks in the diaspora. For example, a Norwegian security analyst wrote in a report:

> The Internet is of major importance to the global jihadist movement today. It facilitates ideological cohesion and network-building within a geographically scattered movement, and all levels of the jihadist network are present on the Internet.
>
> (Rogan 2006: 8)

The messages of Islamist groups dedicated to *jihad bil-sayf* (jihad by the sword) are amplified and appropriated across various media platforms and formats. Encouragement to conduct jihad is widely circulated to young Muslims. Material often includes subtitles in English to target youth in the diaspora (Cheong and Halverson 2010: 1105). Sites promise youth a victory in the final battle. They are invited to become 'pious and heroic cadres'. Through jihad they will 'redeem the suffering and humiliation of their fellow Muslims through faith in God, sacrifice on the battlefield, and righteousness in their cause' (Hafez 2007: 96). They are promised it is simply a matter of time before the just 'cause' wins victory. The sites emphasise the dedication and skill of young jihadis, the brilliance and courage of their leaders, and the 'potency' of their tactical, operational and strategic plans (Samuel 2012: 50). Not only can Islamist extremists now reach out to every Muslim-owned smart phone (in principle), but a few clicks enable a young person to respond.

In all these ways radical sites provide propaganda and materials encouraging mobilisation. They try to fuel anger among young people in the diaspora by perpetuating the idea that Islam is under attack. They integrate multiple Muslim grievances into a single offence of global proportions (see Zackie 2013), and thereby construct the logic of violent jihad.[3] Security analyst Rogan identified typical contributors to online jihadi sites: *'leaders'* who communicate through audio and video files; *'clerics'* who provide theological guidance for jihad; *'strategists'* who give tactical advice on waging individual and group jihad; *'militant organizations'* who spread propaganda globally; and *'grassroots supporters'*. They use the sites to keep themselves updated on developments in the jihadi world (Rogan 2006: 15).

Yet these are not the only visitors. A jihadi site might be visited to get a laugh for instance. It certainly does not mean a young Muslim will be instantly motivated to take direct action and launch a physical or virtual intervention. In fact, Bigo et al. (2014) emphasise that violent action is very unlikely to occur based purely on visual cues and virtual ties. Pantucci (2015) strongly emphasises that recruitment takes place when young people already want to join up, so pro-jihad sites mainly amplify an existing desire for extremist actions.

Yet the conduct of jihad does not necessarily entail physical combat. Torres Soriano (2012: 770) claims 'virtual jihad' is now just as important as young volunteers picking up a gun or strapping on a vest. Jihadi mobilisation is vitally important for the radical Islamist cause and therefore requires engaging net-savvy volunteers to conduct active recruitment activities in the virtual realm. Such volunteers are almost always young and have established themselves as expert hackers and bloggers. They write complex code with ease. Jihadi groups try hard to recruit them because they use 'media battalions' to present technologically sophisticated material to their supporters and to potential adherents (Rogan 2006: 18). They also rely on them to operate effectively in the 'darknet'[4] where terrorism financing transactions take place. 'Virtual' jihadis are apparently very well treated compared to less skilled volunteers for the cause.

Propaganda and recruitment

Recruitment through social media expanded rapidly after 9/11 (Zammit 2013: 742). Carefully selected phrases from the Koran are calculated to fuel both pride and anger. Recruiters encourage thirst for vengeance by uploading videos of Western atrocities against Muslims (Haider 2015). Filmed suicide bomber testimonials are also disseminated. According to Pantucci (2015), the most viewed British jihadi video was that of '7/7' (2005) suicide bomber Siddique Khan. In the pre-recorded video, he says quietly to camera, 'your democratically elected governments continuously perpetrate atrocities against my people all over the world', adding, 'and your support of them makes you directly responsible, just as I am directly responsible for protecting and avenging my Muslim brothers and sisters' (Silber 2012: 111). Khan's uploaded message on YouTube attracted many comments at the time and even more recently, for example:

> Is it okay for Israel as a country to kill innocent Muslims in Palestine, kids who were playing on a beach and then drop a bomb and wipe them out? They're the ones who are the terrorists, may Allah destroy Israel and America, the truth is to prevail *inshallah* the Islamic *Khalifah* is to come *inshallah*.
>
> (vicky7866[5])

As we can see, in 2014 'vicky' clearly voiced agreement with the sentiment of righteous vengeance originally voiced by Siddique Khan in 2005. However, we should not assume that 'vicky' went from that stated position directly to the actual conduct of violent jihad. It is statistically likely that he/she did not. However, vicky's comments written so long after the event still point to a significant issue because extremist groups rely on a base of supporters, 'many of whom may never actually commit acts of violence' (Davies et al. 2016: 53). Propaganda is not just about direct recruitment, but maintaining a support base.

Propaganda formats

Rieger et al. (2013) report on visual formats for Islamist propaganda/recruitment online. The first is the talking head format. The authors offer the following example. The uploaded video depicts a young German militant. He describes for camera how badly Western powers treat the global *ummah*. As he talks, images appear from Abu-Ghraib prison that present the story of how a Muslim woman was raped there. 'He asks his mother while looking into the camera, "How shall I sit still?"' (Rieger et al. 2013: 51). This representation echoes the righteous vengeance discourse of the Siddique Khan video mentioned above. The allegation of bad treatment of the *ummah* by the West is a trans-historical claim that matches a key plot element of the radical Islamist meta-narrative (Zackie 2013; McCauley and Moskalenko 2014; Savage and Liht 2009; Roy 2008). 'Proof' is offered in images from Abu-Ghraib and the story of the sexually assaulted Muslim woman. The story symbolically renders the threat of '*extinction*' (Zackie 2013: 15). The young man asks his mother – a Muslim woman and therefore under threat of rape/extinction – how he is supposed to sit still in the light of such atrocities (implying: … while you whom I honour are vulnerable to these barbarians?). In that sense, his 'story' contains only one good character – the Muslim, and one bad character – the West. All the people of the world, and all the events that happen in the world, are implicitly poured into those two opposed signifiers, with no other relations of power constituted in the hinge between them. The only logical position is that of the Muslim hero who fights for justice and avenges the sufferings of the *ummah*. Thus he positions himself – and potentially the young male audience for the video – as the brave defender (Roy 2008: 20).

Another format of propaganda uses the movie clip technique. Rieger et al. (2013) describe an uploaded video called *The Attack on Our Siblings in Iraq*. It depicts suffering Muslims, non-combatant victims of the Iraqi war. The soundtrack is the *Lord of the Rings* theme music. The voiceover asks who will protect them from the infidels. Images of dead children and crying mothers are shown. The caliphate is presented as the only answer, referencing the global organisation *Hizbut Tahrir*. At this point the soundtrack is the *Pirates of the Caribbean* theme music (Rieger et al. 2013: 55). This example demonstrates plot elements of the radical Islamist meta-narrative – vulnerability, binary world view, avenging warrior – but mixes in an appealing popular culture intertextuality. First, *Lord of the Rings* theme music implies the civil victims of the Iraqi war are like hobbits, simple people who need to be saved by their heroic superiors from the forces of evil sweeping the land. The desired heroic intervention is flagged by the question of who will offer protection from the infidels (read orcs). The caliphate is proposed as the solution, and radical Islamists are depicted as the pious heroes who will save the day and bring it about. Overdubbed music from *Pirates of the Caribbean* then constitutes the character of the righteous 'avenger' as a swashbuckling hero who is not afraid of a fight against the odds. This example shows the use of popular culture in sugar-coated calls to jihad. It suggests the youthful subject positioning of neo-tribal 'cool' – synthesised with the moral high ground of the righteous fighter.

Both the propaganda examples above project the radical Islamist meta-narrative and invite the young person watching/listening to position him/herself as the avenging warrior in the plot; to make the heroic personal distinction from lesser mortals. The first example uses familial discourse as persuasion. The second example invites a positive response, in part through overdubbing theme music that conjures up the heroic world-saving plots of *Lord of the Rings* and *Pirates of the Caribbean*, movies with which the viewer is presumed to be familiar. Cheong and Halverson (2010: 1106) argue that through such intertextuality, radicalised Muslim youth in the diaspora can come to see themselves in the heroic tradition of their favourite secular fictions. In a similar vein, Sageman (2008: 59) reports that Facebook sites urging radicalisation strive to represent 'jihadi cool' and use street-inflected 'jihadi talk' to make engagement seem like a daring form of fun. This is most important for understanding the affective appeal of radical Islamist discourse for youth in the diaspora.

In fact we cannot really grasp the attraction of the radical Islamist meta-narrative for young Muslims in the diaspora without taking into account the affective domain. Once an Islamist position is assumed online, affective inflections in blogs and comments imply fraternity, superiority, joy in the meeting of minds, feeling valued, belonging, recognition, and sense of pleasure and purpose. When the gloss wears off, a later phase may see affect expressed in the form of disillusion, disappointment and seeking to retreat. Online propaganda and the fiery speeches of certain preachers unify and glorify the struggle for caliphate. However, in ground-level conflicts in MENA countries, warring Islamist militia factions fight each other. They splinter and form new hybrids. In uniting temporarily to fight a common enemy, they competitively employ varying degrees of brutality against Muslim civilians and foreigners. When Western recruits enthusiastically make their way to battle fronts, they confront this kind of reality, as well as the language barrier, and the risk of standing out ethnically, or in terms of lack of battle experience. In short, the imagined glorious struggle inevitably breaks down into the paralysing fear and mundane brutality of civil war in the heat and dust, with atrocities on every side. It is not surprising that many Western recruits want to go home. Disillusioned Western fighters may launch compelling stories of their experiences online (see Husain 2007). These 'real-life' stories act directly as counter-narratives to jihadi recruitment.

Islamist celebrity and fandom

The same slick new logic of morality evident in glossy Islamist magazines applies to depiction of key figures and big personalities in the struggle. There are celebrities and fans in this field just as there are in secular youth culture. According to Van Zoonen (2005) celebrity politics is first constituted in the idea that a charismatic figure is both ordinary and extraordinary at the same time, and second, that they are promising something special that connects to the ordinary citizenry. Furthermore, an individual does not become a fan of a celebrity purely through viewing or listening. An individual becomes a fan by translating that viewing into a cultural activity (Jenkins 2006: 41); a distinctive act of choosing. Through fandom they become constituted as a 'participatory community' (Jenkins 2006). Online fandom means that anyone anywhere can participate.

We know that one of the effects of 24/7 'presentism' (Rushkoff 2013) in digital space and communications is to enhance celebrity and fandom around specific taste cultures of young people. Islamist extremism is no exception. Sensational press coverage, video uploads, Facebook activity, likes, Tweets, blog comments, discussion board threads, online claims and counter-claims, create and build the jihadi celebrity profile and garner fans. For example, Furnish (2002) maintains that '[Muslim] terrorists are media celebrities par excellence', giving the example of Osama bin Laden. Driscoll (2015) finds that Islamist warriors can seem attractive to women. 'To them [Muslim girls in the West obsessed with ISIS men], jihadists are like Brad Pitt, only better because Brad Pitt is not religious'. Sheffield (2015) speaks about the inspirational effect in the UK of 'celebrity warriors' like Jihadi John.[6] Across the channel, France is no exception. Following the terrorist murders at the office of the tabloid *Charlie Hebdo* in Paris, French newspaper *Le Monde* published an article titled 'The Kouachi Brothers and Coulibaly, Pioneers of French Jihadism.[7] These 'pioneers' were recognised as creating the mass effect of plunging the whole country into anxiety[8] (Follorou et al. 2015). Whether well-intentioned or not, such coverage contributes to the potency of the jihadi celebrity profile.

However, as Driessens (2015) points out, celebrity by its very nature is fleeting and unstable. The online/social media visibility of political celebrity in particular does not endure. Last week's man (or woman) of the week is rapidly superseded by a new face and a new set of soundbites. The same happens in the radical Islamist field. A Western recruit like Jihadi John (British) or Jihadi Jake (Australian) might overnight become a pin-up boy for fans of Islamic terrorism, but once he is dead his celebrity fades out. Of course a martyred death can create celebrity, but when there are many such martyr deaths this effect diminishes. Along with the fading of the celebrity factor may come the diminishing significance of a group and the quantity of its fan base. This means more celebrities are eagerly sought by radical Islamist groups to encourage their 'fans'. It is worth noting that online now there are now many more references and posts about IS/*Daesh* than about the Taliban and *Al-Qaeda*. This is not to say those groups have actually ceased their activities, but they do not have the same sensational profile they once had in the virtual world. To maintain profile, something new has to be promised.

End of days – the *Mahdi*

One of the enduring 'hooks' of cyber-Islam is the idea that the world-saving *Mahdi* will come soon and oversee the end of days. It is a specific offshoot of the Islamist meta-narrative, one characterised by strong elements of magic and fantasy. Apocalyptic millennial websites offer supernatural stories based on the mythical figures of the *Mahdi* and the *Dajjal*. They are popular with young Muslims worldwide; operating as a 'transnational imaginary' (Werbner 2004: 451). Yet millennial discourse stands on traditional ground, since Islam has had 'a strong apocalyptic and messianic character throughout its history' Cook (2008: 1). A dramatic end-of-days scenario – the apocalypse, the day of judgement – is equally present in Islam as it is in Christianity. Modern millennial discourse is based on centuries-old Islamic prophecies. For example, many online sites anticipate the coming of the new messiah, the *Mahdi*, the second coming of the Prophet Isa (Jesus Christ), and the dawning of a new golden age of Islam (Drissel 2011: 145). The *Mahdi* and Isa will do battle with the evil *Dajjal,* a kind of 'Antichrist' (Werbner 2004: 454).

While conservative Muslim authorities generally do not endorse millennial sentiments – preaching orthodoxy/piety for its own heavenly reward – messianic Muslims scour the landscape of world conflict for evidence of the Lesser and Greater Signs of the Hour that herald the beginning of the end-of-days (Cook 2008). Drissel (2011) studied 150 apocalyptic Facebook pages popular with young Muslims. They avidly debated the relevance of prophetic signs and symbols presaging *aher al-zaman,* 'the end times' (Drissel 2011: 146). In their likes and comments, they talked up the metaphysical powers of the *Mahdi* and the *Dajjal.* They supported a range of conspiracy theories and utopian imaginings. In site comments, orthodox Muslim youth pointed out that the Koran does not mention supernatural figures, but this did not dissuade the fans of millennial Muslim apocalypse.

The story goes that the *Mahdi* will not only re-establish the caliphate, but 'obliterate the hegemonic power of the *Dajjal*' (Drissel 2011: 162). The *Dajjal* constitutes a focal point for conspiracy theories, especially about the events of 9/11. For example, a millennial blog titled 'Story of World Trade Center' presents a detailed version of the 9/11 attacks, involving the *Dajjal* working secretly through the US government, Freemasons and *Al-Qaeda* (Drissel 2011: 166). There was quite a detailed conspiracy story on some millennial sites, for example:

> The *Dajjal* will emerge out of Israel before taking charge in the United States and Great Britain. After solidifying his power base in the West, he will proceed to conquer the rest of the world, though eventually the *Mahdi* and the Prophet *Isa* [9] (together with their assembled army) will stop his advance.
>
> (Drissel 2011: 165)

On other sites, the *Dajjal* was construed as the Dark Messiah or even a *jinn,* the demonic shape shifter of traditional Arab mythology (Drissel 2011: 165). In those respects the mythology of the *Dajjal* embroiders the radical Islamist meta-narrative, especially the Crusader-American-Zionist-West conspiracy component identified by Zackie (2013). Moreover, the *Dajjal* story rehearses the core claim that the history of humankind is a tale of conflict between the truth of Islam and the falsehood of the infidel – 'the *Kufr*' (Mendelsohn 2012: 606). However, millennial discourse does not usually infer individual Muslims personally taking up arms, because the time is not yet right. They must wait for the coming of the *Mahdi.* In that sense this is really counter-jihad discourse, despite appearance to the contrary.

Cook (2008) advises us to make a distinction between millennial Islamists and Islamists who preach violent jihad. It seems they apply a different logic. He claims most Muslim apocalyptic writers subscribe to the notion of an international conspiracy against Muslims. They concur with the idea that the best way to defeat the conspiracy is to unite all Muslims into a caliphate. 'This goal is closely parallel to that of globalist radical Muslims; the only difference is that globalist radical Muslims appear to believe that this should be achieved by fighting' in the here and now (Cook 2008: 17). In other words, apocalyptic Islamist enthusiasts see their worldly mission not in taking up arms but in spreading the word to fellow Muslims about the *Dajjal* conspiracy, the appearance of the *Mahdi*, and other aspects of the end-of-days. They are immersed in the scholarship of excavating interpretive details. Referring to the *hadith*, they minutely examine motifs in current world events that signal the persecution of Muslims and the signifying evil of Western and Semitic oppressors. In short, they are looking for signs of the second coming, rather than justifications for killing. They are embarked on a jihad of knowledge rather than a jihad of militant action. This is a counter-narrative to the radical Islamist meta-narrative because it argues that the *Mahdi* must arrive before action is taken (Drissel 2011: 172). In that sense, the mythical figures of the *Mahdi*, the *Dajjal*, Gog and Magog, Isa and so on are woven into an apocalyptic tale that effectively removes the requirement to personally engage in violent struggle. Werbner (2004: 451) supports the idea that Islamic millennial discourses do not infer immediate militant mobilisation. Since the story is both millennial and redemptive, no immediate action is needed.

The distinction between millennial Islamists and Islamists who preach violent jihad is often seen in blogs and online comments. YouTube is a popular place for millennial speeches and sermons by clerics. An example was uploaded on YouTube in July 2014. It was titled 'Islam & Black Flags/*Al-Mahdi* & *Dajjal*/ Islamic Reminder'. The video featured talks by three clerics about the coming of the *Mahdi*, pointing to varied eschatological motifs in current world conflicts. This video elicited intense exchanges of commentary. For example, Aysha Shammama (no photo – rose picture[10]) posted: 'so many signs we are seeing now!' A similar sentiment was expressed by Daniel: 'most of these things are happening right now in the Middle East and almost all of the minor signs have passed. *Imam Mahdi* will come very soon *insha allah*' (Daniel Yusuf, no photo[11]). These two comments support the millennial Islamist position. Fervent sentiments in favour of the video upload attracted the ire of jihad sympathisers. Supporters of millennial discourse like those above were deemed to be infidels because of waiting to take action, for example:

> Islam is ISIS and ISIS is Islam. All infidels like you will die by the swords of the caliphate. You are *Haram* because you are an infidel ...
> (hoopmillionaire2, photo-back view of male bodybuilder[12])

There were other postings that articulated the same militant position. However, the militant position was then contested in a subsequent post:

I know what shit ISIS is as well as Taliban and other forms of terrorist groups, including US and Israeli govts. ISIS fought America when they invaded Iraq? Who told you this BS? How trustable are your sources? These shit ISIS can't even survive in front of any army of any world trained country. These morons only can kill innocents.

(Faizan Ahmed, young male photo[13])

Faizan's reply uses some of the same meta-narrative materials to challenge the accusations and threats of hoopmillionaire and the authors of similar posts. However, another commentator offered a more distanced counter-narrative to the original millennial video, one that rests on refuting authenticity:

None of these stories in this video are in the Quran. God tells us in the Quran our origin, our mission of life, our destination. But didn't tell us about *Mahdi, Khilafah, Dajjal,* or Black Flags. All of these stories were attached to Islam by some liars about Prophet Muhammad. I'm a Muslim and respect my religion.

(Ahmad Assaf, young male photo[14])

Another filmed teaching titled *Imam Mehdi [Mahdi]* will come after the *Khilafah* [caliphate] was uploaded to YouTube on 21 October 2012. It quickly attracted commentary from an Islamist who was in favour of violent jihad:

Our *chaliefa Ibrahiem* – come join the *Mujahadeen* – they are fighting the whole *kufar* world – from Russia to USA – EU to Israhel – even all corrupt Arab governments fight them.

(Mohammed Abdullah, no photo[15])

This recruitment invitation works by aligning *caliphate by end-of-days knowledge* – the millennial discourse of Islamism, with *caliphate achieved by violent jihad* – the extremist discourse of Islamism (Cook 2008: 17). It implies that the automatic corollary of millennial discourse is to take up arms. However, other commentators on the same video quickly voiced their opposition to the pro-jihad position, for example:

ISIS is fake *dajjali khilafat*!!! They [are] *khawarji*. Dogs of hell. May Allah curse them to death.

(Fatima Khan, young female photo[16])

As Drissel (2011) points out, Islamic apocalyptic discourse is far from monolithic. It is frequently the site of spirited contestations among diasporic Muslim youth.

Overall it is clear that the internet has had a profound impact on the articulation of not only religious debate (Turner 2007), but on apocalyptic discourse (Drissel 2011: 179). Yet the attempted grafting of jihadi discourse onto the millennial fantasy framework is far from welcomed by many. In short, there is plenty in the Islamist millennial material online to fire up contestation between young Muslims. In itself this is one of the 'hooks' that keep them engaged.

Young Muslims debating online

Drissel calls young Muslims in the diaspora a 'Facebook generation' (2011: 152). They are fully engaged in all forms of online activity and social media. Given the extensive and diverse nature of this engagement, it is obvious that interpretations of (cyber-)Islam made by young Muslims will be highly varied. Even on Islamist sites, their interpretations will not simply reproduce a mimicry version of the standard Islamist meta-narrative. The internet itself is 'an inherently polycentric' technology (Drissel 2011: 150), so cyber-Islam (like cyber-Christianity) can be found to contradict itself abundantly along factional and even idiosyncratic lines.

A frequent discussion thread on Muslim discussion boards[17] is whether or not there is a global conspiracy against Muslims so they will turn against each other – divide and conquer. Claims in the debate address the plot elements of *injustice* and *distrust* in the radical Islamist meta-narrative (Zackie 2013: 15). It is alleged on one side that the West (variously imagined) conspires to divide Muslims and sow mistrust between them. The other side counters that Muslims themselves are constantly disagreeing, conspiring and fighting each other rather than uniting in common cause. Debates on this particular topic are aired for years at a time on popular sites such as islamicity.com, engendering hundreds and hundreds of comments. For example, one follower of islamicity.com posted this explanatory comment on the conspiracy thread of the site:

> It's a war against humanity plain and simple (…) They just have to pull stuff like that to breed paranoia. Poking minorities (…) Why? To create diversity and mistrust. Regardless of our political, religious, spiritual, whatever standpoint, we need to come to understand that we are all the target.
>
> (Noah, 8 August 2007[18])

We can read this comment to infer it is the West that conspires to create division by targeting minorities. The West – variously imagined – usually sits at the heart of *conspiracy-against-Muslims* discourse (Cheong and Halverson 2010).

In the following year, another strident declaration about the 'divide and conquer' conspiracy appeared:

JUST BE A MUSLIM, NO POWER WILL OVERPOWER ISLAM,
WHEN WE ARE OPPOSING EACH OTHER, THIS CREATES A
WAR INSIDE ISLAM, THEN HOW CAN WE BE ABLE TO
DEFEND WAR AGAINST ISLAM.

(Syed Nasrullah, 7 July 2008[19])

Here the West is not the main protagonist in creating internal division, but
Muslims themselves who do not realise what they are doing by opposing
other Muslims. The West is still in there though, as the exterior perpetrator of
the 'war against Islam' against which all Muslims need to unite.

In 2009, a further posting referred to millennial ideas in explaining the
anti-Muslim conspiracy:

[This is] a preferred tactic of the evil one and his servants (…) The Muslims were separated then enslaved to the falsehood of political strife and
oppression {divided by politics}.

(Nazarene, 27 February 2009[20])

In this version the imagined perpetrator of conspiracy has shifted yet again,
this time to 'the evil one', who over centuries has twisted the word of God
and thus enslaved the non-Muslim people of the world to false faith. Subsequently he/it has divided Muslims using their pride, and caused conflict
between them. Here we see the ubiquity of apocalyptic discourse. Mentions of
the 'evil one', 'the devil' and 'Satan' were frequent in posted comments for the
conspiracy thread on islamicity.com.

Later in 2012 a further post offered yet another take on the 'divide and
conquer' conspiracy:

Blame is not on the Muslim community, or the Christian community, but
on the implicit perpetrator only (…) or at least one of them. Before Bin
Laden the world took little notice of Islam (…) 'live and let live' was the
way. After Bin Laden everyone was asking 'Why?' Now everyone has
suspicion and blame.

(Caringheart, 7 July 2012[21])

Notably, the imagined perpetrator of the conspiracy in this particular account
is Osama Bin Laden, constructed as a great enemy of Islam.

It is evident from the comparative critical readings above that while there is
shared assumption of conspiracy, the imagined perpetrator of that conspiracy
is not consistent. Each variant beyond the first is, in its own way, an implicit
counter-narrative to the radical Islamist meta-narrative claim that specifically
names 'the Crusader-American-Zionist-West' (Zackie 2013: 15) as the main
enemy which must be bitterly opposed.

Another compelling discussion thread on islamicity.com was titled 'who is
the enemy?' A provocative question was asked by a non-Muslim in 2011, and
provoked a flurry of replies on the same day. The question was:

> Are Muslims on a quest to take over the world? Yes or No?
>
> (Douggg, guest, 26 May 2011[22])

A female member wrote back almost at once:

> Are you kidding me? Who would say no if you are a practicing Muslim?
> (...) Allah (SWT), says to spread Islam throughout the world (...) Does
> that mean that we do not respect other people's man-made beliefs and that
> we do not acknowledge them? No. Does that mean that we cannot learn
> from man, man-created religions? NO. As Muslim we are not supposed
> to force someone to practice Islam.
>
> (Lady, 26 May 2011[23])

So in other words, yes, Muslims are on a quest to take over the world, but not
by force, because everyone should embrace Islam willingly (show true submission). As previously stated, Islam is a proselytising religion like Christianity, so Lady's sentiments primarily express a missionary-like zeal. The
next post quickly appeared, taking a humorous angle:

> Yes, Douggg. We are going to take over the world and will employ you as
> our court jester! (evil laugh).
>
> (Islamispeace, 26 May 2011[24])

The next post took the same affirmative approach as Lady's, but was more
careful about it:

> Surely Muslims would like to see the entire world following Muhammad,
> but Muslims will never desire to achieve it by force. Islam has enough
> good things in it to attract logical and blessed people.
>
> (nu001, 26 May 2011[25])

Reading this set of comments in sequence, Dougg's initial question encodes a dual
discourse – the fear-filled Western idea that Muslims are trying to take over the
world, and the Islamist view that Muslims have a sacred duty to make the whole
world follow Islam. The first and third replies negotiate these dual discourses
by referencing the proselytising yet tolerant nature of Islam, while the second
uses humour. All three replies though, cast Dougg as the outsider, just as he
himself did in posing his question. This negotiated positioning in the text
illustrates how the internet facilitates Muslims locating themselves within a
re-imagined global *ummah* as a mediated community (Mandaville 2001: 184).

As a final point, online sites offer the technological affordance of persona-lisation, which encodes the operation of exclusion (of specific others). Legit-imate users become ever more connected with their in-group, with whom they share (or believe they share) similarities, and at the same time, become more and more isolated from other groups and peers who have different points of view or who do not share a similar identity (Pariser 2011). While personali-sation has contributed in a democratic sense to the development of new 'imagined' communities on the internet, it has also encouraged exclusionary practices. Pariser (2011: 125) argues that the technological affordance of per-sonalisation creates a 'filter bubble', a self-contained loop of inclusion which may perpetuate fantasy ideas about the nature of reality, and guide choices.

Humour

The jihadi may be a figure of fear, but becomes a figure of fun in humorous counter-narratives. Online posts from the diaspora often mock and satirise the juvenile jihadi. For example, the London-based satirical blogger and tweeter Karl Sharro (@KarlreMarks – more than 60,000 Twitter followers) writes about two Islamic State recruits keeping guard on a remote outpost in Iraq. A spaceship lands and two aliens get out. He writes, 'sadly for everyone involved, Abu Abdullah's career as a drug dealer-turned-Muslim-turned ISIS fighter didn't prepare him for the complexities of a theological discussion with visiting aliens. Then he remembers his copy of "Islam for Dummies"', and so the comedy continues. Another of Sharro's satires depicts the self-declared caliph Abu Bakr al-Baghdadi confiding in his psychiatrist about his declara-tion of caliphate, 'I am wondering if I rushed into this'. The psychiatrist advises him to take it step by step, and remember the exercises he gave. The self-styled caliph replies, 'I keep wondering if I should get a turban. One of those big ones in mauve or pistachio, with a silver clip ...' It seems IS and its declared caliphate attract much satirical attention – in cartoons, on YouTube and in satirical sketch shows on television (Pollard 2015).

Making fun of IS happens even right next to war-torn Syria. Letsch (2015) describes the comic films made by exiled Syrian video artists in Turkey. Four young Syrian refugees decided ridicule was an effective way of responding to the extreme violence of IS. A spokesman said, 'the entire world seems to be terrified of ISIS, so we want to laugh at them, expose their hypocrisy and show that their interpretation of Islam does not represent the overwhelming majority of Muslims'. He added, 'the media, especially the Western media, obsessively reproduce IS propaganda, portraying them as strong and intimi-dating. We want to show their weaknesses'. Their film 'The Prince' shows self-appointed caliph Abu Bakr al-Baghdadi drinking wine, listening to pop music and exchanging selfies with girls on his smartphone. A new Moroccan jihadi arrives. The caliph swaps wine for milk and switches the sound system to Islamic chants praising martyrdom. He hands the Moroccan a suicide belt and sends him off. After the explosion the caliph reaches for his wine again and turns the pop music back on. The film-making group has received hate mail and threats via social media. Yet they are keen to continue their satirical work, 'expose their lies and laugh at them. When people laugh, they lose their fear' (quoted in Letsch 2015).

A more recent example comes from Anonymous.com hackers who 'hijack' Twitter accounts belonging to supporters of IS. In the aftermath of the 2016 massacre at a gay nightclub in Orlando, USA by a shooter who pledged allegiance to IS, the hacker WauchulaGhost replaced a jihadi Twitter message with 'Hello World. It's time I share with you a little secret … I'm Gay and Proud!' The same hacker claims to have hacked over 250 Twitter accounts associated with IS members. The IS flag is replaced with the rainbow flag. He also takes down IS accounts.

The possibilities for satirising Islamist extremism are endless. Memes, for example, offer a new way of civic participation in important debates for internet users who eschew airing opinions in the traditional mass media. Memes that mock the Islamist meta-narrative and the idea of jihad are readily found in social media.[26] The meme-creating/viewing/sharing process consolidates the alternative identity of Muslim youth who find them meaningful and funny. While Pantucci (2015) found that jihadi images and messages disseminated online primarily target those who already agree with the radical Islamist position, the same can be said for young Muslims who are looking for amusing counter-discourse that mocks hardline extremism.

Conclusion

In summary, the online environment provides a means for the radical Islamist meta-narrative to be emotively disseminated in a bounded environment from which opposing viewpoints can be excluded. When this occurs, 'the mutual validation of ideas among the participants may not only lead them to develop ideas at odds with the rest of society, but also harden their beliefs' (Sageman 2008: 117). In terms of counter-narrative though, the same technological affordances of freedom of association, rhizomatic spreadability and personalisation invite the assembly of virtual communities of like thinkers who want to contest that same meta-narrative, and develop counter-narratives. This is the dynamic phenomenon of neo-theo-tribalism made manifest.

I conclude this chapter by suggesting that the sheer number and diversity of Muslim-based websites frequented by youth constitutes a heterogeneous and non-stop deluge of claims and counter-claims in relation to the Islamist position and to exhortations of extremism. In fact, the proliferation *in itself* constitutes a form of counter-narrative to the singular radical Islamist meta-narrative. There is also the millennial trend. It is not only extraordinarily contentious to start with, but the terms of debate keep changing as world events unfold. Of course I have been able to represent only a small sample of the dynamic diversity of counter-narrative in this chapter. Each Muslim ethnic group in the worldwide diaspora has its own set of websites through which current issues affecting Islam are constantly updated and debated. I am only able to read websites in English and two other languages, neither of which is Arabic, so my lens is inevitably limited. Yet the diversity and plenitude is there for anyone to observe. It is very easy indeed for any young Muslim in the diaspora to find a version of Islam online that specifically suits their religious beliefs, ethnicity, gender, worldview, hobbies, interests, and so on. On Muslim websites across the board we can find many instances of comment or discussion that reflect on the double positioning of Muslim youth within the faith (be pious!), and within Western societies (fit in!).

In fact both of these discourses exhort Muslim youth to present themselves as 'good'. It is just that 'good' does not have the same connotation in the Muslim and non-Muslim fields. To be a good Muslim theologically means to observe the five pillars of Islam, to follow the rules in culture and social relations, and to focus on pious practice rather than hedonism and consumption. To be seen as a good Muslim in the Western diaspora implies restricting pious practice to the private domain and embracing some of the manifold 'freedoms' of secular democracy. Although these two ideas about what it means to be a 'good' Muslim are not necessarily incompatible, there are certainly tensions that arise. It can be argued that for many youth in the diaspora, it is hard enough just following the *basic* obligations of faith as they go about their everyday lives in the secular West. So to push their piety towards the strictures of Islamism makes it harder and harder for them to fit in the Western society where most of their other life domains – education, friends, family, romance, career – are located. In short, to take up a hardline Islamist position risks condemnation from *all* sides.

It should be evident by now that the radical Islamist meta-narrative is not consistently told the same way everywhere. In the diversity of re-tellings, re-writings and re-readings there is potential for counter-narrative intervention and comic reversal. Moreover, there are myriad points of contention in polyvalent Islamic discourse about the how, who, what, when and why of caliphate, and even of *ummah*. Certainly the meaning of jihad is a source of ongoing fervent debate. It can be argued therefore, that in moments of appropriation, when certain young Muslims in the diaspora imaginatively take up and personalise aspects of the Islamist meta-narrative, there is still ample capacity for counter-narratives to emerge, even from that point.

Finally, we should not lose sight of the fact that, relative to the radical Islamist meta-narrative, there are trends of revitalisation, resacralisation and re-enchantment in Islam itself that engage directly with desire/affect for Muslim youth in the diaspora. That engagement may inhere in meeting with youthful vigour the challenge of achieving caliphate, while confounding the 'wicked problem' of local Islamophobia. This could be realised in some cases by joining *Hizbut Tahrir*. That engagement could also be realised in a 'deviant career', where a young person assumes the assigned negative label and reverses the moral polarity so that bad becomes good – a swaggering jihadi. Finally, that engagement may see the young person aligning with one of the neo-theo-tribal groupings in the global contemporary popular culture of Muslim youth, and expressing a ludic orientation. In my view that is the majority position. It points directly to the wider frame of youthful Islam where expression of piety is part of the new 'cool'. The next chapter looks in depth at that phenomenon.

Notes

1 Others are Snapchat, Pinterest, Instagram, VK, Flickr, Vine, Tagged, Ask.fm.
2 Sermons.
3 Pantucci (2015) argues that it is not only Salafism that encourages Islamist extremism, but the *Deobandi* movement in Pakistan.
4 'Darknet' refers to a virtual realm beyond conventional search engines that works primarily for illegal peer-to-peer file sharing. It uses anonymising software.
5 www.youtube.com/watch?v=HserMrLh7wg.
6 Jihadi John was Mohammed Emwazi, an Iraqi Briton who became an ISIL jihadi and was videoed beheading a number of captives before he was killed.
7 Translated by the author from: 'Les frères Kouachi et Coulibaly, des pionniers du djihadisme français'.
8 Translated by the author from: 'de plonger le pays tout entier dans l'inquiétude'.
9 Isa is the revenant Jesus, who is explained in the Koran as a prophet.
10 www.youtube.com/watch?v=FD-El2HNkaE.
11 www.youtube.com/watch?v=FD-El2HNkaE.
12 www.youtube.com/watch?v=FD-El2HNkaE.
13 www.youtube.com/watch?v=FD-El2HNkaE.
14 www.youtube.com/watch?v=FD-El2HNkaE.
15 www.youtube.com/watch?v=EPS8EHTNaZw.
16 www.youtube.com/watch?v=EPS8EHTNaZw.
17 These sites are popular with idealistic young people, see Drissel (2011).
18 www.islamicity.com/forum/forum_posts.asp?TID=8814&PD=1.
19 www.islamicity.com/forum/forum_posts.asp?TID=8814&PN=2.
20 www.islamicity.com/forum/forum_posts.asp?TID=8814&PN=2.
21 www.islamicity.com/forum/forum_posts.asp?TID=8814&PN=3.
22 www.islamicity.com/forum/forum_posts.asp?TID=20853.
23 www.islamicity.com/forum/forum_posts.asp?TID=20853.
24 www.islamicity.com/forum/forum_posts.asp?TID=20853.
25 www.islamicity.com/forum/forum_posts.asp?TID=20853.
26 www.examiner.com/list/top-10-muslim-memes-for-all.

Chapter 5

Counter-narratives of the new Muslim 'cool'

Introduction

This chapter considers how the parallel world of Muslim youth popular culture generates a range of counter-narratives. Against radical Islamism, the counter-discourse of popular culture expresses the ideal of trendy Muslim 'cool'[1] (Herding 2013), in consumption and neo-tribal choices. This active self-styling pertains to the many in the diaspora, rather than the few who take an Islamist path. As Wright (2012: 42) points out, 'counter-jihad is reflected both in the mundane and the remarkable'; in both overt articulation of counter-discourse through cutting edge style, and through quiet discretionary choice that represents internal piety. Muslim youth culture in the diaspora synthesises transnational Islam with popular culture influences from a variety of global and national cultural flows, as well as local conditions (Herding 2013). However, this is not represented in just a single style or a single set of preferences. Rather, style choices are aligned with the varied discursive positions offered by the observable neo-theo-tribalism of Muslim popular culture, a continuum which ranges from the near-secular to the highly ascetic. The concept also builds on the observation that 'postmodern [religious] fundamentalism is neotribal' (Taylor 2008: 158). For example, peppering the phrase *inshallah* (if God wills it)[2] throughout everyday conversations with age peers includes fellow Muslims and excludes non-Muslims.[3] Yet the person saying it may not be particularly devout. The practice might be operating primarily as a mechanism of distinction (Bourdieu 1984). The discussion below explains the material and discursive engagement of young Muslims with fashion, consumer products and leisure pursuits (see Khabeer and Alhassen 2013), practices that also realise the mechanism of cultural distinction. To choose aesthetically is to distinguish oneself from others (Bourdieu 1984). Consideration is also given to the gendered nature of these discourses and practices of distinction.

Where Islamism provides a meta-narrative of rigidly controlled pious conduct, Muslim commercial interests provide a counter-narrative of guided pleasurable consumption (Starrett 2003). Producers in the Muslim world are keen on targeting the youth market. For example, from a business viewpoint, Muslim

Generation Y in the West has been described as 'looking for opportunities to show that it is possible to be a cool, fun, and hip Muslim' (Javed 2013: 41). For hard-line Islamists this is anathema (Herding 2013). From their position all popular culture is judged *haram* (not allowed within the faith). So Muslim popular culture is *haram* (Alagha 2011). As a first point of definition:

> The opposition in Islamist discourse between '*haram*' and '*halal*' – or more specifically with regard to art, '*fann al-habit*' versus '*fann al-hadif*' – stretches the meaning of 'low' toward 'vulgar' in the sense of 'corrupt' or 'immoral'.
>
> (Van Nieuwkerk 2012: 236)

Thus conservative Muslims often avoid popular culture altogether, including secular music, and even sport, because it distracts from pious practice and might encourage immoral behaviour. However, that ascetic position presents a challenge for the vast majority of young Muslims who want to have fun and be entertained while following the faith (Bayat 2007). Those who strongly support the radical Islamist meta-narrative take an even more extreme view; young Muslims who waste their time on frivolous pursuits are holding back the Islamist revolution of hearts and minds that should be taking place. They may even be judged as *khafr* (infidels) for doing it. Nevertheless, the Muslim youth market worldwide generates staggering amounts of profit.

I argue that the engagement of young Muslims with popular culture constitutes in itself a nascent counter-narrative. Islamism is not fun (Bayat 2007) and popular culture is:

> There is a very basic fact about extremist Islam that is almost never mentioned in the scholarly literature. It is not fun and extremists seek to eliminate most parts of Muslim cultures that are. Having fun in a Muslim way is not counter-radical discourse. It is counter-radical action.
>
> (Woodward et al. 2010: 44)

Nevertheless, Muslim youth wanting to have fun need not take up secular practices. There are plenty of Muslim youth culture products around (see Nilan 2012b) and some of these are described below. In fact, consumption of contemporary popular culture products by Muslim youth implies a high level of reflexivity in the matter of choice distinctions, since they commonly aim to enjoy themselves while remaining within the permitted moral boundary of *halal* (Khabeer and Alhassen 2013). Business interests endorsing 'brand Islam' are ready and waiting with a range of *halal* products and services (Starrett 2003) express their belonging to global Muslim youth culture. However, as Paul Willis pointed out, young people are creative with popular culture. They not only consume it, but produce it interactively in ways that are aligned with clusters of taste preferences among youth. Thus the global neo-tribes of Islamic youth culture include Muslim hipsters in the great cities of world (Cevik 2015), Muslim hip-hop fans (O'Brien 2013), and even Muslim punks (McDowell 2016). Music taste cultures are discussed in a later chapter.

Cevik (2015) views contemporary Muslim style choices as reflecting an individual orientation filtered through the notion of faith as *chosen rather than forced* through regulation, or by submission to fixed tradition. This is the practice of everyday Islam guided by a conscious moral self rather than adherence to restrictive guidelines. Moreover, for Muslim youth in the diaspora, their religious sense of self is inflected by mobility, a kind of postmodern nomadism accelerated by online technology. They can move between different versions of Islam, venture into Sufism (see Chapter 2), go *'fatwa*-shopping' for the ruling on popular music that suits them, and so on. This is not radical disjuncture but a flow between sites and sources of relevant discourse, telling a mixed story of conformity and subversion. In so doing they continue to negotiate along the good Muslim–bad Muslim continuum that is propagated variously by Muslim community voices, the radical Islamist meta-narrative and Western states dealing with the threat of terrorism. They deal daily with the risk of being judged as immoral from the religious side, and as potentially immoral (dangerous) in a different sense from the non-Muslim side.

Global discourses of Muslim youth culture

In Muslim-majority countries and in the diaspora, Western influences are often regarded by older generations as a great source of danger to susceptible youth. They perceive risk primarily in terms of premarital sex, drugs and even satanism, so film, music, radio, TV and the internet are regarded with great concern (Swedenburg 2007). In a similar way to moral panics in Christian-majority countries, youth are defined as in need of supervision, instruction and protection. Yet despite some concentrated efforts at control, even youth in Muslim-majority countries are participating, 'to various degrees and in various ways, in a globalized capitalist youth culture' (Harb 2014: 2), and the trend seems unstoppable. In other words, there is generational conflict in regard to popular culture but young Muslims find ways around it. For example, Varzi (2006: 11) describes how secular-oriented middle-class youth in Tehran rely on the discretion and permission of liberal parents to organise private parties for mixed-sex socialising, live music and alcohol.

It is probable that online sites generated in Muslim-majority countries influence discourses of *halal* and *haram* for Muslim youth living in Western countries through ethnic community links. Thus some Muslim youth in the diaspora might choose to be more ascetic in their lifestyle choices than many urban youth in the country of ethnic origin. Yet in the secular West they can also participate more freely in the neo-theo-tribalism of Muslim popular culture as it is expressed in trendy consumption. In fact, the sheer range of versions of Islam offered online means that any Muslim anywhere can almost always find a theological ruling to suit their lifestyle choices. Islamic law as represented on the internet 'offers a pick-and-choose, do-it-yourself brand of self-help' (Zaman 2008: 471). Media of all kinds constitute the voices of Islamic law, because religious authority is now achieved more by popular recognition than anything else (Mandaville 2001). In the online/offline pleni-tude of voices and forces, competition for creating Muslim identities goes hand-in-hand with competition for religious authority. The ensuing debate about right and wrong in versions of Islam is prolific on social media plat-forms and also in YouTube uploads. For example, Mosemghvdlishvili and Jansz (2013) report that Islam was one of the most hotly debated topics on YouTube by the middle of the first decade of the new millennium. Almost 5,000 clips a week tagged with the word Islam were being uploaded. The most common motivations for YouTube postings on Islam were: 'communicating Islam, self-expression and social recognition' (Mosemghvdlishvili and Jansz 2013: 494). This cultural saturation both reflects and constitutes the religious domain and its various articulations for young Muslims. It is fertile ground for counter-narratives of all kinds.

The most comprehensive study of Muslim 'cool' to date is the admirable ethnographic work by Maruta Herding (2013) in Western Europe. Herding describes Muslim youth culture as a combination of religion and general youth culture; 'it manifests itself in explicitly religious rap, Islamic comedy, young urban fashion with pious slogans or media products' (Herding 2013: 10). These performative expressions are inflected by the norms of the country in which they live, the national language and the customs, even as their style choices refer to global tribes that embody youthful Islamic cool. It seems that in their repre-sentations of identity, young Muslims in Western countries are producing not only counter-narratives to the radical Islamist meta-narrative, but counter-narratives to the war-on-terror narrative too, by blending trendy youth culture with piety.

In summary, Muslim youth in the diaspora inhabit primarily urban domains connected through information technology and social media to the world. They negotiate an offline and online environment culturally saturated with competing discourses of who they are and what they should be doing – or not doing. Here the plurality of contemporary Islam can fit quite well with the contingencies of a fast-moving urban social existence. There is a strong link between religious awareness and post-traditional lifestyles (Turner 2011; Cevik 2015), manifesting in the search for religious guidelines that construct for the individual a morally defensible identity and life pathway (Beck 2010). Yet as this chapter indicates, religious orthopraxy for Muslim youth in the diaspora would seem to be primarily anchored in the contemporary material and tribal world of youth culture, and not so much in traditional ascetic practices and cultural piety. An intriguing example is the advice given in one online com-ment: 'Trouble with being a Muslim hipster is that you can look like a jihadi instead! Keep the beards trimmed, dudes!' (DrAshSays in Taylor 2015). If a young Muslim man is not careful about the length and style of his beard, he risks being read by peers and the public as belonging to the 'wrong' tribe.

Muslim youth culture and counter-narrative

I define youth culture as the set of meaningful things that young people consume and practice which defines them as an age cohort exposed to similar discourses, images, messages, demands and expectations. Across the world, studies of youth culture include popular music, film, media, fashion, distinctive ways of speaking and writing, risk-taking, grass-roots creativity, leisure and social media. In other words, there are some similar features of youth cultures everywhere now in the networked world of late modernity (Nilan and Feixa 2006). Muslim youth culture is no exception. Across the world young Muslims use the same popular culture symbols such as distinctive headwear and clothing, chin-beards, sacred music tracks and Arabic script graffiti – 'to identify themselves and to claim power and space' (Moje 2002: 105).

The Islamist meta-narrative seems to promise revitalisation and re-sacralisation through engaging with extremism. However, Muslim youth in the diaspora construct other attractive stories about Islam where a carefully chosen and externalised expression of piety becomes the new 'cool'.[4] This is especially so for covered female attire and the headscarf, where a vast fashion industry is at work providing style choices. For their part, young men might opt for collarless shirts, chin beards and white skull caps, along with shortened trousers to facilitate pre-prayer washing of feet. Arabic calligraphy and devotional chanting are customised to act as screensavers and ringtones. Roy (2004) might see such choices as evidence of 'deculturation'; the decontextualisation and deterritorialisation of religious practices within youth culture. However, it can be equally argued that the religious symbols taken up by Muslim youth in their fashion choices still have a theological meaning for them, even if it is one that an older generation sometimes fails to grasp. In that respect we can read the category *Muslim youth* as a transnational 'project identity' (Castells 1997: 8) which requires constant collective re-assertion. For example, the most common explanation from Indonesian Muslim-majority youth for the 'new' Islamic cultural expressions of identity – such as Middle Eastern dress and the ubiquity of Arabic script – is that these things signal belonging to the *ummah*. They are also understood to confer blessings. They signal not only dignity, strength and 'moral purity', but resistance to Westernisation (Nilan 2006: 93). The symbols themselves exclude those outside the faith. The logic goes like this: if you don't get it, you don't belong in our youth culture tribe.

Muslim youth popular culture generates a range of counter-narratives to the hardline rigidity of an Islamist position. As implied previously, a counter-narrative can be playful or satirical. For example, Joosse et al. (2015) studied young Somali Canadians dealing with approaches by peers recruiting for the militant jihadi group *Al-Shabaab*. One of their humorous come-backs to

Al-Shabaab recruiters was to say: 'you may think you're cool, but actually you're a tool' (Joosse et al. 2015: 12). Not only do they infer that religious extremism is not cool (because the speaker knows what is really cool), but the term 'tool' is a double-edged insult. The pejorative label 'tool' is a slang term for someone deemed stupid, socially inept, even gullible. Yet recruiters are actually 'tools' – doing the work of those conducting a faraway war. The insult infers that you would have to be a 'tool' to become a 'tool' for the recruiters. Another informant described the militant group *Al-Shabaab* as 'a small fringe group of religious nutjobs' whose members actually know little about Islam. In saying this, the speaker took 'ownership of condemnatory narratives' usually articulated by non-Muslims, and applied them to militants (Joosse et al. 2015: 14). In another example, a study of working-class Pakistani-American youth found them to be keen on presenting the public image of pious but cheerful, public-spirited, cool young Muslims (Ghaffar-Kucher 2015). Both studies imply the new Muslim 'cool' that refuses to be either categorically 'good' or 'bad' in stereotypical terms.

Regrettably, the melodramatic Islamist meta-narrative of militant retribution seems to be the main story told about Muslims throughout the diaspora. The epic tale is favoured not only by extremist groups but by sensationalist Western media sources. As Wright (2015: 9) points out, it yields 'good copy'. However, a melodramatic narrative – by its very hyperbolic and hyperreal nature – is wide open to comic reversals, irony, satire, parody, mockery and other forms of humour that constitute amusing and entertaining counter-narratives within particular youth cultures. As stated previously, the Islamist meta-narrative and jihad are favourite targets of young Muslim satirists. Memes, gifs, mods, skits and satirical tracks, jokes and cartoons all represent forms of 'restyling'; a reworking of both aesthetics and identity in response to an important public narrative – or moral panic – that pertains to the self and its broad political framing (Corner and Pels 2003). Restyling the Islamist meta-narrative through satire means Muslim youth redirect the narrative and recast the main roles (Wright 2015: 13). Many have commented on the rich vein of this humour:

> There is a new weapon: comedy. As ISIS continues their brutal offensive in Syria and Iraq, many throughout the Islamic world have begun parodying the terror group on social media. Dozens of hilarious campaigns have been launched on Twitter and Facebook, ridiculing the extremist group.
>
> (Counter Current News[5])

Mocking and ridiculing are powerful elements of anti-jihad counter-narrative. When this is done by young Muslims themselves it constitutes their identity as both theologically aware and cool. They actively demonstrate their digital literacy in displaying knowledge of Islam. At the same time, since humour is a vital technique in publishing a digital account of the self, they create a satirical product that is recognised and found funny by others who follow the paradigm of Muslim cool, who distinguish themselves by following that style tribe.

Muslim celebrity culture

The previous chapter took a brief look at how the cult of celebrity operates on the Islamist terrorist front. Here I turn to celebrity in Muslim youth culture. The celebrity is an ambiguous but ubiquitous figure in contemporary culture (Marshall 1997). It has been argued that the intensity of celebrity fandom signals an ontological shift in popular culture. 'The celebrity becomes a key site of media attention and personal aspiration, as well as one of the key places *where cultural meanings are negotiated and organised*' (Turner 2014: 6, my emphasis). The Muslim public sphere is no exception (Van Nieuwkerk 2011). Celebrity in the sphere of popular culture is a prime location for struggles over what it means to be a young Muslim in the diaspora.

Who you follow is a clue to how you position yourself relative to the major shaping discourses of Islamism on one side and Islamophobia on the other. Celebrity Muslim preachers are a prime example of how this works. For example, the Egyptian tele-evangelist Amr Khaled inspires young Muslims to be proudly pious in both the Arab world and the West. Prominent preachers such as Pierre Vogel in Cologne and Abdul Adhim in Berlin attract young Muslims in Germany because they are charismatic and profess a strict moral orientation as a brave standpoint in the face of national Islamophobia. For all three celebrity Muslim preachers, their websites are flooded with praise and testimonials from young followers who feel a deep connection to what they are saying. There is no way of knowing though, whether some of those same young fans of Muslim preachers express an equal amount of adoration for different kinds of Muslim celebrities that they admire on television and in popular music. In all probability, many will be fans of both.

In the arena of popular music, many young Muslim fans seem to think that British celebrity Zayn Malik is the embodiment of Muslim 'cool'. Zayn left the famous boy band One Direction in 2015 to pursue a solo singing career. He has 'والتر' – his grandfather's name – tattooed on the right side of his chest and ليكون صحيحا من أنت – 'be true to who you are' – tattooed on the left side.[6] Although he is much loved by young Muslim fans he is much criticised by Muslim conservatives for contradictions between doctrine and his perceived lifestyle. As a Muslim youth culture celebrity Zayn endures criticism from both sides. 'Either Bill Maher is comparing him to the Boston bomber, or conservative clergy are criticising him for not being devout enough' (Samie-zade'-Yazd 2015). In 2012, high profile American blogger Debbie Schlussel accused Zayn of 'boyband jihad' and 'pimping Islam', claiming he was chosen for One Direction only because 'Islam sells in Britain'. In 2013 a non-Muslim US rapper released the track 'Zayn did 9/11', with Zayn's silhouette superimposed over the burning Twin Towers, and lyrics blaming him for the

9/11 attacks. In 2014 Zayn received death threats for tweeting #FreePalestine. From the other side, hard-liners reject his Muslim identity all together. '@zaynmalik needs to join jihad', @ISILCats tweeted, 'not be another dumb sissy celebrity'. To many, Zayn Malik is just *haram*, for example:

> He smokes, he drinks, he has tattoos, he sings, he's dated girls/kisses them etc, all of which are strictly forbidden in Islam.
>
> (Anon[7])

In summary, it seems that 'anything he does in public, any stance he takes, any music he performs, any beard he decides to grow, will always be portrayed as a direct result of not his personal choices, but his degree of Muslimness' (Samiezade'-Yazd 2015). However, the publicity from all sides has only served to enhance Zayn's image of cool among young Muslims.[8] Recently, he was used as a celebrity role model by UK anti-IS campaigner Nurun Ahmed, who wants to dissuade Muslim girls from going to Syria by showing them opportunities for young Muslims in Britain. It can be argued that Zayn has been pressed into service as an embodied counter-narrative to extremism.

The article on Zayn in the *Guardian* by Samiezade'-Yazd (2015) attracted quite a number of comments on the site from young Muslims in the UK. The following posted comment has much to tell us about how expressions and representations of a youthful Muslim identity in the diaspora are constituted through the trope of celebrity. The comment begins as follows:

> I have been able to see bits of myself reflected in Zayn (...) that sort of representation in the media is important for any Muslim.
>
> (Diyana[9])

In other words, Diyana identifies the celebrity representation of Zayn as positive for supporting the legitimacy of her own non-mainstream identity. She then went on to explain her own subject position as a woman from a Muslim background who is no longer religious but believes in some kind of a higher power. Yet even though she now longer follows Islam she still finds prejudice due to her ethnic background. She then returned to the topic of Zayn, reflecting on how he is condemned by voices on both sides:

> People may love the fact that he is Muslim or they hate it (...) a spokesperson for, or a shame to, the name of Islam.
>
> (Diyana[10])

Diyana draws our attention to the fact that as Zayn's celebrity status has increased, so have accusations and threats that concern his profession of Muslim faith. She added that this is wrong because only Allah has the right to judge.

Diyana makes a number of significant points about the utility of celebrity in the Muslim public sphere. She uses the counter-narrative of Zayn to construct her own counter-narrative to those Muslim authorities who would judge him, and by extension, she herself. Read as counter-narrative, her commentary admits local experience of intolerance while challenging radicals who think they have the right to judge. She condemns the moral purity campaign within contemporary Islam which judges Zayn harshly. In other comments she implies that Muslim celebrity in the public sphere of youth culture achieves a victory for 'brown' young Muslims such as herself. Diyana's statements gained a very quick response from Umer Farooq who commented not on Zayn, but on Diyana's admitted non-religious position:

> Your response is running away from religion? Seems like the easy way out right? I've known people that did the complete opposite, born and raised in the west were indifferent towards the religion (...) only studied Islam after the hatred was directed at them and as a result completely submerged themselves into it and fell in love with it.
>
> (Umer Farooq, 9 April 2015[11])

Umer's proselytising response tells a story of disbelieving young Muslims in the diaspora who reinvent themselves as committed believers after the experience of local intolerance drives them to fall 'in love' with Islam. However, Diyana was not convinced. She replied, 'it is not "running away" so much as it is being honest with myself'. The opposing viewpoints aired above point to the diversity of subject positions in the diaspora. The fact that the discussion grew from a posting about Zayn Malik demonstrates the extent to which discussion about Muslim popular culture celebrities has become a key site for cultural meanings to be expressed and negotiated.

Popular culture negotiating *haram* and *halal*

In the Muslim diaspora, businesses have rushed to fill the possible gap of moral doubt with *halal* products including clothing, food and cosmetics (Sobh 2014), as well as matrimonial matching sites (see below). It is estimated the US Muslim consumer market alone is worth billions (Sobh 2014). Advertising emphasises Islamic rectitude. 'Prophet Muhammad [peace be upon him], was the living embodiment of *the brand of Islam*' (Janmohammed 2010: 1, my emphasis). This claim encodes the following (counter-) narrative: If you as a Muslim practise *halal* consumption of products and services, you will be blessed and live a prosperous life on earth, as well as receiving heavenly rewards afterwards. In contrast, the radical Islamist meta-narrative implies ascetic self-sacrifice to a hard life on earth as a militant or fugitive, and even a martyred early death, with only heavenly rewards to follow. It is not surprising that so few Muslim youth are persuaded to take up radical Islamist recruitment invitations.

Under the *halal* label, Muslim consumers can buy not only fashionable clothing, specialised food and pious books, but perfume (men and women), skin and hair products (men and women), cosmetics, jewellery (men and women) and personalised prayer mats (men and women). There are Muslim wristwatches for men and women, and toys, dolls and board games for children. There is even a *halal* online sex shop that claims its products and advertising do not contravene *sharia* law (Payne 2014). In short, brand Islam can be used to sell almost anything, from *sharia*-financed home loans to covered talking dolls and Zam-Zam Cola. In some countries there are Muslim cars with an inbuilt Koran and navigation tool for the direction of Mecca, and Muslim-themed laptops with similar features. In Indonesia, even bottled drinking water is sometimes labelled *halal* for marketing purposes. *Halal* branding imprints products as permitted for Muslims, as 'morally good' (Van Nieuwkerk 2012: 251).

For Muslim youth in Western countries, consumption of such products intensifies the feeling of belonging to a community of young Muslim believers worldwide who have their finger on the beating pulse of style in late modernity. Moreover, such consumption allows them to live the normatively framed Western 'good life' (Mandaville 2007a: 105), while following the Islamic moral code. Finally, purchasing from within a limited selection of Muslim products signifies a form of successful struggle against the temptations of a secular life. In short, *halal* consumption establishes their moral purity within a relational framework of orthopraxy. Guided practices of observance under brand Islam constitute them within the community of God's chosen people (Zackie 2013: 15). Through the praxis of blessed purchase they locate themselves in a parallel world of elevated moral conduct where judiciously chosen luxuries of style are still permitted. This is a targeted, homogenising commodification – 'McIslamisation' perhaps – that parallels the process George Ritzer (1993) describes as 'McDonaldization' in Western culture. Hybrid products, images and text blend the sacred and the profane in the popular culture of Muslim youth – a parallel world of *halal* consumption.

Halal *fashion*

Javed (2013: 41) implies that brand Islam promises young followers of the faith that they can be 'cool, fun, and hip' Muslims. Nowhere is this more evident than in fashion products. For example, in Germany, Nordbruck (2010: 3) found that Muslim youth enthusiastically purchased *halal* clothing and accessories. The study sample consisted of young people who were not raised in strict Muslim families but later embraced global Islam. He terms them 'neo-Muslims'. They wanted to engage in youth culture like their non-Muslim age peers, but on their own terms. Thus they were attracted to German labels such as 'Style Islam', which distributes fashionable street wear and accessories with Islamic messages. In simple terms Muslim youth fashion is booming. For example, trendy printed Muslim t-shirts for both sexes play humorously on Western slogans such as:

Salah. Prayer: 5 a day keeps the *shaytan* away [shaytan means devil]
Ramadan: time to recharge [with an iPad battery recharge image]
iFast [with the iconic apple symbol]
Hungry for the truth? Shahada.[12] *Why wait?* [plays on the Snickers chocolate bar slogan 'Hungry? Why wait?']

(Javed 2013: 41)

The t-shirt slogans above synthesise Islamic identity and Western popular culture in a material commodity. As lightly humorous fashion items they constitute the identity of the wearer as both theologically aware and cool (see Herding 2013). Other examples of humorous synthesis include the Mecca Cola slogan *Ishrab Multazim* – 'drink faithfully', and the popular European clothing franchise Muslim Gear slogan, 'believe in what you wear'. In terms of the cultural imaginary of *ummah* in the diaspora, it is important these consumption choices are not only made by the individual, but then publicly displayed as pious performance of self. Boubekeur (2005) argues that Islamic streetwear and Islam-branded merchandise offer a comfortable consumerism which permits Muslim pride to be quietly demonstrated. For example in the world of sport, the '*Dawah* Wear' jogging suit (for men) was launched by Muslim NBA star Tarik Abdelwahad. The logo is a series of numbers that signify for Muslims the four positions of prayer. On the female side, a Dutch enterprise has manufactured a velcro *hijab* that suits skating, tennis and aerobics (Boubekeur 2005: 12). In the world of fashion, Melanie Elturk in the US started clothing line 'Haute *Hijab*' because she did not feel that upmarket mainstream fashion caters to the young American Muslim woman who wants 'classy' but modest apparel (Sobh 2014).

A more recent Islamic fashion sensation is 'Hipster Hijabis', initiated by Syrian-American Summer Al Barcha, aged 18, when she started the enterprise in 2012. Summer said she began from her own personal dress standards and incorporated the hipster concept because 'hipsters are people who like to dress differently from the crowd and still appear modest, and hijabis represent people like me who wear the hijab and/or want to be modest. I wanted to inspire both' (Summer Al Barcha, 22, quoted in El-Saeed 2015). In an interview she stated she was aiming for:

A way to inspire women to embrace dressing modestly, especially in a society where it is not customary, such as in the United States. I wanted to show that it is possible to still take part in the same mainstream fashions and *just adjust them to fit*.

(Summer Al Barcha, 22, quoted in El-Saeed 2015, my emphasis)

Here it is the idea of 'adjust to fit' that signals an important counter-narrative constituted in the 'cool' of Muslim youth culture. The concept of adjustment (negotiation, synthesis) runs right up against a rigid hardline view that there is only one way of being a legitimate Muslim and that should have nothing to do with secular norms. On the other hand, the 'Hipster Hijabi' suggestion of adjustment does not apply to the extent that all visible signs of a Muslim identity are erased.

Middle-class prosperity

The glimpses above of marketing and consumption under 'brand Islam' imply a middle-class income and lifestyle. The ideal of middle-class Muslim life represents an important element in claims for a moderate Islam and is an important counter-narrative to Islamist ideas of stark asceticism and personal self-sacrifice. Nasr (2010) directly promotes middle-class prosperity as the solution for Muslims worldwide. He believes the new Muslim middle class is the ultimate answer to extremism because it gives equal emphasis to the pious and the material. It constitutes a counter-discourse of comfortable Muslim prosperity that undermines terrorist rhetoric. However, it is not just any commerce that will change the Muslim world, he believes, but 'business with a small "b"' (Nasr 2010: 11), conducted by pious conservatives who favour moderation and a tidy profit. Yet Nasr's (2010) argument for Muslim small business and middle-class prosperity will not be immediately relevant to the poor and marginalised, and it will not be appealing to idealistic pious youth who look to asceticism for self-expression. They decry Muslim businesses marketing *halal*-endorsed commodities. For example, the Islamist group *Hizbut Tahrir*, which attracts many Muslim youth looking for answers, is strongly opposed to any form of capitalism on theological grounds. Their proffered solution is the re-establishment of caliphate based on pure Islamic principles of justice and faith, not the logic of the market and the motive of profit.

The Muslim 'selfie'

Hizbut Tahrir and other Islamist groups condemn the influence of Western individualism on youth. They consider the basis of Islamic sociality to properly inhere in a 'collectivistic self' (Kabir 2012: 43). This is challenged by emphasis on the individual self in secular conditions of late modernity (see Beck 1994). For example, 'selfies' taken by young Muslims particularly attract their ire. The selfie is a self-portrait photograph sometimes posed with friends, celebrities or in front of an important attraction, building or landmark. It is usually taken on a smartphone and shared proudly through social media. Although the selfie trend is certainly not confined to youth or to Muslims, it is taken as a signal for hardliners that young Muslims today are excessively individualised.

Perhaps inevitably, the selfie trend has intruded into the annual *hajj* pilgrimage to Mecca in Saudi Arabia. The *hajj* is a religious obligation of all

Muslims if they can possibly achieve it. Photography used to be officially banned, but now everyone needs their phone. Selfie images from Mecca are abundant online. Criticizing 'selfie fever', Muslim scholars have begged pilgrims not to indulge because it disturbs the spiritual journey. A teacher from Riyadh said he had seen pilgrims taking selfies with the sacred *Kaaba* in the background. He added that the 'selfie is then posted on Facebook'. This makes it a social media event and 'ruins their act of *ibadah*'[13] by bragging. A Saudi Sheikh added that on return they say: 'Come look at me, this is me on Arafat, this is me in Muzdalifah!' (OnIslam 2014). In other words the practice of selfie posing and taking at Mecca is theologically deplored. Not only does it emphasise the individual, it is used for boasting, it creates digital imagery, disturbs other pilgrims, commodifies the spiritual experience, and so on.

However, there is a counter-opinion on selfies taken during the *hajj*. Benoit (2014) argues that looking at personal *hajj* photos will intensify motivation to make the pilgrimage. She adds that while she understands some of the concerns about boasting and diminishing the sacred nature of the event, 'people may be so busy shaming the Hajjis that they are missing the greater picture' (probably no pun intended). Referring to various *fatwa* against digital imagery she adds, 'they are just commemorating their experience and potentially even making *dawah* [religious teaching] to *those of us left behind*' (my emphasis). This refers to the fact that there is now a considerable gap between Muslims who want to make the *hajj* and those who can actually make it. Given the extraordinarily high demand, the number of pilgrims who visit Mecca each year from countries is strictly controlled by Saudi authorities. So throughout the world there are very long waiting lists to make the *hajj* pilgrimage, and some younger Muslims fear they will never get to the top of the list in their lifetime. Moreover, women and the poor are less likely in percentage terms to make the *hajj* pilgrimage (Bianchi 2004). So Benoit (2014) adds that seeing a truly diverse set of photos, 'including women and children, will cement for them the idea that Hajj really is an experience for everyone'. This is an intriguing counter-narrative, because it implies the *hajj* has subtly become primarily a goal for prosperous adult men. The wide dissemination of a *hajj* selfie has the potential to unsettle this underlying discourse of privilege.

Fatwa-shopping

As the example above suggests, religious rulings (*fatwa*) are a moveable feast because quite different theological opinions can readily be obtained by the searching individual. *Fatwa*-shopping is a part of the process described by Lawrence (2002) as 'Allah online'. One of the reflexive strategies for self-identity of Muslim youth in the diaspora is searching for an online *fatwa* that permits a comfortable synthesis of piety and popular culture. Hardline authorities will typically rule out such a synthesis, while liberal authorities will try and accommodate it as a piously negotiated choice. Islam online

consists of many question-and-answer sites because Muslims want information about how to lead a pious yet prosperous life (Zaman 2008). For example, the popular portal 'Islam Online'[14] is a transnational resource that offers
live *fatwa* on everyday matters such as celebrating birthdays, watching television, following sport and plucking one's eyebrows. Yet this is only one site
among hundreds that allow the young Muslim consumer to find a ruling that
permits their lifestyle choice.

The number and variety of online *fatwa* judgements on any issue is
impressive. Young Muslims can take their pick. It is not just liberal interpretations that gain attention. For instance, if a hard-line Muslim cleric wants
to attract pious young followers with a taste for the dramatic, he might produce sensationalistic *fatwa* to gain their attention. Thus self-styled Sheik
Omar Bakri Muhammad, who left *Hizbut Tahrir* to establish the London-
based ultra-hardline group *Al-Muhajiroun*, made outrageous claims to get
free publicity and attract youth. 'In order to attract media attention, Bakri
tended to make violent statements and issue unconventional fatwas' (Mariani
2011: 154). This example draws our attention both to the cult of (tribal)
celebrity in Islam worldwide, and to the fragmentation of religious authority.
It seems the sheer proliferation of rulings invites ever more subjective interpretations to be made. None of the rules or visions/missions offered by online
guides are exactly alike, thus readily permitting the construction of Muslim
youth counter-narratives in the gaps between them.

Muslim youth 'neo-tribes'

Despite some obvious shared points of reference, Muslim youth culture is not
a unified set of cultural practices. There are sub-divisions according to ethnicity, gender, class and so on, as well as style tastes. Bennett (1999a) has
argued that the set of highly diverse youth cultures in late modernity is like
neo-tribalism, following the logic of *tribus*, a concept he borrowed from the
European sociologist Michel Maffesoli (1996). As explained earlier, this logic
can be productively applied to the phenomenon of multiple Muslim youth
cultures through the concept of neo-theo-tribalism. The following discussion
looks at some of those neo-tribal configurations that suggest different counter-narratives to extremism. There are complex configurations of distinction
evident in both consumption and representation.

Billaud (2015) offers selected snapshots of young Muslims in Birmingham,
England. One snapshot is of an arts centre – The Drum – which was set up to
promote British African, Asian and Caribbean art. The Drum promotes
moderate Islam under the umbrella of the Preventing Violent Extremism
(PVE) program (see Davies et al. 2016). Billaud (2015) describes a film night
at the centre when the documentary *Deen Tight* was shown. *Deen Tight* deals
with the positive and negative effects of pop culture on Muslim youth. It
features devout Muslim hip-hop artists. The film night was well attended by

fashionably dressed young Muslims from the middle-class arty/trendy youth scene – or neo-tribe.

A contrasting snapshot from Birmingham at the same time references a different socio-economic category of young Muslims, specifically young men. The Inner City Guidance Centre is also part of the PVE program. The Centre aims to give moral re-education to Muslim 'youths at risk' – young men on the margins of the labour market. Here they can get 'free Internet access, a milk shake bar, giant play stations, pool tables, and counselling "*salafi* style"' (Billaud 2015: 11). The latter claim indicates that the centre favours an Islamist position. The target group is young Muslim men who might be persuaded to join gangs or pro-jihad groups. Masculine leisure pursuits are carefully mixed with new technologies and Islamist doctrine to bring about a moral transformation in young men at the lower socio-economic level so they become more religious. The centre's leader Abu Hakeem is a former local gang member who converted to Islam in prison. He wears a strict '*sunnah*' dress that contrasts with the 'body language of street culture detectable in each of his moves' (Billaud 2015: 10). Abu Hakeem condemns the film *Deen Tight* as *haram*. In making this judgement he positions his own neo-tribe at the Inner City Guidance Centre as morally superior to trendy young Muslims who attend The Drum. Yet his own centre offers opportunities for online video gaming and playing pool, activities which frequently attract the ruling of *haram* from Islamist hard-liners.

A further example comes from Germany. Soliman (2016) studied the visual art of Tasnim Baghdadi, aged 25. Tasnim engages critically and creatively with the issue of the headscarf. In her female-centred art she wants to 'counter any form of categorisation and judgment, whether it comes from the Muslim community or the non-Muslim community' (Soliman 2016: 11). For example, her piece *3 Women × 3 Projections* depicts Baghdadi and two friends dressed up in different ways, some quite unsettling, including the use of *hijab*. As counter-narrative, the artwork speaks about the experiences of young Muslim women who straddle the secular and Muslim worlds in ways that constitute their identities through choice. It is clear that showings of this kind of artwork would attract a similar kind of arty/trendy audience to that of The Drum in the Birmingham example, although primarily female in this case.

Soliman (2016) also studied 'I-Slam', a Muslim youth poetry performance platform founded by two young German Muslim men. At I-Slam events, performers present their own poetry in rounds. The audience votes for the winner in each round who then proceeds to the next round. At the end, three finalists compete against each other for the competition prize. The I-Slam community coaches and supports young Muslim poets for national and international events. The founders of I-Slam emphasise the creative capacity of spoken poetry to address issues relevant to Muslim youth 'in a satiric or humorous way, to speak about certain taboos' (Soliman 2016: 13). Soliman points out similarities in the playful praxis of artist Baghdadi and I-Slam. Both not only represent self-expression of Muslim youth, but aim in an open way to make other young Muslims think about their lives through creative expression. 'Thereby messenger and receiver are both important entities' (Soliman 2016: 13). They mutually constitute counter-narrative through ludic engagement in an artistic event.

Matrimonial sites

The final section of this chapter considers online marriage selection for young Muslims in the context of a rejuvenated Islam. These are counter-narratives of choice mediated through digital technology. Negotiated choice in marriage is anathema to Islamist hardliners, who are firm on the topic of family-arranged marriages with little or no prior contact between the young spouses. However, fully arranged marriages are definitely not considered 'cool' by most young Muslims in the diaspora. Not only do family-arranged marriages refute the important discourse of romance, they often result in separation and divorce due to incompatibility (Rozario and Samuel 2012). Thus seeking a suitable marriage partner is a key concern for young Muslims of both sexes everywhere, including the pious. Muslim matrimonial sites promise to deliver a *halal* compromise that effectively synthesises piety, choice and romance through introducing young people on the basis of matched compatibility.

Getting married successfully is vitally important for young Muslims in making a good adult life for themselves while keeping the faith. Islamic tradition emphasises the necessity of marriage since the family is the fundamental unit of the Muslim *ummah*. In one *hadith*, marriage is called 'half the faith' (Lo and Aziz 2009). Yet for both sexes in the diaspora, actually finding a suitable Muslim spouse can prove challenging. As Rozario and Samuel (2012: 32) point out, 'marriage is a major problem for British Muslims'. Young Bangladeshi women in their study were found to be caught between Western models of a romantic love marriage and wanting to behave in a properly Islamic way. The extended family exerted pressure for female conformity in a traditional marriage, while young women in paid employment wanted to exercise choice. There was a well-known high rate of breakdown in arranged marriages. So young British Muslims and their families were conducting innovative yet pious ways of locating a suitable spouse.

One measure was for groups of young Bangladeshis to get to know each other face-to-face at morally 'safe' matrimonial events. Yet relevant to my arguments here, the researchers also acknowledge that:

> Young Muslims are as familiar as their non-Muslim peers with online dating agencies and sites, internet social networks such as Facebook or MySpace, mobile phones, online video sites such as YouTube and the whole associated new culture of electronically-mediated personal relationships.
>
> (Rozario and Samuel 2012: 33–34)

As this suggests, Muslim matrimony-seeking websites have become popular worldwide (Al-Saggaf 2013). They blend Islamic marriage culture and modern aspirations of individual freedom and personal choice (Lo and Aziz 2009). In keeping with the tenets of faith, the sites reflect the desire for a Muslim spouse. Yet both sexes are equally represented as engaging choice (Badahdah and Tiemann 2009: 88). Matrimonial sites promise – to both sexes – individual choice and self-expression in a modern 'partnership' marriage that yet remains true to the tenets of Islam.

Even so, Muslim matrimony-seeking sites are not generally endorsed by conservative *ulema*. [15] The sites challenge the tradition of arranged and controlled marriage driven by family interests. It is claimed they also make it easier to break the law of *khalwa* (privacy/separation) between men and women who are not married. The law of *khalwa* is also frequently applied in *fatwa* against chatting between unrelated men and women on social media (Larsson 2011a: 158). Some authorities claim matrimonial sites encourage the sin of *zina* – entertaining impure sexual thoughts before marriage. Nevertheless, meeting a suitable Muslim marriage partner online is clearly a popular practice, to judge by the sheer number of sites now on offer.

On the international site Qiran.com, a smiling success story photo depicts Nour and Hiba – in traditional Muslim attire. The testimonial reads:

> My name is Nour, 23 year old Albanian Muslim who has been living in Denmark since I was a very little kid (…) My wish was to find a true Islamic young woman (…) The problem was that I was Albanian and Hiba was Iraqi (…) [Luckily] our families didn't want to stand in the way of our wish to live an Islamic life together.
>
> (Nour, Denmark, 2008[16])

This testimonial illustrates their mutual membership of the transnational *ummah* that transcends ethnic difference. A few pictures away, a different, but apparently equally loving couple are posed for the camera in Western summer attire, showing lots of skin. The testimonial reads:

> Craig and I found each other on Qiran.com and it's the happiest and most real thing we have both found in a long time.
>
> (Sharon, Australia, 2009[17])

As both testimonials imply, internet depictions may have an effect on the way contemporary young Muslims see and practise Islam in forming a marriage. For example, on Muslim matrimonial sites there was no mention of female virginity, or polygamy – both topics of debate elsewhere. The focus is always on piety and compatibility.

Marriage to a fellow Muslim may represent a safe haven in an uncertain world. The ideal of security was a most 'important reason for looking for a

genuine Islamic marriage with a life-partner who shared one's Islamic values'
(Rozario 2012: 160). Rozario's female informants felt that in reinvented
(transnational) Islam they had found a proper life path. This was positioned
against their parents' restrictive versions of Islam, and also against a
secular Western lifestyle which they identified as immoral and un-Islamic.
They viewed marriage as a partnership, rather than a hierarchical relationship between male breadwinner and female housewife. Their accounts
indicated that, unlike their parents' generation, they want relative 'equality'
with their husbands (Rozario 2012: 170). To some extent this means negotiating the theological injunction for a Muslim wife's submission to her
husband:

> Although Islam tells women to obey their husbands, she said, this is only
> 'as long as a husband doesn't go against Islam and God's law'. In other
> words, if one marries a man who follows the Qur'anic injunctions to be kind
> and merciful to his wife, the latter will be treated well in every respect.
>
> (Rozario 2012: 165)

This constitutes not only a counter-narrative to old-fashioned restrictive ideas
about Muslim marriage for women, but to extremist thinking. Their take on
Islam had little in common with conservative Islamic organisations, but none
had an interest in 'extremist' forms of political Islam either (Rozario 2012:
172). Rather, they embraced a modern revitalised Islam that encourages
companionate marriage anchored in the security of faith.

Some in the diaspora are moving to develop quick and easy means of assessing
potential marriage partners. So for example, a young Muslim in Canada is pioneering 'Salaam Swipe', a mobile dating app for Muslims. Like popular dating
app Tinder, users swipe right on someone's profile if they're interested, and
swipe left if they're not interested. App creator Khalil Jessa says that growing
up in North America, he and his friends face 'a very big irony when it comes
to relationships and marriage'. First, young Muslims are discouraged from
getting to know young people of the opposite sex until there is urgency in
their twenties to find a marriage partner. Second, they are supposed to follow
the traditional practice of sending their details to grandmothers and older
female relatives so they can find a match. He finds this 'artificial for many
young Muslims in the West who are looking for love' (Jessa, quoted in Taylor
2015). In a similar way, a group of young Muslim friends in the US have
launched the Muslim dating website Ishqr. One of the taglines reads, 'If you're
a feminist looking for your bold, humble, feminist brother or a Rumi-and
granola-loving-Muslim, Ishqr is the place for you.' Young female creator
Mubeen said:

> Yes, we're proud Muslims but we're also very proud Americans and it is
> very possible to live with these two identities together (...) We've created

our own unique narrative and hybrid identities and that is why there is a marriage crisis.

(Mubeen, quoted in Taylor 2015, my emphasis)

If 'counter-jihad is reflected both in the mundane and the remarkable' in the diaspora (Wright 2012: 42), then this perhaps serves as an example of the former rather than the latter. The new emphasis on Muslim matrimonial choice mediated through technology allows young Muslims to not only find a compatible partner for themselves, but to find one who inhabits the same or a similar neo-tribe of Muslim youth culture.

In short, online matrimonial matching is an important contemporary counter-narrative because it confounds the traditionalist claims of Islamism where arranged marriage is often the norm. The sites are clearly popular, providing young Muslims with new ways of 'exploring and breaking established cultural norms and adopting new forms of behaviour' (Larsson 2011a: 159). Here both sexes are given choice. In principle, while searching for a suitable husband or wife on these sites, the online technological affordances permit them, as 'digital natives', to synthesise Islam with the career and lifestyle aspirations of both partners.

Conclusion

This chapter has offered a broad gaze over the 'parallel world' of Muslim youth popular culture, including preparation for marriage. A synthesis of piety, ludic concerns and late modern pragmatic subjectivity is evident in the new Muslim 'cool' so prevalent in the contemporary diaspora. It stands in the face of radicalisation trends without moving to secular norms. We took a brief tour of young Muslim fashion, consumer products and leisure pursuits, noting the gendered nature of their engagement. The debate about Muslim popular culture as either *halal* or *haram* was also aired. To maintain both piety and 'cool', Muslim youth exercise a strong practice of reflexivity in regard to the popular culture products they consume and utilise. This was identified as a form of counter-narrative in praxis, framed up against condemnation by hardliners on one side and local intolerance of Islam on the other. The next chapter examines some of those same concerns in online video gaming.

Notes

1 I recognise that 'cool' is now a rather dated term among young people themselves, including young Muslims. Nonetheless, I use it here for heuristic purposes. Most of the relevant academic literature to date uses the term 'cool' and it is therefore easier to make a sequence of arguments, rather than switching between terms.
2 And *alhamdullihah* – praise be to God.
3 Much as devout Christians might add 'praise the Lord' to sentences in ordinary conversation with fellow followers.

4 Islam is not the only world religion where this new 'cool' of piety has appeared among youth. For example, Christian rock music is a growth industry in the United States, and the direct appeal of Hillsong Church is to trendy youth.

5 http://countercurrentnews.com/2014/09/muslims-around-the-world-are-making-parody-videos-to-mock-isis/#.

6 He has many other, very different tattoos as well.

7 https://answers.yahoo.com/question/index?qid=20120405194128AAQw6oZ.

8 At the time of writing (2016) Zayn was dating Gigi Hadid, an American model who is the daughter of a Muslim Palestinian refugee. This intensified his celebrity status even further among young Muslims.

9 www.theguardian.com/music/musicblog/2015/apr/07/zayn-malik-muslim-pop-star#comment-50086049.

10 www.theguardian.com/music/musicblog/2015/apr/07/zayn-malik-muslim-pop-star#comment-50086049.

11 www.theguardian.com/music/musicblog/2015/apr/07/zayn-malik-muslim-pop-star#comment-50086049.

12 *Shahada* is the spoken profession of faith, expressing the two fundamental beliefs of Islam: There is no God but Allah and Muhammad is the prophet of Allah.

13 Worship.

14 www.islamonline.net.

15 Religious scholars.

16 www.qiran.com/SuccessStories/story_200812_Nour-Hiba.asp.

17 www.qiran.com/SuccessStories/story_200904_Sharon-Craig.asp.

Chapter 6

Gaming and the young Muslim self

Introduction

This chapter considers how Muslim youth engage with video games.[1] Once again the potency of the Islamist position is illustrated as the young people reflexively negotiate the conduct of leisure. Here the focus is on counter-narratives and counter-practice that allow piety and video gaming to co-exist, and thereby constitute claims to a viable Muslim youth identity. It is clear that 'game-devoted areas of the Internet such as blogs, chatrooms, online periodicals, wikis, and forums can provide unique insights into hot trends' in the gaming community (SAIC 2007: 65). Accordingly, comments from young Muslim game players themselves enrich the arguments presented below. The first section of the chapter provides some background on video gaming.

A caveat: The author readily admits that as a youth sociologist she is far from a games scholar. Therefore the chapter pays due homage to the wisdom of published experts on video and online games. Moreover, since there are so many games available, a carefully limited selection has been made for relevance and popularity in the time period. However, by the time you read this, many new gaming products will have been developed.[2] Finally, this chapter does not rehearse at length the usual issues of contention for young people and gaming – first, whether game violence increases real violence; and second, gender patterns in game play (Gee 2003: 10). It is timely to give some other accounts of this important leisure practice.

Background

According to an original definition, game play of any kind is 'a voluntary activity or occupation executed within certain fixed limits of time and place, according to rules freely accepted but absolutely binding' (Huizinga 1955: 28). Players experience tension, joy and awareness of difference from ordinary life. Like other games, video games provide ludic experiences ordered by rules and limits. They are learned by trying, failing and trying again. Gaming is a dynamic and engaging experience because 'the player feels [ever more] emotionally attached to the outcome' (Juul 2005: 36) as the game becomes increasingly complex through ascending levels of skill. Playing properly requires significant commitment of time. For example, Gee (2003: 5) maintains that online games can take '50 to 100 hours to win, even for good players'. Play also makes high demands on the 'situated cognition' of gaming literacy; the capacity to 'read', decode and reflect (Gee 2003: 8). While pleasurable, this is demanding and serious play.

In the 1950s computer developers devised simple games to test efficacy. Arcade video games and home computer games were common by the 1980s. Given technological improvement, the world market has grown exponentially. In the US, games are played on a PC (56 per cent), a dedicated game console (53 per cent), or a smartphone (36 per cent) (ESA 2016). In 2015, the total amount spent by consumers on games in the US reached 23.5 billion US dollars (ESA 2016).[3] Although there is much greater female participation now, some genres remain largely male-dominated, especially First Person Shooter (24.5 per cent of the US market), and action genres (22.9 per cent of the US market). It is sometimes claimed that online gaming encourages isolation and anti-social behaviour. However, the most popular games are highly social recreational activities (Gee 2003; Gosney 2005; Flew and Humphreys 2005). According to ESA (2016), 54 per cent of the most frequent US gamers play with others, mainly friends. Indeed, 'a key pleasure, motivation and appeal of online gaming is its communal nature' (Crawford et al. 2011: 14). Video gaming enriches the lives of young people because it extends their sense of social belonging (Geser 2007). This insight is most important for the arguments about young Muslims and gaming that are presented in this chapter.

Gaming generates an 'affinity group' of other players within the semiotic domain of the preferred game genre (Gee 2003: 27). At the simplest level, gamers talk to each other, locally, nationally or from another continent. Gamers search online for tips from others on how to pass through levels and they organise online to play in teams and tournaments. They create inter-character dialogue, and blog critically with other gamers. Notably, it appears Muslim male and female gamers do sometimes play together online (Rogers and Johnson 2016). In exchanges between Muslim gamers, and between Muslim and non-Muslim gamers, the technological affordances and creative potentials of gaming itself enable the generation of counter-narratives to the radical Islamist meta-narrative and also to its morally reversed counterpart, the war on terror.

Video gaming and the politics of the self

Video games are readily accessible.[4] There is extensive choice. They offer diverse opponents and challenges. They are visually compelling. 'Today's gamers expect a more photorealistic gaming experience' (Monson 2012: 52). Sophisticated 3D animation means that 'players become the story' (Rushkoff 2013: 64) ever more effectively. It seems most urban youth in the world engage in some form of digital game play at some time. Multiple platforms enhance broad access. For example, phone apps allow the playing of complex MMORPGs (Massively Multiple Online Role Playing Games) like 'World of Warcraft' anywhere, 24/7. Most of the over-15 global population has access to a mobile phone (ESA 2016), and transnational mobile phone game revenue was calculated in billions of US dollars in 2016 (SBS 2014).

Kirkpatrick (2013) proposes that in the digital age, video games have fundamentally altered the relationship between self and society. For instance, in a public place someone can be more involved in a game with online peers than with surrounding people. In other words, the immediate material conditions of society can, at times, be far less important than what is happening in the virtual world. Some young people immersed in the digital world have come to refer to the face-to-face world as AFK (away from keyboard).[5] While games don't force us to do anything, they can affectively 'shape our values' (Wagner 2014: 22). They are specifically designed to elicit intense emotional engagement so that the player will spend the time to learn, to win, and then purchase further games in the series. Game designers make assumptions about the 'ideal' player for maximum profit. Thus RPGs (Role Playing Games) and MMORPGs are intended for fantasy enthusiasts – old and young, both sexes. In contrast, military FPS (First Person Shooter)[6] games seem to be more narrowly targeted at men, and younger men in particular. Niche or 'indie' games target a smaller market slice, such as 'Monster Truck Curfew' (which allows frustrated motorists to play with a dramatic solution to traffic jams), 'Wonderputt' (a golfing game for aficionados), 'OlliOlli' (a skateboarding game for youth), and 'Cis Gaze' (a political awareness game in which the player experiences the aggressions that trans* people face). Yet despite the niche targeting, in principle anyone can play any game. If they want to, and have enough technical know-how, they can 'mod' (modify) the game to suit their own story.

In fact, like all texts, video games can be read 'against the grain' (Chien 2010), according to the subject position of the player (Gee 2003). For example, while an FPS game would seem to appeal primarily to Anglo males, female and/or non-Anglo persons can certainly play it and experience themselves as powerful within the game, even while the meanings of the game shift about in relevance to their framing of self (Patterson 2015). Such alternative readings might be linked to 'owned' identities consolidated through affinity groups. For example, there are female gamer groups such as womengamers.com, where players directly address playing 'against the grain' for game enjoyment. Similarly, in war-on-terror FPS games where the 'hostiles' are Muslim, players identifying as Muslim themselves must read against the grain, and play against the grain, thus shifting the narrative of the game itself (Wagner 2012). In that sense they engage a subtle form of embedded critique (Butler 2004), which pertains to Gee's (2003) argument about decoding and critical literacy in gameplay. In other words, how differently-aligned gamers play the game, and the subject positions they take up, strongly constitute the actual narrative they make for themselves out of the gaming experience.

Muslim youth 'belonging' in gaming

It seems there might be some special value in games for contemporary youth who follow a religious faith (Campbell 2013, 2016). This might be the case for example, for Muslims playing heroic games, or a game in which they learn about the 'Golden Age' of Islam (see Ahmadi 2015). In video gaming, 'the modular, customizable, and participatory culture of the ludic century converges with the broader transformation of contemporary religiosity, which emphasizes the role of the individual and privatization of faith' (Šisler 2016: 3). This claim echoes Cevik's (2015) proposition that contemporary Muslim youth choices reflect an individual orientation filtered through the notion of faith as chosen rather than forced. Like other forms of popular culture, video games offer an imaginative and creative space where cultural meanings of faith and identity can be negotiated (Turner 2014). This is because games communicate through experience; they 'invite players into the creative process' (Rushkoff 2013: 59). MMORPGs in particular encourage the creation and maintenance of substantial 'imaginary' lives (Monson 2012) in which players feel they belong in the neo-tribal sense. Rollings and Adams (2003) identify an initiating 'mono-myth' in many games. The protagonist exists in an 'ordinary world', but receives a 'call to adventure' prompted by something external (Šisler 2013: 141). This initiation helps players enter and belong to the story of the game (Newgren 2010). Yet the story is not just constituted in plot and characters, but in the actual playing of the game, a mediated process where strategies and experiences are shared online with fellow gamers. This amplifies the sense of belonging to a small, defined group.

In summary, the online game environment can operate as a convivial space where a sense of shared identity is demonstrated by Muslim youth who play together and contribute to transnational blogs, such as muslimgamer.com. In the sense of 'situated cognition' (Gee 2003) they are actively learning things not only about gameplay, but about who they are – and might be – as young Muslims who choose to play video games. This argument can be illustrated by briefly examining various kinds of games that offer an identity 'handle' to Muslim youth.

Arabian Nights

Many high-selling fantasy genre games produced in the West draw on the stories of the *Arabian Nights*.[7] Transmuted into cartoons and films they evoke the exotic/dangerous and the mysterious/magical qualities of the idealised Middle East (Jenkins 2003). The visual signifiers that create this exotic Middle East impression are: headscarves, turbans, scimitars, ornate tiling, soaring archways, camels, caliphs, bedouins, genies, belly dancers, desert landscapes, oases, date palms, minarets, bazaars and harems (Šisler 2008: 207). Although the Middle East is certainly not synonymous with 'Muslim' *per se*, the Middle East is semantically the heartland of Islam. Thus Middle Eastern imagery can be highly redolent of assertive symbolism for Muslims living outside the Middle East (Nilan 2016b).

One of the first games in the *Arabian Nights* genre was titled 'Arabian' (1983). The hero was a turbaned, scimitar-wielding youth who conquered castles and ships, battling *jinn*[s][8] and monsters. Later came 'Sinbad and the Throne of the Falcon' (1987), with the *Arabian Nights* hero ridding the land of a Dark Prince. In 'Talisman: Changing the Sands of Time' (1987) a Persian hero seeks a legendary talisman to destroy the evil *jinn* ravaging the land. The very popular 'Prince of Persia' (1989) concerns the triumphant adventures of a warrior prince mentioned in the Bible. Yet despite exotic, orientalised settings and characters, such games follow a standard adventure-quest format, with much use of magic.

This popular sub-genre continued in the 1990s. In the strategy game 'Khalaan' (1990), four caliphs who control vast armies and treasure battle for supremacy in the Middle East. In 'Arabian Magic' (1992) the king is changed by black magic into a monkey. Four heroes with special powers seek the Jewel of Seven Colours to release the hex. In 'Arabian Fight' (1992), players use magic to save the princess, defeat the tyrant and save the world. 'Magic Carpet' (1994) offered a 3D simulation where players flew on Persian carpets. In 'Persian Wars' (2001) a seeker must find the ring of Solomon before rival seekers. Later came the 'Breath of Fire' series (from 2003) in a setting of desert, minarets and bazaars. 'Silkroad' (2005–6) linked the Middle East and Far East with travelling characters and exotic locations, including the standard deserts and minarets. In 2007 Sega released 'Sonic and the Secret Rings'. Sonic's quest is to stop the evil Erazor Djinn from erasing the contents of the *Arabian Nights* book. Sonic's assistant is a benevolent *jinn*.

In terms of the nexus between 'situated cognition' (Gee 2003) and identity, it seems likely that the orientalised *Arabian Nights* play environment provides niches where Muslims, a 'marginalized minority group in many Western communities' might go to find others 'like them' (Mandaville 2001: 183). In those imaginary play worlds, cultural affinity is signalled by readily identifiable symbols, myths, and rituals from the Muslim world (Šisler 2013: 136). Obviously game producers go on developing these kinds of games because players (not just Muslim) like them (Reichmuth and Werning 2006). Stylised orientalism extends into MMORPGs. For example, in 'Nadirim' (2011) a new player, equipped with just a small weapon, is introduced to a world where the sun never sets. A powerful *jinn* has raised a lowly thief to rule a vast empire. The trigger point of the quest is the *jinn* returning with a demon army to take back his empire and banish the sun. Players must build up strategic capacities and defeat the forces of the *jinn*. The imagery is stereotyped Middle Eastern throughout.

In the famous MMORPG 'World of Warcraft' we find a more subtle example of the trend. Blood Elves are one of the races of the fantasy world, and their lands are depicted visually using Middle Eastern imagery:

Elaborately curved entryways, long flowing silky curtains, a deep red and blue color scheme, hookah pipes, lamps, and magical brooms sweeping the pathways give these lands a notable Walt Disney's 'Aladdin' feel.

(Monson 2012: 62)

However, the Blood Elves themselves are physically perfect, light-skinned and show contempt for other races, so some contributors to 'World of Warcraft' forums read the Blood Elves as Germanic rather than Middle Eastern. Monson (2012) suggests the 'race' of the Blood Elves could be read differently by Muslim players, with the elves' attractive appearance and sense of superiority forming key components of an empowering transposed identity.

Affirmation of identity for young Muslim players is constituted not only in the Middle Eastern imagery of such games but in the evil-defeating and world-saving quests that characterise the genre. There are powerful world-saving elements in both religious narratives and digital games. Both celebrate the hero/heroine who makes a sustained effort to overcome forces of evil (Grieve and Campbell 2014). Thus digital gaming offers the opportunity to 'play' with religion where relevant symbolism is present. Yet given the creative nature of 'play', we cannot predict exactly how a young Muslim gamer might 'decode' and imaginatively operationalise such gameplay in relation to the self. As Šisler (2016: 12) points out, even if a game represents Muslim heroes, narratives, and audiovisuals, on a structural level it retains 'the rule-systems and game mechanics' of typical Western-developed games. So the reward of 'winning' is granted only within closed parameters of possibility.

Even so, while 'just a game' in one sense, *Arabian Nights*-themed fantasy quest products offer a generally positive, attractive view of the Middle East, which few other popular media texts do. In summary then, it can be argued that the benign *Arabian Nights* gaming environment in principle allows young Muslims to find affirming visual representations of places and people that speak to them symbolically in terms of identity, and where they can play the hero in legitimising adventure/quest narratives. Such games do not compel young Muslim gamers to play against the grain *per se*, even though avatars are usually Westernised. Rather, they provide cultural resources for constructing a heroic story of the self. This is an important aspect of self-esteem for young Muslims living in the diaspora who may be struggling against negative stereotypes of Islam.

Finding myself in the game

Constructing a heroic story of the self for young Muslim gamers means some element of 'finding' themselves in the game. One MMORPG quite popular with Muslim players was 'Khan Wars' (2009), in which twelve nations join battle, including Persians, Byzantines and Arabs. The special Arab unit is the *mujahideen*. They are described as great leaders in battle who know the art of war to perfection. In other words the Muslims can win. Another popular game with Muslim youth is the 'Prince of Persia' series which features a hero from the Golden Age of Islam. They also like the spin-off 'Assassins Creed' series, which includes the Muslim character Altaïr Ibn-La'Ahad, a disgraced assassin working to redeem himself during the Third Crusade. Here are some self-identifying comments on 'Assassins Creed':

> Did anyone know that Altair from 'Assassins Creed' is a Muslim? Wow, I am a Muslim. I can finally relate my self to videogames.
>
> (furqan2006[9])

> It is the only game my parents pay attention to when I'm playing, as they always want to see the mosque and Jerusalem and other Muslim icons like Prophet Solomon's grave.
>
> (joshF2295[10])

> I love this game. It makes Muslims look really cool.
>
> (Simba, Sunni Muslim[11])

These comments strongly demonstrate the Muslim identity-affirming qualities of 'Assassins Creed' in regard to my arguments above. The first and second comments above bear out the claim of Boellstorff (2008), that intense playing of online games can mean in-game and out-of-game identities become blurred. Furqan's self-affirmation of identity occurs precisely because of the 'matched' Muslim identities of the player and the hero.

First Person Shooter (FPS) games

As a genre, FPS games provide simple 'black and white' contests in which the player takes up the position of hero (Vergani 2014) and kills the enemy. 'Typical player actions for first-person shooters are movement, shooting, and taking cover' (Šisler 2016: 13). FPS games are relatively easy to program and there is constant fast turnover of new offerings (Gee 2003). In the way that the Middle East is depicted they are unlike the fantasy games described previously. The landscape is not benignly exotic. Rather the Middle East is a stark theatre of war, the landscape and people scarred by conflict. Arabs and Muslims are depicted as enemies (Šisler 2008: 214).

After 9/11, FPS games 'reflected the Zeitgeist of the War on Terror' (Ibrahine 2015: 209). Action/battle games in the FPS lineage such as 'Call of Duty', 'Battlefield', 'Command and Conquer Generals', 'Spec Ops: The Line', and 'Splinter Cell' depict Middle Eastern 'hostiles' to be wiped out so as to preserve world order. The hostiles exhibit violent threatening behaviour in the field which categorises them as 'unlawful combatants' (Šisler 2008: 208) and therefore legitimate targets. For example, 'Call of Duty 4: Modern

Warfare' (2007) presents a scenario where an implicitly Muslim terrorist group has obtained a nuclear bomb. The mission of the US Marine/British SAS soldier is to prevent its detonation, utilising the latest surveillance and weapon technologies, and wipe them out. Ibrahine (2015: 210) maintains that games like that have rendered the Muslim world a 'site of perpetual war'; Muslims are depicted as 'villains, terrorists and thus public enemy number one'. 'Muslim Massacre' (2008) was particularly offensive. The American hero shooter must slaughter all Arabs that come into view, whether terrorists or civilians. At higher levels the shooter gets to kill Osama bin Laden, Mohammed and then Allah (Wagner 2014: 27).

Shaw (2010: 799) argues that playing war games such as the militaristic FPS 'Call of Duty' franchise is 'locked within a violent imperial topos'. In his view, such games reveal an 'entrenched colonial logic' geared to military mobilisation. Certainly both sides are aware of the recruitment and training potential of FPS battle games (Klopfenstein 2006). For example, by 1998 the US military was using modifications of popular games like 'Doom' for recruitment and training purposes (Courmont and Clément 2014: 38). Given this fact, some scholars claim a shrinking distinction between the real and the imagined in the virtual realm of war and terror (see Žižek 2002; Baudrillard 1991). However, there is nothing really new in the principle of this claim because battle stories throughout history have always downplayed details of suffering and misery and played up heroic deeds. Moreover, richly gory war stories have long been used for military recruitment to armies. So it is possible to over-interpret the specific political potency (either way) of military FPS games in the context of encouragement to war. After all, they are just games to be played, as many bloggers insist.

'It's just a game'

There is much anecdotal evidence that FPS games of all kinds are just as popular with Muslim male youth as they are with non-Muslim male youth. An anonymous gamer commented – in relevance to Muslims – on the some-thingawful.com games forum, 'I personally do not care who I'm murdering, as long as it's fun'. Although there is a great deal that might seem highly objectionable for young Muslim gamers in Western military simulation products since 9/11, it seems they keep playing. However, this is not without a critical edge. One website posed the question of how Muslim/Arabic gamers feel about playing such games. Three replies are worthy of unpacking to emphasise the implied counter-narrative:

> *Video games are games, it's fun, not real.* Shooting the living crap out of everything that moves is great for stress relief after a long day, and that's irrelevant of religion, nationality or whatever. Especially in modern FPS, you don't play these for the scenario, the background or the characters,

you just shoot. You don't care if you're shooting at Muslims, Russians, Americans.

(Mouad Akrim, 24 March 2015,[12] my emphasis)

Muslim gamer Mouad explains how he likes playing on the terrorist and the counter-terrorist team in 'Counter Strike' since both are 'fun'. He justifies his stance in terms of the 'stress relief' offered by simulated combat. For him, the game narrative is not important. His position avoids the geopolitics of the game (Schulzke 2013), and emphasises its recreational value. As Šisler (2013: 136) points out, Muslim gamers can always read 'against the grain' in the gameplay to position themselves as the powerful first shooter and hero, regardless of who they are shooting at.

The next quote comes from a non-Muslim gamer:

I know many Arab/Muslim guys who enjoy playing these games and do not get conflicting feelings. *They are just games.* I even saw radical Islamist teenagers playing them. However, in many games you can choose between different armies or militant groups, so you can play the 'bad guys'.

(Sammy Thatcher, 30 March 2015,[13] my emphasis)

In other words, Sammy assures us that the Arab/Muslim guys he knows do not feel conflicted because they play the games with obvious enjoyment. He claims that he has observed this even for radical sympathisers. Like Mouad, he emphasises that they are 'just games'. However, he adds that if players do mind about the negative geopolitical depiction, they can choose what he calls the 'bad guys' – the terrorists – the Muslims.

A similar tactic is implied in the third relevant quote from the same site, talking from a specifically Muslim gamer perspective about 'Counter Strike':

I *let it be fiction.* Those who want to portray let them portray, why feel guilty by their scheme to humiliate us rather feel happy and spoil their plans by playing. If u wanna, do more play as a terrorist and u will get the bomb and an AK47 which is the best gun in the game.

(Faizan Ahmad, 23 March 2015,[14] my emphasis)

Muslim gamer Faizan implies that Muslim players of 'Counter Strike' should 'let it be fiction', as he does. In other words he supports the view that it is just a game. However, he then develops a more complex position. He acknowledges that there is a potentially humiliating Western portrayal of Arabs/ Muslims as terrorists, but urges his peers to 'spoil their plans by playing'. He advocates refusing the offered abject position by happily seeking to win. 'Counter Strike' makes this possible because either team can gain victory. He also advises playing more often for the terrorist team, which has the bomb and the 'best gun' anyway, a claim which returns us to the powerful identity meanings that can be generated in the actual mechanics of gameplay.

From the posted responses above, it seems that Muslim players deal with the problematic depiction of Muslim hostiles in FPS games by ignoring, or discursively remaking, the geo-political narrative (content + gameplay). It can be argued that, given a Muslim identity location, their cultural practices of interpretation and affect 'systematically form' (Foucault 1972) a counter-discourse or counter-narrative to the ostensible intent of the game – in the act of playing. They may refuse the offered geopolitical meanings in favour of just savouring the ludic experience, or deliberately play against the grain of the stereotype. In that sense, online FPS gaming by Muslim youth can be read as a kind of subversion; an act of distinction made by using existing popular culture resources. With reference to Willis' (1990) argument, they are using the cultural material on offer for creative acts of reclamation.

Video games: *haram* or *halal?*

As pointed out previously, all forms of popular culture are anathema for hardline Islamists (Herding 2013). As a component of popular culture, video games are frequently judged *haram*, so not allowed within the faith. In online rulings, various theological reasons are given as to why video games are *haram*. One reason is encouragement of violent tendencies. There are *fatwa* on this issue, for example:

Q: Should I allow my child to play violent video games in which you 'kill' people?
A: [No. They may] exhibit a glorification of violence (...) the best of games are those that are aimed at enhancing a child's intelligence and instilling in them noble virtues that will serve them well later in life (The National[15]).

Another *fatwa* concerns the depiction of living things, for example:

Q: What is the ruling on electronic video games?
SHEIKH: What are they?
Q: They are games played on a screen. They possess pictures, sounds, etc.
SHEIKH: Pictures (of living things) are totally forbidden. The Messenger – *salallahu alayhi wa salem* – said: 'May the curse of Allah be upon the pictures makers/takers'. They are not permissible (*Salafi* Talk[16]).

It is notable that the Sheikh in question did not seem to know about electronic video games when the question was first posed. This suggests a generation gap.

A highly posted reason for banning games is immoral content. The following warning is from an online *mullah* [17] about 'The Sims':

> There is no evil action or immoral deed but it exists in this filthy game
> (...) We do not know, by Allah, how any Muslim could accept to allow
> his daughter or his wife or even his son to play this evil game (...) it is not
> permissible for a Muslim to upload this game or play it.
>
> (Mullah[18])

A fourth reason for the judgement of *haram* is that video gaming distracts
Muslim youth from pious practices:

> Islam has permitted recreation and kinds of entertainment provided that they
> are in conformity with the Islamic requirements, such as not distracting the
> person from remembering Allah, offering the prayer or any other obligation.
>
> (Islamweb English[19])

For the young Muslim gamer seeking an overview, one site offers the following
summary:

> Playing video games is not *haram* as long as the game does not contain
> sexual themes, excessive violence or other *haram* things. Also, playing
> time should be limited so that it does not affect other aspects of life such
> as worship, study etc.
>
> (Ask the Sheikh[20])

Music is deemed *haram* by many Islamic theologians, and games employ
music in their soundtracks. However, players can turn off the sound. For example,
a site specialising in games for Muslim youth included the following warning:

> Notice: If the game has music, we highly recommend to turn off the
> music, then benefit from the game without music.
>
> (Muslim Video[21])

Games are a leisure activity, and the concept of leisure occupies a somewhat
ambiguous space in Islam. Various sporting activities and other pastimes are
mentioned in the *sunna*, so leisure pursuits are not out of the question for
Muslims. On the other hand, the conduct of leisure pursuits for relaxation and
for refreshing mind and body should be regulated to produce the moral self.

Contesting the rulings

As indicated earlier in the book, young Muslims who engage with popular
culture must negotiate the risk of being judged immoral, and video gaming is
no exception. Debates about gaming were readily found in online Islamic
discussion sites. On one site a young man wrote about creating a gaming blog.
He found condemnation:

The fact that it is *haram* to help others commit sin [for u by creating a gaming blog] is indicated by the verses in which Allaah says: 'Help you one another in *Al Birr* and at *Taqwa* (virtue, righteousness and piety); but do not help one another in sin and transgression [*al-Maa'idah* 5:2].

(Muslim49[22])

In other words, if someone believes that video gaming is already a sin then creating a gaming blog is an even greater sin because it encourages other Muslims to indulge in the sin of playing. The blog creator was later assured by Muslim49 that he will be harshly punished by God.

Yet no consensus of ruling was found on the topic of video games *per se*. For instance, another young Muslim gamer posed the following question on another site:

I am a person who loves to play video games, although I do not let it get in the way of my Islamic practices. I do occasionally play violent video games, but I consciously tell myself that violence is not okay. Is it *haram* for me to play video games?

(Bladeknight[23])

A senior site contributor replied to him:

No, they're not *haram*. If you think that the games' violence is affecting YOUR own behaviour and making it violent, it's better to avoid it, though it's not *haram* as long as it does not get in the way of your Islamic practices.

(Basim Ali[24])

Here we may contrast the two different framings of a moral Muslim self, outlined by Cevik (2015) and also by Šisler (2016). The hardline ruling exemplifies the forcible imposition of faith-based regulation so the person remains within the moral code. Conversely, the advice from Basim Ali overtly references an individual orientation to Islam filtered through the notion of faith as chosen rather than forced. The young Muslim must therefore decide for themselves whether the practice is adversely affecting the moral self.

Later on the same site a quasi-theological discussion ensued when Bladeknight responded to a post from a hardliner who claimed games were *haram* because they had immoral content. Bladeknight replied that games like 'Final Fantasy', 'Kingdom Hearts', 'Mario' and so on do not feature immorality. He added:

You can't seriously believe in consuming yourself in religion all day and night? I don't believe that video games are non-religious.

(Bladeknight[25])

Fellow games blogger Akbarhassan concurred, subsequently posting: 'I'm obsessed with video games. I don't really believe we should dedicate 101% of our life for Islam'. In other words, both young men construct counter-discourse to an Islamist position by expressing a viable Muslim youth identity constituted in discretionary choice.

A similar discourse was expressed on the destructoid site in reaction to a post titled 'Muslims shouldn't play games urges Islamic writer'. One young Muslim gamer wrote:

> This article makes Islam looks even worse. We won't mind any sh*t just to hit the pause button or close our 3ds system immediately for 5 minutes and pray. *We could be true worshipers and badass S-RPG maniacs at the same time.* I even pray for a while before dispatching my party into battle LOL.
>
> (indonesianRPGgeek,[26] my emphasis)

This implies a dual constitution of Muslim youth subjectivity; a 'true worshipper' and a 'badass S-RPG maniac' at the same time, which challenges the hardline Islamist view. Moreover, the young gamer describes praying before an online battle. This illustrates how 'gaming may lead players to draw on broad religious narratives to explain their emotions and experiences' (Grieve and Campbell 2014: 59). It seems to be not so much a case of faith *versus* fantasy in gaming (Bainbridge 2013), but faith *combined with* fantasy.

There were plenty of posts on similar Muslim discussion sites that advocated that kind of productive synthesis. For example:

> The gaming aspect of my day always comes last. I make sure that my homework/studying is finished when I come home from school (after I do my *salaat* [27] *al-hum-du-illah*). I guess the only thing I do is hang off of a tree in the back of my house pretending to be Nathan Drake[28] from the 'Uncharted' series.
>
> (GamerNarion[29])

Here we can see GamerNarion reflecting on how he balances gaming and piety in his life. He claims the only possibly detrimental impact of video gaming is on his use of free time. However, he assures his peers that his education and faith responsibilities are placed before his leisure conduct of gaming. His revelation that he hangs off a tree pretending to be a favourite game protagonist is interesting because it reveals the creative/imaginative aspect of gaming (see Bogost 2007). This further illustrates Willis' (1990) claim that young people use the cultural resources on offer for creative acts of reclamation. Moreover, GamerNarion subsequently added that he believes all of 'us' (young male video gamers) pretended to be Nathan Drake when growing up. In other words he refers to a young male Muslim gamer neo-tribal formation (fans of Nathan Drake while young) in his inclusive talk at this point, in part by reflexively locating himself as older now.

After analysing numerous popular sites, it seems that as often as an Islamist ruling condemns gaming as *haram*, a counter-argument is offered to construct gaming as *halal*, provided certain limitations are observed. Accommodation always seems possible. We may take the example of 'Command and Conquer: Generals' (2003). The player can choose to fight for the US, China or the Arab/Muslim Global Liberation Army. In the game the US team is handicapped due to a slow economy – so they have only a small army but more technology. The other two sides in the conflict command higher numbers of fighters but have less advanced technology and weaponry. One young Muslim player informed his fellow gamers that he was looking forward to passing time playing the game during Ramadan.[30] He apparently sees no contradiction between playing this game and the holy month of fasting. Possibly he will always play for the Arab/ Muslim 'Global Liberation Army', but this is by no means guaranteed in a game which any side can win. This exemplifies the counter-narrative of an easy-going accommodation between religious observation and video gaming. There is even an online gamer group called 'I'm Proud to Be Muslim' which listed 4,415 members in 2015. The group claims to blend piety and gaming – 'feel free to join the group to share beneficial knowledge and be on the straight path, *InshaAllah*'.[31] The group abjures radicalism. For example,

> Strange Group Invite: Slm [*salam*] all, I got an invite from troll group, not sure if others are getting it too. Feel free to report them for encouraging terrorism.
>
> (Hamza,[32] 4 May 2016)

As Šisler (2016) points out, when the 'participatory' culture of Muslim youth meets the 'customizable' capacities of online gaming, there can be a transformation in the direction of counter-radicalism.

'Counter Strike: Global Offensive'

To further my argument, it is instructive to look at the way Muslim gamers negotiate playing the popular game 'Counter Strike: Global Offensive' (CS:GO), which is a 'symmetric' game[33] (Bornemark 2013: 3) in the 'e-sports' canon. A team of (Arab/Muslim) terrorists and a team of (Western) counter-terrorists try to eliminate each other. In their avatars, players speak to each other in character. The following post exemplifies general collective enthusiasm for the game:

> I want to take my hobby to another level with my brothers and sisters. Become the best in the video game community (...) *AllahuAKbar! Asa-laam Alaikum* bro's and sis's! *Bsmila Ar Rahman Ar Raheem*! 'O you who have believed, seek help through patience and prayer. Indeed, Allah is with the patient' (Qur'an, 2:153).
>
> (Noor * 3 * بسم الله February, 2014[34])

Noor blends video gaming slang and a Koranic quote in his post. The 'patience' he attributes to the Koranic verse refers to the patience needed to master CS:GO when someone (like him) is a newcomer (noob), which is how he described himself earlier. Another site member demonstrated the same kind of synthesis while urging CS:GO gameplay: '*Al Salam alykum* :) CSGO people add me :) *inshallah* we can play together and get to a new Level' (pa1N 13 March, 2014[35]). Muslim gamers can and do constitute an 'affinity group' (Gee 2003) in which individuals synthesise viable identities as pious players.

In 2011, one member on the 'Proud to Be Muslim' site put out a call for teams to play CS:GO[36]:

> Slm [*salaam*] guys, we are setting up a CS:GO server this week *inshAllah*. Will post the details on the forums.
>
> (Hamza[37])

Clearly, both teams in the projected bout of the game will be 'played' by Muslim gamers. However, disputes can arise. After one game on 2 June 2011 a 'Proud to Be Muslim' player posted:

> WE DONT WANT TO HEAR YOUR ♥♥♥♥ING '*ALLAHU ACBAR*' ALL THE TIME.
>
> (Fulgur[38])

His peer retorted, 'I like to yell "*ALAHUU AKBAR*" when the bomb goes off. just sayin' it's fun ... jeez' (Daredevil[39]). Yet another player added:

> Dude calm the ♥♥♥♥ down ... Its not 'the Muslims' don't be a stereotypical ♥♥♥♥ who thinks this. My friends who are not Muslim, say *Allah Achbar* when joining the T [terrorist] side just so there is more excitement in playing the role of a terrorist.
>
> (Clor[40])

It is intriguing to note that players on the terrorist team (whether Muslim gamers or not) enhance the pleasure of a hit by shouting *Allahu Akbar*, which means 'God is Great' in Arabic. It is the cry usually associated with jihad warriors. This perhaps indicates that the play is ludic rather than geopolitically aligned. Another CS:GO player on the same site on the same day pointed out that, 'if a 16 year old living in a Western country says *Allahu Akbar* he doesn't automatically become a Muslim' (Hakob[41]).

More or less the same issue of contention about shouting *Allahu Akbar* was aired on YouTube on 5 February 2015.[42] Regular non-Muslim CS:GO player Destiny uploaded footage and soundtrack of the time he found that, 'CS:GO gets a little "too" real when I find I may have an actual terrorist on my team'. The upload shows a moment in the game when Destiny's terrorist avatar and a fellow terrorist avatar are making their way through the backstreets. Suddenly the other terrorist avatar/player rushes forward. He starts speaking very rapidly in a foreign language and shooting enemy combatants, yelling *Allahu Akbar*. In the inset image, Destiny is seen laughing uproariously at what just happened on the game screen.

This upload received a great many comments from young Muslims. Quite a few took the position of 'don't laugh at my religion'. Others thought more respect should be shown for the victims of Islamist terrorism. Some struggled to understand what had been said by the player in the game. For example, Alyeldin Mohamed asked 'is he even speaking Arabic, I don't understand a word'. Another commentator added:

> Just to make it clear; This guy is just jabbing around. He didn't say a single word that made sense but *Allahu Akbar*. Second: He is not making fun of Islam or anything related to Islam! (...) I'm a Muslim and I laughed my ass off when i saw this!
>
> (Sheik, 5 February 2015[43])

Some commentators took the matter quite seriously:

> To all Muslims and Islam followers, this video isn't making fun of you. It's making fun of the extremists, terrorists (...) Stop being so butt hurt about it, no one is making fun of your religion.
>
> (Alex Luna[44])

A more recent comment on that same YouTube upload maintains that 'making extremist Muslims look like a joke is one way of ruining extremist Islam' (Kessler Hassenstein[45]). In this statement we see once again the discursive remaking of the radical Islamist meta-narrative; one that systematically (yet humorously) forms a counter-narrative in the act of play.

Muslim games and gamers

The gaming field is highly diverse and getting more so all the time. Indie game designers and 'modding'[46] specialists are increasingly producing games and game variants that cater directly to niche markets, including Muslim youth. The opportunities for Muslim youth afforded by 'Islamogaming' (Campbell 2013) are significant. This is because:

> 'Most video games on the market are anti-Arab and anti-Islam,' says Radwan Kasmiya, executive manager of the Syrian company Afkar Media. 'Arab gamers are playing games that attack their culture, their beliefs, and their way of life.'
>
> (Roumani 2006, online)

As indicated above, playing online games from a powerful position can boost the self-esteem for Muslim youth (Wagner 2014). When a gamer plays a purposed Muslim shooter or avatar, he/she potentially engages the construction of a victorious Islamic identity (Šisler 2013). Certainly Campbell (2013) found that young Muslims achieved 'digital dignity' through games that enact counter-stories. One boy aged 14 on the West Bank is reported to have said after playing a Muslim battle game:

> I know this is not real. But it feels good to pretend. It feels good to ... imagine that we are not victims, but we are conquerors.
>
> (Tawil Souri 2007: 540)

In the new millennium Muslim game designers have intentionally subverted and refashioned standard Western stereotypes of the Arab/Muslim enemy (Machin and Suleiman 2006) to create games that appeal to the cultural identities of the young in both Muslim-majority states and the Muslim diaspora. Theological grounding and religious pride is provided through battle strategy metaphors:

> Playing Islamic video games is an act with double dimensions, one that enhances one's own identity and one that denounces neo-imperialism for allegedly attempting to undermine that very identity (...) Players develop a sense of belonging to a civilisation. They cultivate the audacity to win the symbolic battle in a virtual realm.
>
> (Ibrahine 2015: 215)

Yet as pointed out previously, it is relatively easy to reverse the moral polarity of the radical Islamist meta-narrative to become the war on terror because the stories employ the same black-and-white narrative structure. The same is true of Muslim games that reverse the hero/enemy polarity. For example, the explicit war-on-terror FPS game 'Quest for Saddam' (2003) was answered by *Al-Qaeda*'s game, 'Night of Bush Capturing' (2006) which is simply a 'modded' version of 'Quest for Saddam'.[47] Similarly, in 'Special Operation 85' (2007) two young Iranian nuclear scientists are kidnapped by US forces while on a religious pilgrimage, and imprisoned in Israel. An Iranian special agent must extract them. The game mimics the 2006 US game 'Assault on Iran' which has a similar plot structure.

Both Western and Muslim-themed FPS games offer 'a means for gaining self-esteem, to feel as if "our cause" is the just cause' (Hawreliak 2013: 546). For example, in the early pro-Palestine game 'The Stone Throwers' (2001),[48] the young hero must punch, kick, and throw rocks at waves of Israeli riot police. An enthusiastic player commented 'you feel yourself as a stone thrower, killing the Arab's number one enemy, Israel. I recommend that all of you go to this website and download this game and enjoy killing the Israeli soldiers. LOL'.[49]

However, some Muslim games offer more than just a simple moral reversal of Western FPS. For example, in an Islamic war game like 'Special Force' (2003), superiority inheres in collectivism and religious devotion (Hawreliak 2013), while in a Western war game like 'Call of Duty 4', superiority inheres in advanced technology and weaponry. Indeed, in many Muslim games, battle strength 'comes not from technology but from God, as represented by heavenly light' (Machin and Suleiman 2006: 7–8). Moreover, there are 'contrasting cultural hero systems'; different framings of the 'innocent and guilty, those worthy of salvation and those suitable for sacrifice' (Hawreliak 2013: 546). For example, in the Syrian-created FPS game 'Muslim Mali' (2005), players engage in aerial dogfights with French fighter planes. Game-over pop-up text praises the unsuccessful (dead) player as a martyr to jihad. The hero's willingness to self-sacrifice, facing down death in the certainty of immortality, distinguishes the ethos of this Muslim-themed FPS. Except of course we must remember that this is a game. The avatar is respawned to play again.

In another example, the intriguing 'Quraish' (2008) is a real-time battle strategy FPS game that deals with the first 100 years of Islam. The player can choose to command the Bedouins, Arabs, Persians or Romans. At the sixth level the player must choose whether to convert, show respect for Islam, or deny Islam and continue to battle against it (Šisler 2014). This choice assembly engages the 'identity of his [sic] virtual self' (Šisler 2013: 144) as a Muslim. Thus issues of religious and cultural identity are central to Muslim games (Šisler 2013), and many parts of the meta-narrative are referenced, including the anticipated final battle and the caliphate. However, this is nothing new. Popular titles in the general gaming world often refer to a cataclysmic end of days. For example, RPG franchises like 'Halo' (2002–2015) locate humanity on the brink of extinction, facing an end-of-days battle between good (the hero player) and evil (a fundamentalist religious sect) to ward off the looming apocalypse. In a similar vein, the Muslim-targeted game 'Maze of Destiny' (2004) depicts a perfect Islamic world blighted by Darlak the Deceiver who has imprisoned religious teachers and hidden the Koran. The hero-player must find the Holy Book and re-establish the true worship of Allah before the world ends. Similarly, the mid-2000 '*Ummah* Defense' presents a peaceful global caliphate which faces 'an impending attack by infidel space invaders' (Brachman 2006: 156) who aim to destroy the world. Thus 'as a member of the Intergalactic Muslim Council, the player must battle the Flying Evil Robot Armada led by Abu Lahab XVIII, the last unbeliever left on earth' (Campbell 2013: 71). Here we see ample evidence of the world-saving appeal of both religion and epic narrative. In these specifically Muslim video games, they are brought together.

In the role-playing genre, the RPG 'Arabian Lords' (2007) is set during the Golden Age of Islam (550 CE–1250 CE) when merchant trade and growth were at the zenith. The player is an enterprising merchant lord within a range of single player scenarios. The lord starts with one palace and expands to build and rule an entire city by hiring workers, managing and upgrading trade markets and keeping customers satisfied. When the game designers were asked in interview why the game is based on trade rather than battle, the reply was, 'a conflict based strategy game set in that era would have opened up the outcome of documented events in Arab and Muslim history which would not have been received well with our target audience' (Mahmoud Khasawneh[50]). Religion was also handled carefully, in consultation with a team of experts:

> How the Mosque is handled in the game? We knew that culturally religion played a major role during this time span covered in the game, and that it still does today. We wanted to make sure to include this in a way that would honor its significance, while being sensitive.
>
> (Mahmoud Khasawneh[51])

In other words, too much emphasis in the game on Islam as a guiding theology of the times might not have appealed to the target audience of young Arab gamers who wanted a 'World of Warcraft'-type experience set in their own cultural history. 'Arabian Lords' spent six weeks at number 2 in Virgin Megastore's official Middle Eastern charts in 2007. However, as Khasawneh admitted, 'nothing can knock World of Warcraft off the top spot'.[52]

Hoping to corner the Muslim youth market, Middle Eastern corporation Falafel Games has produced the MMORPG 'Knights of Glory' (2011) which once again uses *Arabian Nights* visual imagery and Arabic language during the Golden Age of Islam. The player can lead a multinational Muslim army against the two strongest empires of the period. 'We're the only game where the Arabic player can identify with his own culture, his own history, and say I'm one of the heroes instead of the one being shot at' (Vince Ghossoub, co-founder of Falafel Games).[53] It is available in English and as a phone app.

However, as admitted above, there is nothing so far to compare with the enduring popularity and creative potential of the most famous MMORPG – 'World of Warcraft'. It seems there could be an alignment between the theological position of the good Muslim woman and the avatar of the healer in 'World of Warcraft':

> By day I am your kind and diligent straight A student, trying to be the best *muslimah* [54] she can be, but is there more to Me than meets the eye? By night, I am known as A Great Healer in an amazing guild in the MMORPG also known as 'Wow' ['World of Warcraft'].
>
> (Zahara Osman[55])

This quote provides us with an example of how, in principle, anyone can successfully play any game. The setting, characters and gameplay can be appropriated into a personal story of the successful self. Here the game is read into a narrative that suits the player's own subjectivity as a *muslimah* – a devout young female Muslim, but one who is a role play gamer by night. Her choice of role – healer – is possibly aligned with her moral subjectivity as a *muslimah*. Another posting on the girlgamers site confirms the popularity of gaming for some young Muslim women:

> 16 year old *Hijabi* here! I love playing 'Fallout' (the old ones + 3), the 'SMT' and 'Persona' Series, 'Fire Emblem', 'SSB', the 'Elder Scrolls' series, 'Hotline Miami', 'Nancy Drew' games, and I adore late 90s MSDOS adventure games (especially horror ones), and a bunch of other games!
>
> (Rammundone[56] 2016)

FPS Islamic gaming is often political. For example, 'Under Ash' (2002) and 'Under Ash II' (2005) offered players the experience of destroying Israeli military positions. Similarly, 'Special Force' (2003) and 'Special Force II' (2007) are FPS games created by Hezbollah where players fight the Israeli army with the help of God. A failed player – who 'dies' – is praised as a martyr – *al-shuhada*. Furthermore, players who have the necessary coding skills can take this further and 'mod' an existing FPS game to specifically suit their own story. For instance, IS released a trailer for a heavily modded pro-paganda version of the game 'Grand Theft Auto' in 2014. It was called: *Salil al-Sawarem* ['Sound of Swords']. The trailer featured cruel military tactics that IS uses against its enemies. It celebrated jihad and self-sacrifice. However, the actual modded game does not seem to have been released. More recently, IS distributed a modified version of the popular FPS game 'ARMA III' where gamers role-play militants. Players are rewarded not only for killing Wester-ners but for wiping out Syrian regime soldiers and Kurdish Peshmerga fight-ers. Examining this modded game, Brachman (2006: 157) argues that 'while players may understand that such games are based on fiction, the act of playing them arguably increases their propensity to accept ideologies that consist of extreme goals, such as the establishment of a global Islamic cali-phate'. The game offers a mediated version of jihadi discourse that seeks to appeal to young Muslims who support IS.

As the many examples above demonstrate, young Muslim gamers can creatively reconstruct the world as they want it to be. For example:

> Up until now 'Final Fantasy' is the favorable RPG game for me. (If you don't have any idea what RPG games are look on the net.) I have figured it out by playing RPG I want to do jihad just like what the story in RPG game (...) I want my Islamic life is just beautiful as RPG game. That's what I called the real Jihad.
>
> (Samian, 28 April 2015[57])

The story here is that Samian was inspired by fantasy (possibly apocalyptic) RPG games to follow jihad for Islam (although it is not entirely clear what kind of jihad he actually means). Nevertheless, the point is that he does not refer to a journey from religion to militant action, but from 'playing RPG games' since childhood to a vivid imagining of the heroic nature of jihad. In theory, any popular game can be read, appropriated or even 'modded' to favour a particular story of the self, including imaginative insertion of subjectivity into an Islamist position, and the reverse – the counter-narrative of apolitical ludic play.

Conclusion

This chapter has discussed the field of Muslim youth gaming. It seems that video game-play in itself may offer 'empowerment' (Werbner 2004) to create new hybrid meanings of a Muslim identity (Vergani 2014), or at least to offer some 'persuasion' (Bogost 2007) towards positive self-esteem. A sense of belonging is constituted for the neo-tribe of Muslim young people who make the choice to play video games together and contribute to transnational blogs. For the most part they seem aware that gaming itself is regarded by many of the faith as *haram* but they can go searching online for liberal rulings. Muslim game designers target the collective identity of Muslim players, but tend to do so relevant to gaming as a leisure pastime, not for a political cause. So this is not a networked project identity in Castells' terms (1997) but a networked pleasure identity, like so many in the leisure/entertainment field online. Doubtless there are serious matters of identity and self at stake, but not necessarily in a directly political sense. Like other young people today, the young Muslims cited above are united in their love of playing, and they choose to play a wide range of games (see Detweiler 2010). They clearly take pleasure in the affinity group of Muslim gamers, and many choose to play with teams selected from Muslim gamer sites. Gaming builds cultural belonging as young Muslims, but it does not in principle constitute them as members of a theological/political *ummah* in Islamist terms.

Overall, quite extensive examination of Muslim gaming sites revealed little actual endorsement of a jihadi position per se. Of course it is probable that such sites do exist, perhaps concealed and protected. In such places quite different sentiments might be expressed about the gaming experience, and the narrative of jihad might be stridently upheld. What seems evident, though, is a pervasive love of video gaming. It is a primary component of Muslim popular culture. Despite the fact that the content often stereotypes Muslims, this seems to be constituted as ludic collective practice in the act of playing.

As a practice of popular culture within the framework of *narrative*, young Muslim players in the diaspora reflexively position themselves in the game play, as we have seen. Yet how differently-aligned gamers decode the game, and the subject positions from which they play the game, strongly constitute any possible narrative they might make for themselves out of the experience, especially where there are elements which are, or could be, constituted as belonging to Islam in some sense. With reference to the radical Islamist meta-narrative, the general counter-narrative they construct is a claim for the co-existence of piety and video-gaming. The next chapter examines a similar practice of synthesis in the popular music of Muslim youth.

Notes

1 Various reference sources use different terms, including 'computer', 'digital', 'online' and 'virtual' gaming. I use the term 'video game' to include all kinds of gaming platforms, although games played *only* on mobile phones do not form part of the discussion.
2 For example the current worldwide craze of *Pokemon Go*.
3 In 2015 the most popular non-sport video games in the US were: 'Call of Duty: Black OPS III', 'Fallout 4', 'Star Wars Battlefront 2015', 'Grand Theft Auto V', 'Minecraft', 'Mortal Kombat X', 'Call of Duty: Advanced Warfare', 'Batman Arkham Knight', 'Lego: Jurassic World', 'Battlefield Hardline', 'Halo 5: Guardians'.
4 Games are not only bought, but borrowed, shared and pirated.
5 www.internetslang.com/AFK-meaning-definition.asp.
6 In First Person Shooter games players aim at opponents and click to eliminate them. Success depends on the ability to make rapid visual judgments and responses.
7 The book *Arabian Nights* was originally *One Thousand and One Nights*, a collection of stories and folk tales from the Islamic Golden Age, with some Middle Eastern folk tales added later. Said (1978) was critical of the first translation into English.
8 A *jinn* is a supernatural creature mentioned in the Koran. Often but not always malevolent, they can change form and possess humans. Also *djinn* or genie.
9 www.gamespot.com/forums/games-discussion-1000000/assassins-creed-altair-muslim-26053507.
10 www.gamespot.com/forums/games-discussion-1000000/assassins-creed-altair-muslim-26053507.
11 www.gamespot.com/forums/games-discussion-1000000/assassins-creed-altair-muslim-26053507.
12 www.quora.com.
13 www.quora.com.
14 www.quora.com.
15 www.thenational.ae/uae/uae-fatwa-qas-the-islamic-ruling-on-violent-video-games.
16 www.salafitalk.net/st/viewmessages.cfm?Forum=6&Topic=8928.
17 Religious scholar.
18 http://islamqa.info/en/174522.
19 http://fatwa.islamweb.com/emainpage/articles/ver2/ver2/engblue/index.php?page=showfatwa&Option=FatwaId&Id=259372.
20 www.askthesheikh.com/is-playing-video-games-haram-forbidden/.
21 http://games.muslimvideo.com/35/War-Games.
22 http://turntoislam.com/community/threads/video-gaming-news-blog-halal-or-haram.85541/#post-559841.
23 www.shiachat.com/forum/topic/234967128-lawsare-video-games-haram/.
24 www.shiachat.com/forum/topic/234967128-lawsare-video-games-haram/.

25 www.shiachat.com/forum/topic/234967128-lawsare-video-games-haram/.
26 www.destructoid.com/muslims-shouldn-t-play-games-urges-islamic-writer-179904.
    phtml.
27 Prayer.
28 Nathan Drake is a heroic action game avatar, descendent of Sir Francis Drake, but
    dressed in jeans and a T-shirt. He often jokes and quips, reflecting on the chal-
    lenges he faces. He conveys an everyman character.
29 www.ummah.com/forum/showthread.php?338837-Is-it-Haraam-to-play-Video-Ga
    mes.
30 https://2acd-downloads.phpnuke.org/en/c110868/command-and-conquer-generals.
31 https://steamcommunity.com/groups/al-eslam.
32 https://steamcommunity.com/groups/muslimgamer/discussions/0/364040166693632
    307/.
33 In a symmetric game each player has the same set of actions. The outcome
    depends only on a player's action and that of the opponent, not on whether he/she
    is player one or player two.
34 https://steamcommunity.com/groups/muslimgamer/discussions/0/684839199660492
    988/.
35 https://steamcommunity.com/groups/muslimgamer/discussions/0/684839199660492
    988/.
36 CS:GO has two defining features. First, permanent death forces players to spectate
    until they are respawned in the next round. Second, players purchase weapons and
    equipment at the start of each new round with credit earned from kills and vic-
    tories in a previous round. Either team can win.
37 http://steamcommunity.com/app/730/discussions/0/618463446163177210/?inside
    Modal=1#p2.
38 http://steamcommunity.com/groups/al-eslam.
39 http://steamcommunity.com/groups/al-eslam.
40 http://steamcommunity.com/groups/al-eslam.
41 http://steamcommunity.com/groups/al-eslam.
42 www.youtube.com/watch?v=HphwQNhByOk.
43 www.youtube.com/watch?v=HphwQNhByOk.
44 www.youtube.com/watch?v=HphwQNhByOk.
45 www.youtube.com/watch?v=HphwQNhByOk.
46 'Modding' is modifying a game, using code to change features.
47 Later, Iraqi-born American artist Wafaa Bilal created a further modded version:
    'The Night of Bush Capturing: A Virtual Jihadi' in 2009 as an art piece. The avatar
    Bilal is overcome by grief on the death of his brother by 'friendly fire' (true event).
    He joins *Al-Qaeda*, trains as a suicide bomber and kills President Bush (which did
    not happen).
48 This game is very similar in sub-genre terms to 'Streetfighter'.
49 www.1up.com/features/islamogaming.
50 www.itp.net/500579-arabian-lords.
51 www.itp.net/500579-arabian-lords.
52 www.prospectmagazine.co.uk/world/arab-videogames-quirkat-falafel-games-knight
    s-of-glory-call-of-duty.
53 www.wamda.com/2013/05/falafel-games-launches-mobile-mmo-knights-of-glory.
54 Muslim woman.
55 https://steamcommunity.com/groups/muslimgamer/discussions/0/541906989390842
    210/.
56 www.reddit.com/r/GirlGamers/comments/4atzj3/any_muslim_women_gamers/.
57 www.islamicity.com/forum/forum_posts.asp?TID=28733.

Chapter 7

Muslim youth tribalism in popular music

Introduction

This chapter builds on the previous one to consider Muslim youth and popular music. Young Muslims participate creatively as both listeners and producers. The discussion proceeds from the proposition of Nasir (2016: 2) that 'young Muslims today ought to be analysed through the dialectics of popular culture and Islamic piety'. The field here is popular music. Popular music defines not only eras in human history (Mannheim 1952), but taste cultures, and the cultural identities of young people as they grow up in those eras (Bennett 2000). Young people often say their favourite music speaks deeply to their sense of who they are, and to the problems they face in everyday life. Muslim youth are no different. Bayat and Herrera (2010) argue that no other medium expresses the complex and multiple identities of Muslim youth compared to popular music. Performers and bands can be offensive or outrageous, or build bridges that encourage harmony. Muslim celebrities in the music field can reach out to audiences of millions, Muslim and non-Muslim alike. Moreover, through the consumption and production of music, Muslim youth in the diaspora have a way to 'attain a social capital of hipness and respect on the streets' (Bayat and Herrera 2010: 21).

Music cultures are affective, dialogical and transformative (De Nora 2000). They are also transnational (Khan-Harris 2007). Diverse genres, styles and identity frames cross-influence each other globally according to local inflections of meaning. There is de-territorialisation at work as modes of music dissemination and reception continue to proliferate (Connell and Gibson 2004) in complex socio-spatial relations (Huq 2006) across the world. Like-minded individuals assemble – actually and virtually – around music to share ideas and experiences (Bennett and Peterson 2004; Khan-Harris 2007). This is 'neo-tribalism', rather than a fixed set of taste preferences (Bennett 1999a).

As explained previously, it really is a matter of neo-theo-tribalism when Muslim youth create their own music taste cultures. Globally, there are Muslim versions of almost all genres of contemporary popular music: pop, rock, hip-hop/rap, indie, reggae, folk, soul, punk, heavy metal, jazz fusion and so on. There is even a specifically Muslim straightedge hardcore following.

All these Muslim music genres have been commodified to a greater or a lesser extent by entertainment companies seeking new markets (Connell and Gibson 2004). Companies recognise Muslim youth as niche consumers so they look for new Muslim performing artists who can be lucratively promoted. At the same time though, the production and dissemination of any kind of Muslim popular music must negotiate various theological *fatwa*. Different genres attract different levels of moral disapproval.

In short, the popular music of Muslim youth expresses identity, builds solidarity, articulates outrage and anger, and garners respect. It plays a significant part in the constitution of a 'cool' global Islam, providing a readily accessible resource for youth identities not only in Muslim majority countries like Turkey (Solomon 2011) and Egypt (Van Nieuwkerk 2011, 2012), but Western countries like France (Jouili 2013), Germany (Herding 2013), the Netherlands (Gazzah 2010) and Australia (Nasir 2016). As Detweiler and Taylor (2003: 1) point out, it is possible to 'find God' in popular culture; in this case through performative Islam. Muslim popular music reproduces, informs and reconstructs a sense of collective identity for youth in the diaspora. It can be read as a parallel youth music universe that broadly represents the discursive landscape of migration and diaspora. For example, the rap groups Fun-Da-Mental in the UK and IAM in France were instrumental in the post-9/11 period for positive Muslim identity-building through hip-hop. Yet we should always keep in mind that music is often deemed *haram*,

> Entertainers have historically not been highly respected in Muslim societies, primarily because entertainment itself is seen as unimportant and a waste of time, at best, and corrupting and libertine, at worst.
>
> (Goshert 2007: 91)

In fact, music was totally banned by IS in the Syrian province of Raqqa (part of the declared caliphate) on 20 January 2014. The regulation was supported by promise of harsh punishment.[1] The IS justification is that 'songs and music are forbidden in Islam as they prevent one from the remembrance of God and the Koran and are a temptation and corruption of the heart'.[2] This is a frequently expressed opinion which requires some unpacking.

Theological rulings on music as *haram*

Despite the dogmatic certainty expressed in hardline *fatwa* like the one above, there is no single ruling on the topic of music in contemporary Islam. Instead there are liberal, moderate and Islamist opinions on offer, with the moderate line most frequently expressed. Some moderate scholars permit popular music with 'clean' lyrics and performance, and a simple, 'clean' melodic sound with a pious message, as long as it does not impede regular prayer. Other moderates forbid the use of tuned instruments, and many forbid female performers.

Yet often they do not ban music as such, so long as it is morally sound and not sensual (Otterbeck 2014). And if that ruling does not suit them, young Muslims can shop about online for the theological ruling on music that does.

Muslim youth in the diaspora not only download and listen to music, but play it. Online one can find many requests from Muslim youth for rulings on whether playing the guitar – for example – is *haram*. One strict site, Islamic-Laws.com, judges the guitar *haram*. Music is the fifteenth greatest sin (singing is the sixteenth). Even dealing with musical instruments is forbidden:

> The manufacture, sale and purchase of musical instruments is *Haraam* and the income derived from musical activity is also *Haraam*. The transactions involving these (instruments) are invalid. It is *Haraam* even to keep instruments of music in one's possession. It is obligatory to destroy them.[3]

Yet there is always a conciliatory viewpoint elsewhere on playing music. For example:

> Music and musical instruments as forbidden only if and when they are used for themes or messages that are declared as forbidden or undesirable. Based on the second view, as long as you stay clear of undesirable themes, and messages, then what you are doing can be considered as permissible (...) The Prophet, peace be upon him, has permitted us to have occasional outlets in order to help us recuperate and refresh ourselves.[4]

The following sequence of blog comments by young Muslims themselves demonstrates how contradictory rulings on guitar playing are dialogically expressed and, in the end, subverted by a mildly blasphemous joke. At the start, a young man asks his peers on a video-gaming site what they think about the hardline ruling of his father:

> Is it [a guitar] *haram, mukroo*,[5] or *halal*? I was planning to purchase one and learn to play as a hobby, but my father just said no because, 'It wouldn't make me a better Muslim'. Hate to break it to ya, but a lot of stuff doesn't make a person a better Muslim. Then he goes on to say that stringed instruments are *haram*.
>
> (RayUltimate[6])

RayUltimate implies he was upset by his father's ruling. A fellow gamer quickly offered the moderate view,

> From what I know, it's like video games. If it keeps you away from fasting, praying, devoting some time to God, then yes, it's *Haram*. If it kinda

becomes a hobby, and you can avoid all temptations and resist any wrong intentions, then it's fine.

(AncientZero77[7])

A fellow gamer then attempted to clarify the basis for the hardline ruling:

What he's [your father] probably referring to is Muhammad (saw) and his companions, some did used to practice music and instruments and poetry but the longer they were Muslim and stayed in the company of the Prophet, the further they went away from those things.

(Jediknightkhan[8])

Another gamer, The Battler, then commented jokingly, 'wait, so ... are you saying they're the first Muslim band?[9]' RayUltimate – seemingly cheered up – wrote back 'LOL!'[10]

We can see here the consolidation of neo-theo-tribalism around the question of Muslim youth playing the guitar. These young men are comfortable enough with that identity position to share a joke about the companions of the Prophet. Although this is a mundane, low key exchange, it illustrates the way in which a small counter-narrative, a joking one in this case, is extracted from a ruling on music as *haram*. Rulings on playing music were also challenged on other sites by Muslim youth. For example:

You can't just say *haram* is *haram*; in our society we need an explanation on this. In the time when our Prophet (SAW) was alive, music was associated with adultery, idol worship, dance, and all other actual *haram* acts. But in this age that we live in, music is not like that. We have things like orchestras.

(Abir313[11])

And

I play guitar, beatbox, DJ, piano, and learning other things :) yes i am a Muslim peace, love, and unity I blame my guitar! love you all!

(kik <3[12])

In fact the new wave of Muslim musicians – such as the Outlandish trio in Europe – include in their performances a diverse range of instruments. This has caused some debates within the Muslim community (Nasir 2016; Barendregt 2006), but has done nothing to reduce the popularity of the trio in the diaspora. In general terms the popular music favoured by Muslim youth is fertile ground for the expression of highly mobile Muslim identities that are distanced from a hardline Islamist position.

Synthesising piety and music

In keeping with the dominance of the moderate ruling on Islam and music (see above), many Muslim performing artists try to strike a balance. The UK Muslim singer Sami Yusuf serves as a good example of an appealing synthesis between the pious and the secular in sound, content and performance (Kubala 2005). Adapting the traditional *nasheed* form (see below), Sami sings soulfully in English and Arabic about his devotion to Allah while condemning violence in the name of Islam. In the YouTube video clip of his hit song 'You Came to Me', he is dressed in a soft brown suit (black t-shirt, no tie) and stands in a single spotlight. As he reaches the higher, long notes of the song, he lifts his hand. Silvery Arabic glyphs from the Koran materialise and swirl before dissolving. For the faster, more upbeat parts of the track, he is running through a forest in the rain, symbolically seeking something. The comments appended to his YouTube video indicate the rapture of Sami's fans, who respond to the affective potency of his music. For example,

> Just WONDERFUL Brother :) May ALLAH bless you.
>
> (Emi Rose[13])

> After listening, i feel disconnected with this world ... want to go back to *RasoolAllah. Sallalahu alaihe wasallam.*
>
> (Omar Hasan[14])

> The symbolism in this video is amazing.
>
> (Firas Wahdan[15])

> Please Mr. SAMI, next time make songs less beautiful, it is too much for my heart !!!
>
> (Zahira RACHADI[16])

These comments would seem to bear out Sylvan's (2002: 4) argument that music can offer a powerful religious experience, even an 'encounter with the numinous' (Sylvan 2002:4). They also support Otterbecks's (2014) claim that appealing tonal sounds stir something pre-discursive in people that speaks both to the self and the transcendent. In that way, Sami's music certainly seems to inspire piety.

However, some Muslim commentators judge Sami Yusuf's popularity in highly negative terms. For example, he is strongly criticised by Yvonne Ridley, a British journalist who was captured by the Taliban in 2001 and later converted to Islam. In a media column she claimed that Yusuf and other young Muslim musicians were narcissistically inspiring 'unIslamic' behaviour, especially unruly shouting, singing along and dancing by female fans. Sami Yusuf wrote back to her publicly, explaining how he consults with Islamic scholars to be well informed in his music. However, Ridley was not convinced,

> If he wants this sort of adulation then that's fine but why doesn't he just admit it in the first place instead of responding with a 2,000+ word response on his website (gosh, doesn't he have a lot of pictures of himself on display?).

(Ridley 2006)

As Paul Willis (1990) pointed out, young people do want to have fun, while at the same time they use available popular cultural resources to produce creative acts of reclamation that define identity. We might conjecture that stylistically Sami Yusuf offers a strong identity argument to young fans that you can look hip, sound modern and still be a good Muslim. Despite condemnation by Islamist voices, his fan base remains extensive. Sami Yusuf caters to different kinds of youthful Muslim fans by producing different versions of his tracks. For example, he produced a pared back, percussion-only version of his album *Al-Mu'allim*[17] to cater for Islamist youth, as well as a fully orchestrated version for the rest (Otterbeck 2014: 18). The example shows how Islamic popular music products are increasingly shaped to fit different Muslim youth sensibilities (neo-tribes) as commercial market niches.

In another example, the British Muslim boy band Seven 8 Six also produces pious Islamic music in a modest mode of performance, but they too are regarded with suspicion. In 2006, Seven 8 Six was dropped at the last minute from the line-up for Expo Islamia, a large Muslim gathering in the UK. Their performance was cancelled by Muslim authorities because they were perceived to be too much of a temptation – *fitna* – for young Muslim women and girls 'due to their looks, beautiful voices, and marital status' – single (Goshert 2007: 60). This example emphasises the point that Muslim girls in particular are not supposed to have fun in popular culture because it is a moral risk.

Yet Muslim popular music is important for youth in the diaspora, not only because it constitutes emotive manifestation of faith and *ummah*, but because it is often a plea for social justice (Swedenburg 2010). One powerful way in which a sense of injustice can be redressed is through musical manipulation of symbolic associations that emphasise cultural difference from non-believers. Music is a primary conduit for this symbolic process of constituting an affirming neo-theo-tribalism. In the new millennium conditions of uncertainty, religious neo-tribalism creates an inclusive symbolic enclave in which those who feel embattled can find sanctuary. This is an example of what Hage (2011) calls immune space, a place to pick up the pieces of a self-esteem compromised by intolerance of Islam. While older people might develop or join an inclusive religious community or group to achieve this, young people can create the same outcome of certainty and belonging through affiliation with forms of popular music that categorise them as different to non-believers.

Thus the inclusive neo-theo-tribalism of Muslim popular music partly defines Muslim 'cool' in the diaspora as a form of belonging.

In practice, the re-invention of a faith-based collective belonging makes certain aesthetic styles of music available as 'referents for configuring agency' (De Nora 2000: 124). This often hinges on the thorny issue of authenticity; the question of what is authentically Muslim in content, sound and performance. On a continuum of authenticity we might place the commercialised pop music of Zayn Malik at one end, and unaccompanied devotional *nasheed* [18] at the other.

The pure form – *nasheed*

The distinctively Muslim genre of [popular] music is *nasheed* (also *nasyid, nashīd*). A *nasheed* is an 'Islamic-oriented form traditionally sung acapella in tandem with only basic percussion', or unaccompanied. It is widely accepted as *halal* (Nasir 2016: 5). Islamic worship is rooted in oral and aural experience, for example the term *Qur'an* in Arabic means recitation. Thus the word of God is a text to be recited by believers. So Islamic spiritual expression may take on an oral or musical style,[19] such as *nasheed*. However, for the pious, *nasheed* performance must remain within strict limits, as follows:

> Women should not sing in front of non-*mahram*[20] men, people should not listen in mixed gatherings, and there should be no dancing in mixed gatherings nor any kind of alcoholic drinks or other *haram* behavior.
>
> (*Fiqh* of music, Al-Muhajabah[21])

Despite such endorsements, *anasheed* (plural) still attract the disapproval of those who regard *any* form of music as *haram*. For example, in Ryan's (2014: 454) UK study, the majority of her very pious Muslim youth interviewees (of both sexes) rejected *all* music as 'unIslamic'. However, in the diaspora such disapproving voices are overwhelmed by the voices of young Muslims who are enthusiastic about pious but popular music (Larsson 2011b).

Nasheed are an important tool for proselytising the faith. In Southeast Asia *nasheed* sung by groups of handsome young men in appropriate clothing have encouraged rejuvenation of Islam among the young (Barendregt 2012: 316). It seems the global online dissemination of devotional *nasheed* hits has stimulated 'new imaginaries' of Islam and the meaning of *dakwah/takwa*[22] for young people so they are more aware of behaving in a morally appropriate way (Göle 2002). In many Muslim majority countries there are televised devotional *nasheed* competitions. These talent quests usually feature only male singers – solo, duos, trios, quartets or larger groups – who quickly gather fans and become celebrities. In their rendering of devotional *nasheed* on television the young musicians seek to create a distinctive Muslim 'cool' in their sound and performance (Herding 2013). They may deliver devotional songs without instruments. However, the sound can be made rich and full by operationalising multitrack technology to create a 'complex musical web' of harmony, vocal counterpoint and even vocal percussion (Otterbeck 2014: 18). As counter-praxis, this kind of 'looping' is a tactic that accommodates the *fatwa* on musical instruments while recreating an instrument-like sound vocally, using digital technology enhancement.

It should be noted that the production of 'pure' devotional *nasheed* is relatively rare in Western countries. First, devout Muslim musicians want to communicate directly, so they use the language of their audience rather than Arabic (Goshert 2007; Aidi 2014). Second, their youthful audience expects more in the way of an instrumental sound (Nasir 2016). Third, the musicians want to stretch creative boundaries in producing their own expressive counter-narratives about what it means to be a Muslim youth in the diaspora (Bayat and Herrera 2010). For example, US artist Mo Sabri blends *nasheed*, guitar and hip-hop. His most popular track, 'I Believe in Jesus', has had millions of viewings on YouTube. He says he wrote the song to remind Muslims that Islam reveres Jesus as a prophet. UK artist Dawud Wharnsby claims a good *nasheed* combines both spirituality and human experience, like the hymn 'Amazing Grace'. In a recent *nasheed* he sang about being free, that no-one controls him. He knows he is on the right path and is sure that God is pleased with him. Such forms are sometimes referred to as 'urban nasheeds' (Nasir 2016). The *nasheed* overlap with 'Muslim R & B' is exemplified by the Danish trio Outlandish, which has been extraordinarily popular in Britain and continental Europe. Overall it seems that Muslim popular music has the widest appeal for youth when the songs are not overtly political (Khan 2007) but 'moderate' and affirming. Pro-Muslim narratives created by innovative Western *nasheed* musicians work symbolically and materially as DeNora (2000) puts it – by constituting both aesthetic and affective agency in the articulation of identity, of belonging to a theologically informed neo-tribe of musical appreciation.

On the other hand, *nasheed* are also used in the promotion of violent jihad. 'The vast majority of [jihadi] nasheeds can be subsumed under "battle hymns"' (Said 2012). *Anasheed jihadiya* – jihadi *nasheed*[s] – were first produced in the 1970s when militants in Egypt and Syria started writing them to inspire their supporters. Apparently even Osama bin Laden sang in a *nasheed* group when he was a teenager (Marshall 2015: 215). Since that time, *anasheed* referencing the Islamist meta-narrative have been used to inspire youth to jihad:

> A good nasheed can spread so widely it can reach to an audience that you could not reach through a lecture or a book. Nasheeds are especially inspiring to the youth, who are the foundation of jihad in every age and time.
>
> (Anwar Al-Awlaqi, militant imam and *Al-Qaeda* operative, quoted in Pieslak 2015: 14)

In 2013, IS/*Daesh* produced the emotive *nasheed* امتي قد لاح فجر 'My *Ummah*, Dawn Has Appeared', which became the unofficial anthem of the militant group. It is an infectiously catchy tune with a martial upbeat. Transposed over a still shot from the hugely popular video game 'Assassin's Revenge', the *nasheed* led to some ironic comments by non-Muslims who liked it on YouTube,

> That awkward moment when you are humming this song at work and your Muslim co-worker puts his hand on your shoulder and says 'Soon, brother, soon'.
>
> (Suzuki Nathie[23])

> Really nice music. Oh good morning CIA.
>
> (Wanty[24])

However, it should be noted that jihadi *anasheed* are invariably sung in Arabic. So the message of the lyrics is not immediately accessible to many young Muslims in the diaspora because they do not know Arabic. This tends to counter their direct influence in promoting jihad worldwide. Yet despite the popularity of *anasheed* among pious youth, the most common form of Muslim popular music is undoubtedly rap, and a large portion of this chapter will be devoted to discussion of that genre. First though, it is appropriate to give a brief overview of minority counter-discursive genres of Muslim popular music.

Other hybrid music genres

As mentioned briefly above, there are Muslim versions of most genres of popular music. The discussion below looks at two of the most contested genres to unpack the kinds of counter-narratives they embody.

Muslim punk

Muslim punk draws together piety and protest (Murthy 2013) in a distinctive synthesis sometimes called *taqwacore*.[25] It has been claimed that, first, Muslim punk enables 'a radical individualization of religion'. Second, it rejects preaching and secular judgements. Third, it is 'a community based on freely chosen and freely revocable commonalities'. Thus 'Muslim' is a cultural identity, '*taqwa*' is a private matter, and punk is the common point of '[p]reference' (Fiscella 2012: 278). Not only is the DIY ethos of punk deemed a good match for the mobilising egalitarianism of Islam (see Moore and Roberts 2009), but the incongruity in itself achieves rich iconoclasm. Thus Muslim punk is a strong counter-discourse to the asceticism and rigid boundary maintenance of the radical Islamist meta-narrative. In fact, 'apostasy is not merely permitted in a punk version of Islam but more or less recommended' (Fiscella 2012: 276). For example, from dual personal experience US female Muslim punk fan Tanzila Ahmed writes, 'a punk-rock circle pit is like *tawaf* around the *Kaaba*. It looks like circular chaos of pushing and shoving, but there is an internal order' (Ahmed 2012: 58). Commenting on her own life journey through punk and Islam she adds, at 'the intersection of punk, prayer, and love, I had finally found my people' (63).

McDowell (2014: 256) claims Muslim punk rockers 'make religion their own along two dimensions'. They use 'the oppositional attitude of hardcore punk to understand themselves as religious/punk'. Muslim punks say they feel excluded from their traditional religious communities for being punk, and from mainstream American culture, even punk rock culture, for being Muslim. Yet they find the two compatible. For example, a fan explained that: 'Islam doesn't have any ranking or hierarchies and that's quite essential in punk as well' (Sam quoted in McDowell 2014: 266). Another fan explained it as follows, 'when you take things like Islam and punk which are not supposed to go together, and you put them together, and they marry each other perfectly, I mean, what could be better than that?'[26]

In the punk music genre, the affix 'core' usually refers to a very loud, driving, harsh form such as hardcore or grindcore. So Muslim punk, or *taqwacore*, is 'God consciousness' served up hard and loud (McDowell 2014). In the UK, Muslim punk probably dates back to the 1979 founding of the band Alien Kulture (Fiscella 2012). In Europe, before the idea of punk Islam was formally recognised in the US, it was represented in a 1984 song released by art-punk Italian band CCCP Fideli Alla Linea. There was also Danish-Turkish Tesnim Sayar, who got into punk in 2001 and designed her own hijab topped by an impressive black fabric mohawk. Murthy's description of how the *taqwacore* music scene came to develop in the US points to the significance of creative synthesis in the constitution of Muslim youth cultures. *Taqwacore* began as an invented genre. In 2003 Muslim convert Michael Muhammad Knight self-published a novel called *The Taqwacores*. It tells a story about a group of young 'punk Muslims' who are not comfortable with the Muslim student association at their university and do not want to pray at the local mosque. In their lifestyle they successfully synthesise punk music, the DIY ethos and Islam. The book became a *bildungsroman* for progressive young Muslim Americans (Murthy 2013), and was later made as a film.

Taqwacore as an actual genre took off when Kourosh Poursalehi, a Sufi Muslim teenager in Texas, put to music a poem from the novel: 'Muhammad Was a Punk Rocker'. His band also took the name Vote Hezbollah from Knight's book. The so-named *taqwacore* music scene quickly developed, making use of irony and iconoclasm. For example, Muslim punks in the *taqwacore* tradition created a joke band called Box Cutter Surprise, to challenge pejorative essentialisms of Muslims following 9/11 (Murthy 2013: 174). In another example, a track by the most famous US Muslim punk band The Kominas was entitled 'Suicide Bomb The Gap'. The song simultaneously protested against American corporatist imperialism and the essentialising of Muslims as suicide bombers. 'Rumi Was a Homo', another track by The Kominas, challenged the homophobia of hardline Muslim groups. A later song was titled 'Wild Nights in Guantanamo Bay'. Murthy (2013: 174) admits that the 'extreme progressivism of some of this music ends up drawing fire from both sides'.

The Kominas[27] are the best known US Muslim punk group to date. An early controversial track was 'Sharia Law in the USA' which conjures up the image of a Muslim version of the Sex Pistols (Fiscella 2012: 272). It begins with an audio recording of news stories about 9/11. Against the backdrop of helicopters and police sirens, a rockabilly beat increases in volume. The lyrics establish a semantic link between being an Islamist and the Antichrist. The iconoclastic protagonist is on the 'wanted' list but is still very stylish (McDowell 2014: 270). Kominas member Ali defends the track, saying, 'it's a completely sarcastic song if you break down the lyrics'. Another band member reflected that, 'at different times we've alienated Pakistanis, Muslims, white people. Like everyone. [We're] punks'.[28] In a similar vein, the Canadian female Muslim punk band Secret Trial Five recorded the track 'Middle Eastern Zombies', which played ironically with mainstream stereotypes and upset the Muslim community in Canada.

It is evident that the largest Muslim punk scenes are in Muslim majority countries rather than in the diaspora (Fiscella 2012). Despite notoriety, Muslim punk bands in the West continue to struggle. Their relative alienation from the mainstream punk scene, combined with lack of support from Muslim communities, means that they are not economically viable for much touring or live performance. Instead they devote energy to a strong online presence. This seems to be working. For example, there are many more women tweeting about *taqwacore* 'than you would see at most of their concerts' (Murthy 2013: 164). Yet compared to Muslim rap, Muslim punk has so far gained only a relatively small following in the diaspora.

Muslim metal

Muslim heavy metal has an even smaller following in the diaspora, yet it is even more subversive, attracting a high level of moral panic in Islamic communities because of associations with satanism (LeVine 2009). For example, Mayer and Timberlake (2014: 29) quote a performer from Norwegian black metal band Darkthrone: 'With my art I am the fist in the face of God'. When this implicit message is meshed/mashed with Islam, an extraordinarily unlikely synthesis is created that pushes further than Muslim punk in terms of iconoclasm. The actual sound of heavy metal music seems to be a primary attraction for fans (Weinstein 2011). Mayer and Timberlake (2014: 28) explain that 'contemporary metal music typically uses highly distorted guitars, rapid-fire "blast beat" drumming, complex time signatures, flamboyant instrumental virtuosity, and atonal or dissonant arrangements that are unappealing to many listeners'. Metal vocalists do not so much sing as growl or scream and the lyrics are often unintelligible. This makes heavy metal the genre commonly ranked as most disliked in research on popular music (see Bryson 1996). Muslim metal bands seem to be particularly popular in Muslim majority countries, with only a few succeeding the West. They have a wide online presence, which suggests a transnational audience.

In his book *Heavy Metal Islam*, Mark LeVine observes young Muslims struggling to reconcile their religion with a passion for rock music and desire for change in the conditions of their lives. A founder of the Moroccan metal scene told him, 'we play heavy metal because our lives are heavy metal' (LeVine 2009: 570). Perhaps the same could be said for Iran, since Iranian metal bands are popular there with urban youth, despite a public ban. There is even an underground metal band in Saudi Arabia – *Al-Namrood*. When iconic groups such as Iron Maiden play concerts in Dubai, they are attended by thousands of Muslim metalheads from neighbouring countries where such music is banned. In a similar way, Turkish metalheads have managed to successfully claim some urban space of their own even though sensationalist media reports link heavy metal music with 'satanism, suicide pacts, and perverted sexual practices' (Hecker 2012: 2). Yet at the same time, they are engaging – through concerts, recordings and the internet – in building the kind of solidarity among youth in the Middle East and North Africa that conventional methods seem often unable to accomplish. It appears that Muslim heavy metal music scenes are pushing the boundaries of free expression and association across the Muslim world, despite risks of arrest and imprisonment (LeVine 2008).

Elsewhere, in the perhaps unlikely setting of Brazil, the full *niqab*-wearing performer Gisele Marie[29] plays deafening thrash metal riffs on a polka-dotted Gibson guitar. Originally Catholic, she converted to Islam after the death of her father. She said some people are shocked to see a practising Muslim wearing a *niqab* playing in a heavy metal band, while others find it 'interesting' or 'cool'. She says the music expresses who she is.

Two themes emerge most cogently from this brief discussion of Muslim punk and Muslim metal. The synthesis of Islam with a 'hard' form of popular music is both shocking and iconoclastic. Yet the synthesis seems to express aspects of how the young Muslim musicians and fans feel about their lives. In both cases, the phenomenon of neo-theo-tribalism in these forms of Muslim popular music is expressed in counter-discourse at four levels. First, in the secular youth culture scenes of punk and heavy metal, a specifically Muslim version represents a new, radical offshoot of iconoclasm. Second, in local Muslim communities, youth appropriation of punk and heavy metal music offends the sensibilities of an older generation. Third, since punk and heavy metal are already subversive forms of popular music, when combined with the category 'Muslim' they can engender even more antipathy and anxiety in a national consciousness. Finally, Muslim punk and Muslim metal are loud and fun, they deliver irony and spectacle. Representing not only the forbidden practice of music, but a richly shocking synthesis, they directly challenge the purist asceticism of hardline Islamism.

Islamic hip-hop or rap

Hip-hop (rap) is the world's most common form of Muslim youth music.

> Hip-hop's social commentary and its antagonistic style offer ideal platforms for articulating public misconceptions of Islam as well as the everyday injustice that Muslims face locally or globally.
>
> (Nasir 2015: 1042)

It is an inexpensive form that suits any young musician with few resources because it relies primarily on the voice and a beat; 'a narrative form of vocal delivery which is spoken in a rhythmic patois over a continuous backbeat, the rhythms of the backbeat and the voice working together' (Bennett 1999b: 79). Rap is delivered in all languages, from Swahili to Hindi to Mandarin. Some believe that rap, with roots in Africa, is related to the tradition of (Koranic) recitation, like *nasheed*. For example, Mos Def, a successful US Muslim hip-hop artist, maintains that 'both rapping and reciting have didactic possibilities due to their similar rhythmic qualities' (Rantakallio 2011: 37; Amghar 2003: 81). Certainly both *nasheed* and rap maximise the affective qualities of the human voice. Goshert (2007: 39–40) points out that rap may constitute an outlet for Muslims who are devout but still want to participate in a compelling contemporary music culture.

Muslim rap serves as an especially valuable musical resource for the expression of outraged identity in the diaspora (Saeed 2014; Nasir 2016). The urban young and disenfranchised are particularly drawn to hip-hop (Rose 1994a). According to a French source, rap is a means of channelling negative and destructive forces (anger/shame/fear) into a positive force of celebration.[30] In Muslim hip-hop, Islam emerges transcendentally from the rap itself as a life ideal. This ideal might be unworkable in society at present but it is constituted [performatively] through religion, and realised as a discursive utopia in rap lyrics[31] (Amghar 2003: 80). While the lyrics often directly reference the Islamist meta-narrative, they do so in a flow of embedded critique that works with symbols, irony and affect to constitute multiple counter-narratives of how to understand oneself as a Muslim subject in transnational and local youth culture. For Aidi (2014), Muslim rap therefore resolves the question of 'belonging'. It creates a neo-theo-tribal music space to heal self-esteem compromised by local intolerance of Islam (see Hage 2011). Embracing Islam in hip-hop, disaffected urban immigrant youth regain a positive sense of identity, and assert their legitimate presence in youth culture (Swedenburg 2002). Muslim rap is a worldwide phenomenon. The selective discussion here looks primarily at the genre in the US and France. The iconoclasm of female Muslim rappers is also considered.

US Muslim rappers

In the US the genre of rap has been instrumental in offering young Muslims a sense of valid identity in both Islam and in the American nation (Goshert 2007). Historically, one of the first US Islamic hip-hop groups to put its music on the internet and gain major attention was Soldiers of Allah (2000). However, these pre-9/11 Muslim rappers spoke scornfully of infidels and called for jihad and caliphate. After 9/11, their tracks were not well received by the Muslim community because they encouraged negativity towards American Muslims (Aidi 2004). Some other notable US Muslim rappers who started up early in the new millennium were Black Muslims in the Malcolm X tradition. Some were 'Five Percenters'.[32] The Five Percent Nation was a breakaway movement from the original Nation of Islam organisation whose goal was to improve the conditions of African Americans. The logic of the Five Percenters is that 'only 5 percent of humanity know the truth and understand the "true divine nature of the black man who is God or Allah"'. Thus '85 percent of the masses are ignorant and will never know the truth; 10 percent of the people know the truth but use it to exploit and manipulate the 85 percenters' (Aidi 2004: 111). In this cosmology, black men were 'Gods' and black women were 'Earths'. In transposed Five Percenter utopian theology, Manhattan (Harlem) became Mecca, Brooklyn was Medina, Queens was the Desert, the Bronx was Pelan and New Jersey was New Jerusalem. Some Five Percenters rapped about a 'Mothership of deliverance' which would be 'manned by Allah and Elijah Muhammad coming to destroy America' (Aidi 2004: 113). Such ideas have largely fallen out of favour (Van Nieuwkerk 2011; Fiscella 2012).

After 9/11 there was an increase in Islamic rap uploads as young US Muslims sought to express their anger at mainstream suspicion and intolerance. They were also attempting to construct affirming cultural, social and political spaces for themselves through hip-hop (Swedenburg 2002). For example, US hip-hop legend Mos Def was starting live performances with the Islamic prayer *Bismillah ar-rahman ar-raheem* (In the name of God, the most gracious, the most merciful). Mos Def is quoted by Nasir (2016: 80) as follows, 'If Islam's sole interest is the welfare of mankind, then Islam is the strongest advocate of human rights anywhere on Earth'. The benefits of Muslim rap are threefold. Not only is it an expressive 'way to fight public discourses that stigmatize Islam' (Van Nieuwkerk 2011: 7) but it strengthens the discourse of 'cool Islam' (Herding 2013; Mushaben 2008), as well as urging young Muslims to live morally sound lives.

A striking example is Native Deen, a Muslim trio from Washington who started to rap in 2000 without instrumental accompaniment, incorporating *nasheed* and R&B sounds. 'Their lyrics are positive, inspiring, and a reminder to do good, often in contrast to the material found in much mainstream American rap' (Goshert 2007: 47). For example, they sing about not being afraid to stand alone in their praxis of Islam because God is with them. They maintain their devotions even though non-Muslims may fail to understand, and mock them, as they state in their 2007 song 'I Am Not Afraid to Stand Alone'. In that track the young American Muslim is constructed as standing strong both in American society and in Islam at the same time. Expressing this synthesis, sentiments in the lyrics imply bravery, independence and strength; all elements of the American dream, and also of an admirable American masculinity – one blessed by God.

The Native Deen rappers dress in a very modest way and make only small stage movements when performing. Yet the band still attracts theological condemnation. A young fan asked an Islamist online forum whether it was *haram* to listen to Native Deen. The overwhelming response was 'yes'. One post elaborated further:

> It is *haram*. Full stop. Why don't these 'Muslim rappers' recite their lyrics and spread their message without the music or dancing? Why can't they spread their message via *halal* means? What is stopping them from doing this? Indulging in 'Islamic' hip hop or rap is a slippery slope. Music can be extremely intoxicating.
>
> (S999[33])

According to this hardline position, rap and Islam are just incompatible and that is that. Yet the neo-theo-tribalism expressed by Native Deen fandom would have it otherwise. One way that Native Deen creates this sense of a youthful *ummah* in rap is through symbolic associations that emphasise cultural difference from non-believers. Goshert (2007: 48) points out that Native Deen lyrics often 'contain Arabic words known to almost all Muslims but not, of course, to most non-Muslim Americans'. For example, their song 'Small Deeds' includes the words *sadaqah*[34] and *baraka*.[35] Like many of their songs, the figure in 'Small Deeds' is an ordinary American Muslim youth who can be encouraged to greater piety. He/she is invited into the meaning of the lyrics by the use of words that speak to the inclusivity of faith. The implied constitution of identity scaffolds hipness and orthopraxy at the same time. In short, Native Deen exemplifies the 'moderate' discourse of Islam, producing popular music with a simple melodic sound and a pious message.

Muslim rappers in France

As pointed out in Chapter 1, by mid-July 2016 multiple Islamist terrorist attacks had left more than 230 people dead in France, precipitating a seemingly permanent state of maximum security alert (Fouquet 2016). France today is a confronting place for Muslim immigrants, with strong mainstream political views frequently expressed against them. Muslim hip-hop artists do not have an easy time of it. French Muslim rap is often angry and aggressive, with vocal lines growled and words spat out. Rappers often produce starkly political tracks, 'offering trenchant social critiques of racism, globalization, and imperialism' (Aidi 2004: 117; see also Herding 2013; Swedenburg 2002). Khosrokhavar (1997: 202) puts it this way:; (French) Muslim rappers musicalise their Islamic faith,[36] while engaging in performative critique of the society in which they live. Moreover, French rap engages the public visibility of expressions of faith that offer direct testimony of the role played by emotion[37] (Amghar 2003: 78). There is both expression of faith and the strong *affect* of anger constituted in the performance of the French rapper.

Back in the 1980s, some French politicians courted rap artists like Afrika Bambaataa to come to France and help 'channel youthful rebellion into the aesthetics of hip-hop' (Osumare 2007: 86). However, by the 1990s authorities had come to view hip-hop as a distinct threat, in part because of the mixing of French language with English and Arabic in the urban rap of the *banlieues* (suburbs). The year 1994 saw the passing of the Toubon Law which mandated the legal preservation of French language. This law was used in the successful prosecution of many rap artists (Osumare 2007: 89) on the basis of their lyrics. By 2002, Jean-Marie Le Pen, the then Front National leader, was denouncing rap as 'a dangerous art which originated in Algiers [sic]' (Osumare 2007: 89), thus eliding co-existing moral panics in the country about race and youth. The anger and irony of French Muslim rap appears to confirm Rose's (1994b: 100) argument that 'oppressed people use language, dance and music to mock that in power'. Notably, because so many young Muslims in urban France practise rap to create that effect, it seems inevitable that a few of them would later take action as Islamist terrorists, such as the Kouachi brothers who attacked the *Charlie Hebdo* office. Aidi (2014: 5) found that the situation of suspicion for Muslim rappers worsened after the *Charlie Hebdo* attacks; in the public mind Muslim rappers became terrorists-in-the-making.

In the aftermath of the Islamist terrorist attacks in and around Paris in November 2015, that perception of the Muslim rapper as a potential terrorist threat was intensified. In the days following, it came to light that one of the suicide bombers who attacked the Bataclan music venue – Omar Mostefai – had been a rapper in his twenties. Similarly, footage was circulated of two other Paris terrorists, the Abdeslam brothers, dancing to their favourite rapper Lacrim in a Brussels nightclub two months before the attacks. Thus the proposed link between Muslim rap and progression to Islamist terrorism was strengthened in the public imagination.

A long-term Muslim convert member of French rap group IAM deplored this:

'Every time we see a terrorist now we see pictures of him before, and of course he's rapping,' says Akhenaton. 'So people are like, "He used to rap, curses! First you rap and then you blow yourself up!"'[38]

It therefore seems rather ironic that while the mainstream French media depict the music of rap as a sinister precursor to Islamist attacks, IS partly justified the attack on the Bataclan venue in terms of the music concert being held there. The IS claim for the attack stated that 'hundreds of apostates had gathered in a profligate prostitution party' at the Bataclan,[39] making implicit reference to music as morally *haram*. Thus music is condemned by the jihadi hardliners even though, as a genre of music, Muslim hip-hop has long been an important resource for broad 'mobilization' against Islamophobia (Saeed 2014: 189) in the diaspora.

An example of a French Muslim rapper confronting this dilemma is Médine, 'the wrathful hardcore rapper who plays with Islamist symbols and violent lyrics' (Jouili 2013: 75). Médine offers a stark vision of France oppressing those who follow Islam. His songs appeal directly to angry young Muslims battling unemployment in the *banlieues* of major cities. As part of his general position, Médine was long critical of the *Charlie Hebdo* position in mocking Islam. However, after the Islamist attack on the *Charlie Hebdo* office he took a different tack, according to the following account.

'Basically after Charlie Hebdo there was this hunt to shut people up, to stop people criticising. My album is called *Démineur* [Minesweeper]', he says, which is what he calls 'people who are looking to defuse the situation, who are talking intelligently'.

(Médine 2015[40])

It is possible Médine was shocked that IS attacked the Bataclan venue in Paris where he himself had ten days earlier performed his own Muslim rap songs at a pro-Islam event titled 'Who Is Malcolm X?' This fact points to the challenge of using music as form of pro-Islam protest in the diaspora when music itself is relegated to the realm of *haram* by hardline militants.

Muslim women and hip-hop

There are relatively few female Muslim rappers. This is not surprising. As explained in Chapter 1, young women are not supposed to perform in public. Sametoğlu (2015) uses the Muslim term 'halalscapes' to explain the boundaries drawn by young Muslim women to balance religious exigencies and the desire for fun. If young Muslim women do get involved in hip-hop they must negotiate the accusation that they have crossed a moral boundary. For example, the US rapper Sister Haero reports that she constantly has to battle the view from her own faith that Muslim women should not perform, and from the male-dominated hip-hop scene that female rappers are inferior. For example, Diam's (sic) is a famous French female performer who rapped about social justice in the first decade of the new millennium. She caused a storm of national debate when she suddenly converted to Islam in 2008. Her 2012 television appearance in conservative *hijab* was deemed outrageous by the French press. She also provoked outrage from Muslim hardliners, even though she stopped performing when she converted.

In the UK, two female convert rappers formed Poetic Pilgrimage, and have become celebrated worldwide. Yet throughout their success they have battled prejudice against female Muslim performers: 'people thought that a woman being on stage is her kind of exposing herself. The voice of a woman, they say, is like part of her private parts that shouldn't be seen by the public' (Sukina, quoted in Miyakawa 2015). As an example, an article about the work of Poetic Pilgrimage in *Al Jazeera* online (2015a) drew the following comment:

> This is totally against proper Islamic teachings. Women being in the studio with other men, dancing in public with other men watching? If they wasn't claiming Muslim they wouldn't be in ALJAZEERA.
>
> (Skinny Worrior in Al Jazeera 2015a)

As the disparaging comments show, Poetic Pilgrimage certainly attract suspicion and intolerance, but they are determined to give a female counter-narrative of Islam through music. They feel many of the problems faced by Muslim women across the world are the result of cultural misinterpretation rather than an inherent misogynist bias in the religion itself. So they set out to release their faith from the hands of those who have stolen it, as Sukina conveys in her rap lyrics for 'Aborted Daughters'.

An American solo female Muslim rapper, Miss Undastood, began with secular rap under her own name (Tavasha Shannon) when she was at college. At 18 she became devout and decided to use only Islamic lyrics, but this was not well received (Khan 2011). 'People didn't understand me', she said.[41] So she chose the name Miss Undastood. A 2010 interviewer described Miss Undastood as one of only a handful of hijab-wearing rappers and praised her musicality and piety. However, following the upload of that interview, the following comment appeared on the same site.

> What utter nonsense. Did our Prophet (SAW) approve of women jumping on the stage and singing in front of men as well, *Astaghfirullah*.[42]
>
> (Jhangir[43])

Miss Undastood says she wants her fans to 'feel' her music, yet she also makes strong points about everyday Muslim politics. In one of her choruses she urges followers of Islam to read the Koran carefully rather than listen to some preacher's interpretation. In another song, 'Best Names', she repeats many times that Islam is not a game – but deep faith. In 'Hijab Is the One Thing', she sings that although she elects to wear the *hijab*, that doesn't infer that other Muslim women who do not wear it are less devout. It seems that Miss Undastood has appropriated cultural symbols in Islam, 'recontextualised these symbols' and used them to speak out (Khan 2011: 60). Criticism from within the religion has not stopped her.

So despite the continued battery of negative comments from Islamists of both sexes, this has not stopped young Muslim women from musically expressing their own synthesis of social concerns and piety online through rap. For example, a study of Muslim youth in Australia found one informant and her sister 'wrote poems which they then performed as raps and uploaded to YouTube' from their suburban bedroom (Harris and Roose 2014: 203). It can be argued that given the hardline ruling against participation of Muslim women in music and public performance, any female Muslim rapper is, in her very constitution of embodied expressive selfhood, constituting a counter-narrative to the Islamist position. Her female fans create a similar location of subversive subjectivity.

Rap and jihad

Despite the hardline ruling on music as *haram*, rap is used for jihadi purposes (for example Alagha 2013). It can be used this way because of its flexibility as a 'transnational revolutionary soundtrack' (Aidi 2014). Constituting themselves as 'verbal *mujahideen*', jihadi rappers try to reach out to marginalised youth in the diaspora (Alim 2006). There are many examples on YouTube. For example, Somali American Omar Hammami, who joined the militant group *al-Shabaab* in 2006, produced recruitment videos overdubbed with his own catchy track 'Make Jihad With Me' before he was killed. It has been claimed that propaganda of this kind constructs the recruiter as the epitome of the 'cool older kid' on the street. The jihadi rapper extends a privileged invitation to come within the 'aura of coolness' he invokes. He conveys not only the idea of being 'young, confident', a rebel 'with a cause', but he has a soundtrack! (Joosse et al. 2015: 10.)

Drissel (2011: 175) researched 'jihadist-style apocalyptic lyrics and symbolism'. The example he gives is the catchy acapella rap 'Dirty *Kuffar*', by the British-Pakistani group Sheikh Terra and the Soul Salah Crew, which combines jihadi argot with messianic imagery. The video features ski-masked rappers carrying both the Koran and weapons. Footage shows American soldiers shooting Muslims in Iraq and Chechens killing Russians. The 9/11 Twin Towers explode and collapse as maniacal laughter is heard in the background (Drissel 2011: 176). In Germany, the urging of jihad through rap is expressed aggressively in tracks such as '*Allahu Ekber Bizlere Güç Ver*' by *Sert Müslümanlar* (Tough Muslims). Their rap lyrics encourage Turkish Muslims to take up arms to serve the cause (Solomon 2011). Perhaps the most infamous German Islamist rapper was Deso Dogg, who went off to join IS, where his ability to connect with disaffected youth has made him a key recruiter for the terrorist group.

It is evident that there is tension in the field between jihadi rap, pious Muslim rap and political Muslim rap. Aidi (2004: 19) identifies this as a battle 'for the soul of the Muslim "hip-hop *ummah*"'. Overall, while it is the case that rap can be used for the purposes of protest, moral improvement or Islamist terrorist recruitment, it must be kept in mind that rap is a highly flexible popular music genre. Worldwide hip-hop is not just music but a culture, a neo-tribal configuration that galvanises a sense of belonging to something bigger. Yet there is no guarantee of the direction this mobilisation will take.

Counter-narratives in popular Muslim music

Bringing together the arguments in this chapter, it is clear that Muslim popular music provides ample opportunities to construct counter-narratives, not only in the light of hardline Islamist rulings such as that offered by IS, but in the context of Western states where Muslim youth are reaching for adulthood in conditions of intolerance. Aidi (2014) proposes that contemporary Muslim popular music expresses how young people feel caught between the pull of anger against the panic-affected Western countries where they were born, and the lure of the battle-worn but seemingly heroic Middle East and the ascetic warrior ethos of Islamism. Yet at the same time Aidi (2014) is optimistic that the creative, cosmopolitan Islamic youth identity expressed in the many genres of Muslim popular music constitutes an alternative to puritanical discourse, radical jihad and the pull of hard-line movements like IS/*Daesh*.

Angry music is not the only kind that expresses a youthful Muslim identity in the diaspora. There are plenty of lyrical songs that celebrate Islam as a religion of peace and personal salvation. The affective potency of music is a powerful tool (Otterbeck 2014; DeNora 2000). Music in a religion provides an accessible 'philosophy and worldview' that translates readily into a code for living one's day-to-day life, as well as a cultural identity and a sense of belonging to a community. Thus a musical subculture (of a religion) 'functions in the same way as a religious community, albeit in an unconscious and postmodern way' (Sylvan 2002: 4). This is an important insight because it emphasises the affective potency of music for the affirming religious experience of belonging to Islam. Some musicians adapt 'Muslim' genres and sounds into a Western musical frame, while others 'Islamise' Western musical genres (Goshert 2007: 35). Overall, contemporary Muslim youth in the diaspora can develop – through music preferences – a constitution of self that is both pious and 'cool' at the same time.

Conclusion

Muslim popular music as a youth preference is intrinsically a counter-narrative to the radical Islamist meta-narrative of distance, superiority and vengeance because it makes an implicit statement about the way things should be, and could be, in the diaspora. It also challenges the *fatwa* that music is *haram* (Otterbeck 2008). Put another way, in the music preferences of Muslim youth we glimpse the reflexive co-production of salient identities made possible by neo-theo-tribalism. Collective reinvention of a faith-based self is hinged on the musical manipulation of symbolic associations that emphasise cultural difference from non-believers. It is evident that the confluence of popular music and Islam generates a huge volume of identity resource material for young Muslims in the diaspora. This happens primarily through downloads of music tracks, clips, blogs, forums and zines. Young Muslims who access this cultural material are locating themselves within the *ummah* – generally speaking, but they are implicitly distancing themselves from hardline extremism because they are enthusiastically consuming what hardliners condemn. So in that sense, to be an active fan of Muslim popular music is to position oneself assertively within a counter-narrative of ludic practice. The next chapter looks at a case study of Muslim youth in a nation of immigrants, Australia.

Notes

1 There are unverified reports that IS executed a 15-year-old boy for listening to Western music in Mosul in 2016.
2 www.al-monitor.com/pulse/security/2014/01/isis-raqq-ban-music-smoking-impose-veil.html#.
3 www.islamic-laws.com/musicgreatersin.htm.
4 www.onislam.net/english/ask-the-scholar/arts-and-entertainment/singing-and-music/.
5 Disapproved.
6 www.gamefaqs.com/boards/563727-prince-of-persia/43149398.
7 www.gamefaqs.com/boards/563727-prince-of-persia/43149398.
8 www.gamefaqs.com/boards/563727-prince-of-persia/43149398.
9 www.gamefaqs.com/boards/563727-prince-of-persia/43149398.
10 www.gamefaqs.com/boards/563727-prince-of-persia/43149398.
11 www.sunniforum.com/forum/archive/index.php/t-104106.html.
12 vine.co/u/1208592030977110016.
13 www.youtube.com/watch?v=z2_2cFityc4&list=RDz2_2cFityc4#t=0.
14 www.youtube.com/watch?v=z2_2cFityc4&list=RDz2_2cFityc4#t=0.
15 www.youtube.com/watch?v=z2_2cFityc4&list=RDz2_2cFityc4#t=0.
16 www.youtube.com/watch?v=z2_2cFityc4&list=RDz2_2cFityc4#t=0.
17 *Al Mu'allim* means the teacher in Arabic and symbolises the Prophet Muhammad.
18 I do not discuss the traditional music form *qawwāli* because it is not favoured so much by youth.
19 Chanting is a sacred tradition in the Sufi strand of Islam.
20 Unrelated men.
21 www.muhajabah.com/music-fiqh.htm.
22 *T(d)aqwa* means a shield or protection against wrongdoing that is created by being aware of God in all behaviour and so moving towards the perfected self.
23 www.youtube.com/watch?v=1nIN6Ciw1Ws.
24 www.youtube.com/watch?v=1nIN6Ciw1Ws.
25 God-conscious hardcore.
26 www.fuse.tv/2014/01/fuse-news-islamic-punk-rock.

27 The term *Kominas* implies low-life, scumbags in Pakistani.
28 www.fuse.tv/2014/01/fuse-news-islamic-punk-rock.
29 www.firsthillmedia.com/gisele-marie-rocha-burqa-clad-guitarist-brazil/.
30 My translation of: *il est un moyen de canaliser les forces négatives et destructrices en puissances positives.*
31 My translation of: *L'islam apparaît comme un processus transcendental par lequel l'idéal de vie exprimé dans le rap, irréalisable dans la société, prend forme grâce à la religion, il serait la réalisation d'une utopie discursive décrite dans les textes des rappeurs.*
32 For example, J-Live, Busta Rhymes and Wu Tang Clan.
33 www.ummah.com/forum/showthread.php?197608-native-deen-haram-or-halal.
34 Charity.
35 Blessing.
36 My translation of: *les rappeurs 'musicalisent' leur islam.*
37 My translation of: *les caractéristiques les plus manifestes de cette évolution sont la visibilité sociale de la manifestation de la foi, son témoignage direct, le rôle qu'y joue l'émotion.*
38 www.factmag.com/2015/11/03/franco-arabic-rappers-in-paris/.
39 It is claimed that the Bataclan venue had a Jewish owner.
40 www.factmag.com/2015/11/03/franco-arabic-rappers-in-paris/.
41 www.muslimhiphop.com/Hip-Hop/Miss_Undastood.
42 An Arabic expression of disapproval or shame. The literal meaning is 'God forgive me'.
43 http://brotherdash.com/hijabi-hip-hop/.

Chapter 8

Australian Muslim youth

A case study

Introduction

This chapter is a case study of Australian Muslim youth. It looks at how they take up and construct counter-narratives. Australia is a useful country to examine because it is primarily a nation of immigrants, yet lacks formal provision to protect human rights (Williams 2011: 1169). There is a significant public fear of Islam (Bouma 2016). Broadbent (2013: 189) found widespread support for the idea 'that Muslim Australians are potential terrorists'. Yet Australia has so far seen only a very small number of cases and convictions of Islamist terrorism (Mullins 2011). Nevertheless, public reaction has been strong. Between 2001 and 2014 some 64 separate pieces of counter-terrorism legislation entered Australian law. However, to counter instances of racial-religious profiling in the implementation of these laws, unfortunately Australia has no Bill of Rights to protect human rights,[1] unlike most liberal democracies in the world. Muslims in Australia often feel unfairly targeted by counter-terrorism laws, but it is difficult to challenge the application of them in constitutional terms. There are laws to protect minorities against defamation, and to prosecute hate crime, yet basic human rights are not directly protected. Moreover, despite many cases, there is no public database of hate crimes conducted against Muslim Australians such as that produced by the US Federal Bureau of Investigation (Fry 2016: 123).

In terms of tolerance of Islam, at best there is a binary division of Australian Muslims into 'good' and 'bad' (Patil 2015; Aly 2007). Yet regardless of age, gender or ethnicity, Australian Muslims young and old overwhelmingly oppose terrorism. They challenge the moral panic and interventions that challenge their human rights primarily by asserting a positive image. A common response to negative labelling is to argue back that 'Islam is a religion of peace', so terrorists by definition are not 'true Muslims' (Cherney and Murphy 2015: 10). Even one of Australia's most senior *salafi* clerics has offered this view (Le Grand 2015). Young Australian Muslim journalist Ruby Hamad writes,

> There is no clash of civilisations between Islam and the West for the soul of humanity. There is no existential crisis of contrary religions. There is

no 'us' and 'them'. What there is, is a never-ending battle between progressives and regressives. There are those who advocate for inclusive values, and those who wish to discriminate.

(Hamad 2016)

This is more or less the same point made by Šisler (2016), Cevik (2015), Turner (2014) and many others about the difference between religious observation as forced, and religious observation as chosen and negotiated.

When Islamist attacks take place anywhere in the world, Muslim families have negative experiences. They are 'the first to suffer the consequences of terrorism. The shame of having a member of the faith commit acts of violence in the name of religion, and the subsequent anti-Muslim backlash, affects all Australian Muslims' (Akhbarzadeh 2015). For example:

In the south Brisbane suburb of Holland Park, where a mosque has stood since the early years of Federation, Ali Kadri recounts stories of women [now] being too fearful to go to shopping centres wearing their *hijab*, of second and third-generation Muslims being abused for growing their beards.

(Le Grand 2015)

Every new attack makes their lives even harder. In 2015, for instance, global and local terrorist attacks saw Australian Muslims exposed to twice as much as usual verbal abuse and intimidation[2] (Battersby 2015).

This kind of situation occurs because Australian Muslims per se are routinely demonised in the popular media as dangerously 'backward' people and/or potential terrorists (Cherney and Murphy 2015; Patil 2015; Battersby 2015; Tufail and Poynting 2013; Aly 2007; Bouma et al., 2011; 2011; Poynting and Mason 2007; Rashid 2007; Dunn et al. 2007; Wise and Ali 2008; Sohrabi and Farquharson 2012). They experience everyday discrimination (Sohrabi and Farquharson 2015; Broadbent 2013; Nilan 2012a; Fozdar 2011; Hage 2011; Northcote and Casimiro 2010; Hassan 2010; Noble and Poynting 2008; Poynting and Mason 2008; Dunn et al. 2007; Poynting and Noble 2006; Poynting et al. 2004). In 2014, one in four Australians held a negative attitude to Muslims (Chalkley-Roden 2014), and Muslims experienced discrimination at three times the rate of other Australians (Kearney and Taha 2015). Acts of religious discrimination are prohibited under Australian law.[3] Yet media and political voices still propagate distorted and biased stories about Muslims (Sohrabi and Farquharson 2015: 2) that fuel intolerance.

As for youth, the government has expressed concern about 'the local and national adaptation of young Muslim Australians' (Hosseini and Chafic 2016: 4), implying they pose a direct threat. Policies and interventions target 'better' Muslim youth integration. Their sense of social exclusion is understood as the precursor of radicalism (Akbarzadeh 2013; Broadbent 2013; Hassan 2010). Yet young Australian Muslims are already actively 'including' themselves in all spheres. They have strongly made their views about Islam and everyday life known on social media. New Facebook pages and Twitter feeds have been established that affirm positive Muslim identities within the various neo-tribal formations of the faith. Songs that bridge Islamic theology and peaceful co-existence have been written and performed. This flurry of Muslim identity activity illustrates not only how they react to the moral panic over Islam in Australia but how the moral panic itself forms Muslim youth as particular kinds of subjects at risk. They feel that as young Muslims they are compelled to give account of who they are, and what they are doing in the name of Islam. For example:

If you happen to have been born into a Muslim family and you do not automatically regard this as a source of shame, expect to get called things like 'the perfumed face of a very dangerous ideology', and 'the reason jihad has not stopped for 1400 years'. These types of comments occupy my Twitter.
(Hamad 2016)

As one Sydney musician said,

I feel as though Muslims are always put in a defensive position, they're always being asked to perform their loyalty as Australian citizens, to show that they're not terrorists, to argue that Islam is a calm and pristine and peaceful religion (...) on the other hand that almost legitimises the accusation to begin with.
(Safdar Ahmed, quoted in Chalmers 2015)

The argument in this chapter is that the Islamophobic moral panic in Australia colours the affective atmosphere for young Muslims. Following the global trend of neo-theo-tribalism, they create counter-narratives in popular culture through engaged reflexivity about who they are and where they are heading.

Muslims in Australia

Key Muslim migrant communities are from the Middle East, Asia, Eastern Europe and Africa (Harris and Roose 2014: 799). In the 2011 census Muslims were 2.2 per cent of a population of 21.5 million; with 61.5 per cent born overseas (ABS 2012). Yet a recent poll found many Australians believe Muslims make up at least 18 per cent of the country's population[4] (The Guardian 2014). The margin of the overestimation is illustrative of the pervasive moral panic. Vivid news reports about attacks and atrocities stick, even if they are describing something that rarely happens. As Sherene Hassan quipped (in Sohrabi 2015: 9), 'the worst examples of Muslims are those that make it to the media'. For example, the image of Australian jihadi Khaled Sharrouf's young son posing with a severed head in Syria shocked the world.

Nearly half of all Muslims live in Sydney, with almost a third in Melbourne (Jakubowicz et al. 2014: 9–10). Muslim communities in Australia have been 'traditionally inward-looking and preoccupied with the internal concerns of the community' (Peucker et al. 2014: 296). However, the shock of terrorist attacks has meant reaching out to the wider community and becoming more active in the public domain.[5] For example, Sherene Hassan was strongly affected by 9/11:

> I was living in Adelaide at the time, where the Muslim presence was quite limited, and I was very frustrated with the way Islam was being portrayed in the media, and very frustrated with our Muslim spokespeople. So I got involved.
> (Sherene Hassan[6] quoted in Sohrabi 2015: 5)

Australian media broadcasters with a jaundiced view – 'shock jocks' and conservative politicians – claim that Muslims want to impose *sharia* law and female veiling, that they support terrorist actions, and donate to jihadi groups. There have been avid local protests against the construction of mosques and Islamic schools, imputing that all Muslims are the same (Dunn et al. 2007; Wise and Ali 2008). A group called Reclaim Australia organises rallies against Muslims 'changing our country', as they put it. The Rise Up Australia Party actively lobbies against engaging with Muslims. The United Patriots Front organises anti-Islam street protests. The right wing Australian Liberty Alliance's manifesto demands a ban on Muslims migrating to Australia, and that mosques be shut down. Membership is growing steadily (Bourke 2016). One anti-Muslim street protester said,

> [Muslims] come here to live in Australia and they want to change our values, our way of life, to suit them. They come here for a new life – and they want their old life. So why stay here if they don't want it? They can leave – simple as that.
> (Quoted in Al Jazeera 2015a)

Yet Australian Muslims across the board support the principle and practice of democracy (Rane et al. 2010: 139). As Atie and Dunn (2013: 2) point out, 'there is no compelling empirical evidence in Australia to support the case for widespread radicalisation (or vulnerability to it) among Muslims, nor is there evidence to suggest widespread alienation' (see also Abou El Fadl 2007). A survey by Rane et al. (2010) found Muslims simultaneously value their Islamic identity, and actively seek to integrate into mainstream Australian society. It seems that while negative depictions in the mass media have shaken the confidence of many, their trust in care, education and the judiciary, remains high (Rane et al. 2010). In short, like other Australians, Muslim people just want to get on with making prosperous and harmonious lives for themselves and their families. Sometimes this can be challenging.

One young Australian actor changed his Muslim name to get work. When he first registered as an actor, he used his given name – Mustafa Dennawi – and posted his details. Then he waited, for more than a year, and got no roles. He made the decision to change his name to Tyler De Nawi, while keeping his photo and all other details the same,

> The next day, the messages began to come in – not just replies to my applications but also direct approaches from directors and producers. 'We love your look'; they said. 'We want you on our short film. We want you to do an underwear shoot in Singapore'.
>
> (De Nawi 2016)

It is clear that names matter to potential employers. Booth et al. (2012) measured Australian labour market discrimination using fictitious ethnic names. Compared to 'Anglo' names they found significant differences in employer callback rates, with systematic variation across ethnic groups.

Discrimination against Muslims occurs in employment (Hassan 2010; Fozdar 2011; Nilan 2012a; Lovat et al. 2013; 2015). Muslims in Australia have 'similar or higher' educational attainments, compared to the whole population (Hassan 2010: 575), yet remain disadvantaged in the labour market. In 2011, the national unemployment rate for Muslims was 12.6 per cent, more than double the national average. This holds 'significant implications for the sense of belonging and citizenship' (Peucker et al. 2014: 296; Kabir 2008). Young Muslims may resent others having career and life opportunities which they do not perceive for themselves (Hassan 2010). They are simultaneously promised opportunities and denied chances by institutionalised religious racism, which produces complex feelings of exclusion and self-blame (Hage 2011). Yet the fact that such feelings are experienced does not mean they will turn to Islamist extremism. In fact, they demonstrate considerable resilience, creativity and collective solidarity in dealing with this tension.

Muslim youth in Australia

Muslims in Australia show a young demographic profile (Peucker et al. 2014). Of Australian Muslim youth surveyed in 2010, 72 per cent had experienced discrimination (Jakubowicz et al. 2014: 12). Suspicion of terrorist leanings falls most heavily on male Muslim youth. Muslim leader Berhan Ahmed, 2009 Australian of the Year in Victoria, says that top-down authoritarian approaches to prevent male Muslim youth radicalisation are 'not addressing the root causes'. They sometimes rebel, he says, because 'belonging is more than just waving an Australian flag' (Ahmed quoted in Green 2015). Melbourne Muslim businessman Ali Dirani feels young Muslims need to be reminded of the opportunities in Australia, where they can prosper and worship freely, as he does. Dirani describes sympathising with IS as a kind of illness, since IS is anathema to Islamic values.

> No sane individual would believe that the creator of humanity is going to condone this (...) they want to make God a partner in their crimes. The individuals that are on the ground killing, the way they are doing it they have lost their humanity.
>
> (Ali Dirani quoted in Le Grand 2015)

Dirani says the 'cure' for young people sympathising with IS lies not in punitive measures, but reaching out from the *ummah* by those who live easily in secular democracies. Yet he acknowledges that young Muslims in Australian do not always have an easy time of it. They feel disappointed and resentful (Poynting et al. 2004), as if they live 'under the public gaze' (Cherney and Murphy 2015: 6). This creates pressure:

> Every time I see my religion being vilified in the media, I have to look away or shut it down. I want to do something, say something, defend my religion, but I also don't want to have to do something. I shouldn't have to say something. I haven't done anything wrong.
>
> (Rodoshi Hassan, f, 21, Sydney, cited in Donelly 2016)

Peucker et al. (2014: 283) claim that 'repeated pressure on Muslims to denounce terrorism' has prompted further 'angst and alienation' among them. Young women who wear the headscarf are specifically targeted.

> It's like being an outcast. It's terrorising. I shouldn't have to wake up every morning thinking about how I am going to respond to verbal or physical abuse. I shouldn't have to walk around the streets thinking that my headscarf makes me a target.
>
> (Sarah Shehata, 21, Melbourne, cited in Donelly 2016)

It has been argued that the new Australian counter-terrorism laws and police operations risk becoming counter-productive because they over-reach community norms[7] and create a siege mentality among young Muslims who feel they are being unfairly targeted (Cherney and Murphy 2015). Even well-intentioned counter-terrorism initiatives can generate at the extremes a counter-productive response of resentment.

Australian jihadis

Some young Australians have gone overseas to join jihad and some acts of Islamist terrorism have taken place on Australian soil. It is therefore appropriate to briefly review some of these events.

Domestic attacks

On Australian soil there have been relatively few deadly Islamist terrorist attacks, and intelligence agencies seem to have been quite effective in preventing actual attacks (Mullins 2011). Moreover, Australia has not seen a 'significant presence of active transnational jihadist networks' (Zammit 2010: 14). Most cases since 2003 have involved either self-starter individuals or a small group of local perpetrators. For example, Mullins (2011: 267) mentions the uncovering of the 'Pendennis' terrorist network in 2004 (see also Ali and Moss 2010). In 2014 sole attacker Numan Haider (18) stabbed and killed two police officers in Victoria. He carried an IS flag. In the same year a self-proclaimed sheikh, Man Haron Monis,[8] took 17 people hostage in Sydney. He forced hostages to hold up a jihadist flag against the cafe window. Monis and two hostages were killed, while another four people were injured. In April 2015, five young men were arrested in Melbourne over an Islamist extremist plot to target police officers with 'edged weapons' on Anzac Day.[9] Police were informed of the threat by UK authorities after arresting a 14-year-old boy in Manchester. A few days after the Anzac Day arrests, a propaganda video by senior Australian-origin IS recruiter in Syria, Neil Prakash, urged attacks on home soil. 'My beloved brothers in Islam in Australia ... Now is the time to rise, now is the time to wake up ... You must start attacking before they attack you' (Calligeros 2015). The following month a 17-year-old Melbourne man was charged after police raided his home following a tip-off. They found Islamic extremist propaganda and three pipe bombs.

In 2015 Farhad Jabar Khalil Mohammad (15) shot dead a police accountant outside Parramatta Police Headquarters in Sydney. He came straight from the local mosque dressed in Muslim attire and shouting '*Allahu Akbhar*'. An issue of *Dabiq*, the IS online magazine, praised him as a martyr:

> Amongst these brave knights of *tawhīd* and *jihād* was fifteen-year-old Farhad Khalil Mohammad Jabar, who on '2 October 2015' struck the crusaders of Australia and killed one of their personnel.
>
> (*Dabiq* 2015[10]: 3)

In April 2016, a young Islamic State supporter allegedly attacked a former Australian soldier in a jail cell in Queensland. He used a sharp object to carve 'e4e' into the man's head, in reference to the IS motto of an 'eye for an eye, tooth for a tooth'. According to Zammit (2010: 8) most Islamist terrorist cases in Australia involve young men, with an average age of 27. Very few had a devout Muslim upbringing. This calls into question the demonisation of Muslim youth *per se* as ripe for radicalisation.

Foreign fighters

The majority of Islamist recruits to jihad leave Australia to fight in the Middle East (Jennings 2015). Australia apparently contributes one of the largest number of foreign fighters per capita from the diaspora to regional conflict in Syria and Iraq (Al Jazeera 2015c; Kenny and Allard 2015). More than 100 Australians have had their passports cancelled because they were planning travel to conflict zones, or had returned from them (Le Grand 2015). On average, Australian jihadis now are young and quite well educated (Zammit 2010). 'Gen Y jihadists are mostly born in Australia and have diverse ethnic backgrounds' (Australian Strategic Policy Institute 2015: 7). Media headlines revel in stories of young Australian jihadis.

In 2014 young Australian jihadi couple Amira Karroum and Tyler Casey were gunned down in Aleppo, Syria. Their profiles of radicalisation do not fit the stereotype of the poor marginalised Muslim. Amira Karroum attended an expensive private girls' school in Brisbane before university. Convert Tyler Casey grew up in a fundamentalist Christian home (ABC 2015). However, the fact that neither fits the expected 'vulnerable-to-terrorism' Muslim profile was channelled through radio and television chat shows into the fearful Islamophobic perception that potential radicals are therefore everywhere.

Perhaps the most famous Australian jihadi to date was convert Jake Bilardi (18). A school friend introduced him to Islam. He then actively corresponded online with contacts in the Middle East (Bachelard and Cordoba 2015). Jake bought a one-way ticket to Istanbul. Two months later, he contacted his family to let them know he was in Iraq training for a 'martyrdom mission'. He carried out a suicide attack in Iraq in 2015. Jake's profile on a Livestream site quotes Islamic philosopher Ibn Taymiyyah:

> 'What can my enemies do to me? My paradise is in my heart, it is with me wherever I go. To imprison me is to provide me with seclusion. To send me into exile is to send me away in the Path of Allah. And to kill me is to make me a martyr.'
>
> (Bachelard and Cordoba 2015)

Another young Australian jihadi was Adam Dahman, who left Australia at 17, strapped on a suicide vest and killed himself and five other people near a Shi'ite mosque in Baghdad in 2014. We may surmise that in some cases local contacts nurtured their radical views; in other cases that online media facilitated their radicalisation. Only three of the 16 young Australian Islamist terrorists studied in depth by Jennings had mental health problems. Their search for personal meaning in extreme action is perhaps a better clue. For example, terrorism expert Greg Barton described Australian senior IS recruiter Neil Prakash as a 'desperate kid looking for meaning' who converted to Islam just a year before joining IS (Barton quoted in Greene 2016).

Barton describes the use of young idealistic Westerners by IS as a 'very cynical move from a very cynical operation'. He explains that young Australians who can't speak Arabic and have no combat experience are of no real use, except for propaganda value. 'So many of them become patsies who are told to strap on a vest or hop in the driver's seat of a suicide vehicle' (Barton quoted in Brown 2014). Barton (quoted in Green 2015), believes the problem of Muslim youth radicalisation lies beyond 'dynamics in our suburbs and with our youth'. He encourages looking at 'the way in which the global network of events in Syria and Iraq are energising them', including the declaration of caliphate.

Considering the relatively small number of Australian recruits, their influence is notable. For example, Australians Neil Prakash (previously a rapper), Abdullah Elmir, Abu Yahya ash Shami, Abu Nour al-Iraqi, Tareq Kamleh and Jake Bilardi have all featured in IS recruitment propaganda (Jennings 2015: 20). Moreover, Australian Muslim convert Musa[11] was named by UK authorities in 2014 as the second most influential Islamist preacher for foreign fighters in Syria. An Australian media graduate, Musa was employed by an Egyptian TV channel in 2011 because of his Western appearance (Safran 2015). Musa's televised version of Islamic history included a story about Islamic forces fighting 'Dracula', which ended with the Ottoman leader Muhammad al-Fateh's head on a stick. This is what inspired Bram Stoker, according to Musa. Later he wrote a piece on the American national anthem 'The Star-Spangled Banner', claiming it was an anti-Islamic song 'based on fighting in Libya between Americans and Muslims in the early 1800s' (Safran 2015). Safran describes Musa as 'a total nerd for the more obscure elements' of Islamism, which perhaps explains his appeal for foreign fighters seeking validation in fantasy ideals. Musa was deported from the Philippines in 2014 and his passport was cancelled. In May 2016, he and four fellow jihadi sympathisers (all without passports) were caught and charged after attempting to sail a small boat from northern Australia to Indonesia, from where they planned to join IS in Syria (Mills and Bucci 2016).

Australian female jihadis

Some young Muslim women get involved in terrorist extremism (see Hoyle et al. 2015; Cragin and Daly 2009), including from Australia (Hatch 2015). The positive message from IS is that their women are valued, not as sexual objects but as mothers and guardians of IS ideology. Joining the IS caliphate is framed for Muslim girls as a big adventure (Hoyle et al. 2015), with promise of meaningful romance. Social media often depict a proud lion and lioness standing together (Saltman and Smith 2015: 16) in defence of caliphate. Some push factors for female IS recruitment are:

Feeling isolated socially and/or culturally, including questioning one's identity and uncertainty of belonging within a Western culture; feeling that the international Muslim community as a whole is being violently persecuted; and anger, sadness and/or frustration over a perceived lack of international action.

(Saltman and Smith 2015: 9)

Between 15 and 20 per cent of IS foreign recruits are estimated as female:

Women may account for nearly one-fifth of all foreign recruits. In an address to the Australian Parliament in February 2015, Foreign Minister Julie Bishop advised that up to 40 of the 550 or so Western women taking part in or supporting terrorist activities in Syria and Iraq are Australian.

(Jennings 2015: 16)

In May 2015 at least twelve women, some as young as 18, travelled from Melbourne to join IS. They were not just 'jihadi brides'. Through their online blogs many later actively spread propaganda to attract new female recruits (Saltman and Smith 2015). Tara Nettleton, Zaynab Sharrouf and Zehra Duman are the most well-known Australian jihadi women. Tara Nettleton converted to Islam and married Khaled Sharrouf in Sydney at the age of 15. With their five children they relocated to the IS stronghold of Raqqa when eldest daughter Zaynab was 13. At 14, Zaynab was married as a second wife to her father's jihadi comrade Mohammed Elomar, a former Sydney boxing champion, and bore a child to him before his death. Zaynab remains an avid defender of the radical Islamist meta-narrative in her blog even though her father Khaled Sharrouf was killed in June 2015 and her mother Tara Nettleton died in Syria in late 2015 of appendicitis.

Australian female jihadi Zehra Duman was only 21 when she arrived alone in Syria in 2014. Her trigger was the declaration of caliphate by IS leader Abu Bakr al-Baghdadi (see Chapter 2). She wrote in her blog, 'I couldn't sit back 1 second. I was waiting for the day *Khilafah* returned' (quoted in Saltman and Smith 2015: 31). Zehra married fellow Australian Mahmoud Abdullatif, 23, but he was killed in action. Zehra often expresses hatred of the West, instructing her Twitter followers to, 'kill *Kuffar* in alleyways, stab them and poison them. Poison your teachers. Go to *haram* restaurants and poison the food in large quantities'. She wants to fight on the frontline and has posted photos of herself and other women in full Islamic dress brandishing AK-47s. Another young Australian female recruiter, Shadi Jabar Khalil Mohammad, was killed along with her husband in a Syrian air strike in 2016. She was the older sister of Farhad Mohammad, the 15-year-old Islamist who shot dead the police accountant in Parramatta in 2015 (Greene 2016). She travelled to Syria the day before her brother's attack to marry senior IS militant Abu Sa'ad al-Sudani.

Some claim significant IS female figures like the Australians described above have created 'jihadi girl power subculture', in which becoming a 'caliphette' is empowering (for example Pandith and Havelicek 2015). Yet this seems a large claim. It is quite evident that the women's celebratory blogs are carefully crafted for propaganda purposes. There is little information given about the actual conditions experienced by women from Western countries under the IS caliphate, and there is no real option for them to return home, given their established links with terrorism. The few stories that do get out paint a picture of suffering.

What do these terrorist activities have to do with ordinary Muslim youth in Australia?

The answer to this question is – very little in the direct sense. Most young Muslims do not feel any connection to the violence carried out by domestic Islamist terrorists or by Australian IS recruits in war zones. For example, 21-year-old Ozen is a graduate of an Islamic school in Melbourne. Some of the questions asked by non-Muslim acquaintances leave him speechless. 'It's a bit of an extreme example, but with the beheadings by ISIL, they say, "Is that a norm?" It's just so abnormal to us' (Ozen, quoted in Flitton 2015). Another young man said he knows three peers who have become radicalised by radical preachers and extremist friends.

> A lot of the Middle Eastern people in south-west Sydney feel isolated and alienated in their own city where they've grown up in. It's a shame because a lot of the youth aren't willing to listen to the right people and they're very easily influenced.
>
> (Leith Naji quoted in Taha 2015a)

He said he can understand their motivation to some extent. However, what they turn to is not his idea of Islam, but 'a grotesque distorted version of Islam' (Leith Naji quoted in Taha 2015a). Overall, reported jihadi events and actions do nothing to make their lives as young Australians any easier. Neither do the policy responses of the government that target Muslim youth.

Mainstream responses

The National Terrorism Public Alert System in 2003 set the threat level for Australia at 'medium'.[12] It remained there until 2014, when IS intensified attacks in the Middle East and Al-Baghdadi declared a caliphate. It is currently 'high'.[13] As indicated above, Australian authorities exercise extensive powers of surveillance, entry and detention to combat terrorism. In effect, this is a parallel criminal justice system specifically for 'terrorist acts', broadly defined. In this regard, 'Australia has exceeded the United Kingdom, the United States, and Canada in the sheer number of new antiterrorism laws'

(Roach 2011: 309). In August 2014 government funding for counter-terrorism increased by $630 million. Late 2014 saw new counter-terrorism laws targeting foreign fighters. In March 2015 an anti-terrorism package for Australian schools was launched. In the same year an Australian National Counter Terrorism Coordinator was announced and changes were flagged to citizenship laws (Jennings 2015: 37) targeting dual citizenship holders.

The plethora of new anti-terror laws and policies use neutral terms, yet they are almost exclusively applied to members of the Muslim community and their organisations (Williams 2011; Roose and Harris 2015). Most of the budget is channelled into technology and surveillance, especially for online extremism (Kenny and Wroe 2015). Yet useful intelligence also relies on the family and friends of young jihadis sharing information about planned violence. This points to the need to nurture Muslim community trust and inclusion; to foster a strong sense of belonging. Yet the concept of belonging is often substituted in policy by the very different idea of integration, which connotes bringing people of different racial or ethnic groups together into an equal association in the society; or 'fitting in' with mainstream norms. In 2011 the federal government invested in the Building Community Resilience Program. Counter-radicalisation materials were targeted specifically at Muslim youth to 'guide them away from intolerant and radical ideologies' and build resilience to resist 'violent extremism' (Broadbent 2013: 190). Later that program was replaced by the currently active Living Safe Together program.

Another set of Muslim youth integration initiatives is conducted under the banner of 'Countering Violent Extremism' (CVE), which replicates the PVE program in the UK. Recently a boy aged 16 from suburban Sydney was arrested for planning an attack on Anzac Day 2016. He had previously followed a CVE de-radicalisation program. Akbarzadeh (2013) is strongly critical of the CVE model, arguing that it pathologises Muslim youth and ignores life conditions. Harris (2013) is also critical of such policies. They not only implicitly label Muslim youth as a problem but exclude their voices. Kuranda Seyit, founder of the Forum on Australia's Islamic Relations, said his experience of working intensively with young Muslims showed that most simply got over their extreme views after a few months with the right kind of community intervention (Olding 2015), which is not necessarily the kind of intervention deployed in CVE approaches.

In fact, government initiatives like CVE respond not necessarily to a rise in Islamist terrorism, but to voter trends and conservative voices in Australia that demand political action on Muslim youth radicalisation, which is sensationally exaggerated in many media accounts. One striking example is a 2014 essay in the conservative magazine *Quadrant*. The writers argue that a '*regrettably liberal*' focus on multiculturalism means the government is powerless to deal with people who render 'infrastructure a soft civilian target' (Martin Jones and Smith 2014: 10). The authors detail the ontogenesis of what they call the Islamist youth 'death cult'. First, they claim that 'the militant disciples of the Islamic Internationale, stylishly accoutred in black headscarves and matching Ray-Bans', project an image of radical Islamist chic. Second, the militants' 'heady mixture of posturing and utopian activism' appeals to the younger generation of Muslim Australian youth. Third, the militant message is reinforced by Twitter, Facebook and YouTube; 'the blandishments of a postmodernised call, adumbrated with gangsta-rap-style narcissism and amplified by the intoxicating appeal of a sacralised violence, prove irresistible to a younger, educated, but deracinated generation of diasporic Muslims' (Martin Jones and Smith 2014: 12). Their description of militant appeal to the small minority is not entirely inaccurate. However, their surprising conclusion is that Australian multiculturalism should be entirely abandoned in favour of enforced 'assimilation' through stronger civic controls. In fact, as Modood (2013) points out, Australian multiculturalism has been, and remains, central to economic sustainability and effective nation building (see also Roose and Harris 2015). In principle, enforced assimilation would be counter-productive because it would breed further resentment.

Australian cabinet ministers have challenged Muslim community leaders to do more about Muslim youth who become radicalised. However, as the Islamic Council of Victoria spokesman points out,

> Radicalisation is very complex and doesn't fall directly in the realm of imams, sheiks, or other leaders. It's more about young people who are quite disconnected from the mosque ... these young people are not actually attending the mosque and they are finding different ways to get information.
>
> (Kuranda Seyit quoted in Bachelard 2015)

In fact, the Australian intelligence service ASIO has issued a 'call to arms' for families to spot radicalisation of Muslim youth (Wroe 2015). Yet there is no budget for this. The suggested strategy would appear to be at odds with the current federal government priority for funding surveillance technology and security personnel.

Dealing with the 'war on terror' – Australian style

Despite the less than ideal conditions described above, young Muslims in Australia demonstrate strong aspirations and confidence about their future. Apart from religion, their most frequently nominated life values were found to be: friendship, honesty, trust, family, respect and loyalty (Jakubowicz et al. 2014: 11). Like their parents' generation, they just want to make good lives for themselves while following their faith. This is easier in some places than others. For example, there are concentrations of people from different ethnic backgrounds in some Australian suburbs (Al-Natour 2015; DIAC 2009) where a strong spirit of multiculturalism prevails. Young Muslims attending public schools there are unlikely to experience overt discrimination solely on the basis of religion. For example,

> I find that it doesn't really matter what religion or ethnicity you are in our school (…) X High is very accepting and diverse in its different cultures and beliefs. I think that also being a state school, it gives a chance for all sorts of people to get to know each other and become friends.
> (Salma, quoted in Zulfikar 2016: 4)

Salma's account alludes to the positive multicultural orientation of some inner-city suburbs where young Muslims actively participate in popular culture. For example,

> I can continue wearing my Hijab and putting on my footy top to go to the footy. It's no problem. You don't let people bring you down and feel confident about being a Muslim and an Australian. We must integrate in society but also not sacrifice practicing our religion.
> (Zaynab, quoted in Sheriffdeen 2011: 172)

They effectively synthesise 'Australian' values and Islam:

> I am Australian, and proud to be so. I readily identify with Australian values and identities. I am pleased to say that Islam and Australian values, in a majority of aspects, work together in harmony and without clashes.
> (Rashid, quoted in Sheriffdeen 2011: 139)

A very common response of the young to being associated with terrorism is to take the position of: 'it makes you want to be a better Muslim' (quoted in Cherney and Murphy 2015: 11). For example, the advantages of *salat* (praying five times a day) is celebrated:

> Something that's overlooked about [prayer] is that it gives you a bit of time to yourself. It's refreshing (…) Your mind drifts from what you were doing before, it takes away all your stress. It's beautiful. It's a privilege to be able to pray five times a day.
> (Osama, 15, 2015[14])

This is a long way from a 'death cult'. It is a deeply felt statement about religious affect; the calming emotional/corporeal intensity of prayer. Another young Muslim made a similar point about a life lived in religious intensity, in contrast to the ignorance and angst that informs extremism:

> [IS] is more about power and politics than it is about religion (…) They lack education of their own religion. They get their emotions mixed up

with their religion: 'I'm angry so I want to connect my faith with this anger' (...) Being Muslim, we're just normal people (...) trying to find God in everything that we do.

(Mariam, 19, 2015[15])

Selfless service to the public good is another prized counter-story about Islam. For example, Osama and Mariam both attend SeekersHub, an Islamic community centre in Sydney that encourages harmonious piety. The classically trained leader, Imam Afroz Ali, runs discussion groups and also works directly with young Muslims moving in a direction which might lead them to violent radicalisation (Fife-Yeomans 2013). Imam Ali's dedicated approach demonstrates the Islamic ethic of caring service, which aligns closely with the principle of responsible citizenship.

Roose and Harris (2015: 474) found that volunteering was a critical arena of engagement for young Australian Muslims. In their study, 73 per cent of 80 participants had recently volunteered for community service. Suleiman (2009: 66) confirms that 'civic involvement is an Islamic imperative: the care of the young, the old, the vulnerable, the sick, the disposed and the oppressed'. Volunteering constitutes the virtuous society – *hilf al-fudul*:

I think it's a sense of duty. As Muslims, just as humans we have a sense of duty. [Islam] teaches us that we have a duty of care for – even if – it is our duty, human duty, to look after everybody.

(Charlie, quoted in Roose and Harris 2015: 474)

As a story about being Muslim in Australia, this again is a striking counter-narrative to the radical Islamist position. It suggests the cultural configuration of low-key piety in everyday youth conduct.

Young Australian Mohammed (25) says that there was a time after 9/11 and the Bali bombings when he did not feel like he belonged in his country. 'You don't know where you belong, you don't know where you're from, and you don't know where you're going' (quoted in Bucci 2015). However, Mohammed was not tempted by extremist Islam. Rather, he was inspired by a leadership seminar at the age of 18 to go to university and build a career. He now runs his own construction company. Mohammed believes in treating the lure of IS as a social problem. He argues that any measure which reinforces an 'us against them' mentality is counter-productive and can be used to support jihadist propaganda (Bucci 2015). Another 'answer' is to resist peer pressure towards resentful inwardness. Australian-Pakistani Anooshe Mushtaq's (2015) message on her blog is for young Muslims in Australia to actively resist the need to be accepted in any group that excludes itself from broader society. She urges her peers to take a stand against radical messages that shrink their social horizons.

Finding a job and working hard

A point frequently made by young Australian Muslims themselves is that they are no different to other young people. They just want to get a job and make a good life. For example, Hamza (21) is an apprentice in the construction industry in Western Sydney. He believes Muslim youth in Australia are demonised. In the aftermath of the terrorist shooting outside Parramatta Police Headquarters in 2015, he said 'you still get harassed just walking down the street. Police ask where you're going, completely unsolicited. They give you a hard time'. Hamza wishes he was not targeted because of his ethnicity (Somali) and religion (Islam). He is aware of how 'caucasian Australians' see him. Nevertheless, he is pragmatically getting on with his life goal to get a trade qualification and build prosperity. He doesn't think there is a crisis of radicalisation. He says 'there's a lot of Muslims, and most of us are just hard-working people'.[16]

In a study of Muslim jobseekers conducted by the author and colleagues in New South Wales in 2010/2011[17] there was plenty of evidence of discrimination. For example:

> *Al hijab* is the main problem as employers are afraid of this appearance as it could affect the business or they would think because I am covered I could be fundamental or extremist, especially with this bad reputation of Muslims at the moment.
>
> (Rahimah, f, 25, Iraqi refugee, Sydney 2010)

However, accounts of looking for work in our study revealed a highly pragmatic approach.

> Make sure that you are clean and tidy, speak confident, the way you speak to them and smile. They are gonna see you as one with the custo-mer as well so they know that you have a good personality. Ask about your tasks and prepare for a question from the employer like – why should I employ you? CV preparation is very important. Go to profes-sional advice but write it yourself like what comes first and what comes last. Speak to them normally and imagine you are speaking to them the way you want them to speak to you.
>
> (Amin, m, 25, Iranian second generation, Sydney 2010)

Only one female jobseeker said she had taken off the *hijab* as a strategy:

> I could see people staring at me because of my different look. I used to wear a head cover but now I have to take it off so people could stop treating me in a different way.
>
> (Hikmah, 34, Arab-Iraqi refugee, Sydney 2010)

She was optimistic about the outcome of a job interview she had just conducted. It was definitely harder for young women if they used the headscarf.

> I don't find myself having any problems that others have out there. They have their headscarf on. For example, if you wear a scarf and you are looking for a hairdressing job, it is pretty hard. You have to find someone who does it at home, which is pretty hard to find. But for me I don't really find, I don't think, that people will find that I am Muslim by looking at me.
>
> (Leyla, 22, Lebanese second generation, Sydney 2010)

On the other hand, confidence seemed to be a more important factor. One self-assured young woman who wore the headscarf said, 'usually I work in child care. And now I've changed the business to become an aged care worker' (Munira, 27, Indonesian migrant, Sydney 2010). She found a permanent position. Verbal communication skills were a noted advantage. A young man who came to Australia as a child found that his clear speech and Australian accent outweighed the fact that he had a 'Muslim' appearance:

> When they speak to me they get to know a lot more (...) It doesn't really matter. They see that my English is perfect. I am great, you know, like any Aussie.
>
> (Sabar, 28, Iraqi-Kurdish refugee, Sydney 2010)

However, this was unlikely to be the case for recently arrived young Muslims:

> Actually looking for a job is very hard. Agencies are lying to you. They say yes, look for job, look for job but when you tell them I couldn't find a job, no one answering you, no one giving you a job. If you have a CV or any ability, they don't care. The last job I got, it was through a friend – working in a factory.
>
> (Siddiq, m, 26, Arab-Iraqi refugee, Sydney 2010)

This suggests making an advantage out of being part of the Muslim community. That is, using forms of social capital. It connotes a sense of community belonging and does not match claims of widespread individualised alienation.

Counter-extremist positions in popular culture

Stephenson (2010) found that 'home-grown' Muslims under the age of 25 were active in negotiating both their Australian identity and their Islamic values through creative strategies such as speeches, storytelling and popular entertainment. In his recent study of Australian Muslim youth, Nasir (2016: 4) implies how counter-narrative is reflected in 'their musical choices, use of language, Islamic performativity, and consumption patterns' – in other words, their neo-theo-tribal preferences in youth culture. Below a number of relevant examples are analysed.

Jihadis are ignorant of their religion

The religious ignorance of jihadis is a frequent target of jokes. The following joke was posted on the moderate Australian Muslim Youth Network Facebook site in 2015.

> An IS member stopped the car of a Christian couple.
> IS Member: Are you a Muslim?
> Christian man: Yes I'm Muslim.
> IS Member: If you are a Muslim, recite a verse of the Quran.
> The Christian man recites a verse from the Bible.
> IS Member: Okay, you can go.
> Later his wife says: Why did you tell him you are Muslim? If he knew you were lying he'd have killed us both!
> The husband replies: Do not worry! If they knew the Quran they wouldn't kill people.

In other words, IS recruits are reliably ignorant of the Koran; theologically stupid. In such jokes jihadi militants are constructed as mentally dull and lacking in intelligence. They are frequently depicted as zombies. Yet the creative humour also expresses resentment that poorly informed, violent people have come to represent Islam in the public imagination.

This fact is also deplored in creative expressions such as the popular video of Kamal Saleh reciting a poem by Muslim Belal (Ashley Belal Chin), 'Nothing To Do with My Prophet: Response to the Killing of Innocent Civilians in the Name of Islam'. This moving plea for a compassionate Islam has had millions of hits.[18] The poem/video expresses more or less the same argument as the IS joke above, although in a very different genre. It implies that jihadi terrorists do not know the Koran and neither do they follow the lead of the Prophet.

A similar discourse is often found in social media. For example, following the deadly Man Haron Monis seige in central Sydney, there were fears that ordinary Muslims would be targeted on public transport. The result was the I'll Ride With You campaign of solidarity. There were 40,000 tweets using the hashtag #Illridewithyou in just two hours, according to Twitter Australia; 150,000 in four hours. In another example, during the London Tube stabbing attack in early December 2015, an onlooker yelled at the Islamist terrorist, 'You ain't no Muslim bruv'. The statement was caught on video and quickly went viral, trending strongly among young Muslims in Australia as #YouAintNoMuslimBruv Twitter hashtag. These are networked acts of social citizenship (Johns 2014).

Muslim hip-hop in Australia

As pointed out previously, hip-hop is a popular means of expression for Muslim youth worldwide. To the present time, The Brothahood is Australia's premier Muslim hip-hop group. It formed when the four male members attended a Young Muslims Australia (YMA) holiday camp as teenagers. They reach out to a wide audience of Muslim youth:

> A lot of young kids understand Hip Hop, and they enjoy Hip Hop music, so we thought we'd use Hip Hop music and be able to explain Islam to them instead of them listening to all that bling bling and all the you know, girls and guns and money and stuff that they can't relate to.
>
> (Timur Bakan quoted in Roose 2012: 158)

Using regular hip-hop beats they address issues of concern. For example, in their track 'The Simple Truth' they address issues of avoiding alcohol, tolerating suspicion and blame, regular prayer, and sharing a sense of human solidarity with non-believers. The lyrics are simple and colloquial, designed as Timur Bakan says, to appeal to Muslim teenagers in the suburbs.

Thus The Brothahood engages directly through the medium of youth popular music (Nasir 2015) in the generation of a counter-narrative to extremism. They speak from within, and to, the local neo-theo-tribe of Muslim hip-hop. The Australian Human Rights Commission has acknowledged the value of the group's contribution. The 2007 Australian documentary series *Halal Mate* featured the band. *Halal Mate* depicted 'ordinary' Muslims who work, fall in love, play sport, and have dreams and ambitions while living by the code of Islam in downtown Melbourne. There are other emerging voices in Muslim rap. For example, in Sydney a young hip-hop performer of Lebanese/Palestinian background, NOMISe, is rapping about local racism and world politics. He fuses Arabic lyrics and beats with Western sounds.

Following the Man Haron Monis seige in central Sydney in 2015, a 17-year-old Muslim student from Greenacre in Western Sydney wrote and recorded her rap song 'I'll Ride with You', amplifying the meaning of the hashtag that was popular at the time. She told the press she was horrified that gunman Man Haron Monis had hijacked and 'misused' her religion. She said she felt depressed as an Australian and as a Muslim, adding,

> I'm still baffled by how he would dare use such a beautiful testimony, such beautiful words for harm, it's a beautiful religion and for him to go and abuse it in such a way is horrible. His actions did not in any way represent Islam and what it teaches.
>
> (Amar Hadid quoted in Taha 2015b)

Recently, famous French Muslim rapper Médine (see Chapter 7) visited Melbourne in 2016. He worked with some young Muslim Australian rappers on their self-written tracks, urging them to foreground Islam and daily life in their creative output.

Beyond hip-hop, the neo-tribe of Muslim heavy metal has some following in Australia. For example, Safdar Ahmed plays black/death metal with his band Hazeen, which was inspired by *taqwacore* (see Chapter 7). Whether screamed or groaned, his songs satirise the radical Islamist meta-narrative and depict the personal impact of Islamophobia and racism on young Muslims in Australia. Safdar admits his main tool is irony. The Hazeen duo perform in black costumes, covered in ghoulish make-up – 'corpse paint'. Their very well attended inaugural gig was played in an abandoned theme park in Sydney's west, backlit by 'Muslim zombie' posters. Through the symbolism of the zombie, Ahmed makes an ironic argument about the so-called Islamist 'death cult'. 'It's a way of taking the whole discourse ... of radicalisation and the fear of terrorism and so on, and exaggerating it to the point where you reveal its implicit absurdity' (Safdar Ahmed quoted in Chalmers 2015). For example, one of their songs, 'Beneath the Black Crescent Moon', synthesises Islamic symbolism with the nightmare world of black metal. Like other Muslim heavy metal music, the band pushes hard against restrictive narratives in the Islamic world (LeVine 2008).

Satire

As elsewhere, comedic satire is a popular medium for challenging stereotypes in Australia. Ten years ago the comedy act Salam Café was formed by a creative young group including the now notable Muslim public intellectual Waleed Aly. Salam Café offered humorous skits parodying common stereotypes to mediate between Islamic and Australian identity (Stephenson 2010). The group quickly found television exposure and was nominated in 2009 for a Logie Award, Australian television's highest prize. Members of the original creative team, Nazeem Hussain and Aamer Rahman, went on to make the TV show *Legally Brown*, and also formed the comedy duo Fear of a Brown Planet. They often make stand-up comedy videos about contemporary issues. Their videos go viral when uploaded. Nazeem Hussain is also a host on the mainstream youth music radio channel Triple J.

A less formal example of the satiric medium is provided by the orchestrated actions of Max, Rebeen, and Arman Jalal, Melbourne brothers aged 20, 18 and 16. They dressed up as Islamist terrorists to stage fake bombings and hoax abductions in 2015/2016. Videos of their stunts were posted online and attracted much international attention. One brother told the media 'We have two million fans' (quoted in Cowie and Butt 2016). They wanted to make fun of Australian social attitudes to people of Middle Eastern appearance. In one uploaded clip the three are dressed in white robes, and one fires a replica semi-automatic gun out of a car window at a phone box, causing a man and his young daughter to flee in fear. In March 2016, 30 counter-terrorism police officers raided the Jalal family home and charged the three brothers.

The brothers then made an apologetic appearance on the national television show *The Project*. Host and fellow Muslim Waleed Aly (see below) was critical of the brothers' attempts at satire. 'Isn't it pretty damn irresponsible to make people think they are in the middle of a terrorist attack?' Max Jalal conceded, 'that scene was pretty irresponsible, yes' (quoted in Toscano 2016). Subsequently, the brothers confessed that all their prank terror videos were staged with family and friends acting the part. In fact, the young girl in the contentious shooting video was their cousin, nine-year-old Mary Jalal. This is a counter-narrative, or at least an attempt at one. The brothers set out to pretend, to satirise, to ironically simulate local Islamist terrorism in the sense advanced by Baudrillard (1994: 2): 'it is no longer a question of imitation, nor duplication, nor even parody. It is a question of substituting the signs of the real for the real'. It can be argued that the Jalal brothers were playing with the underlying assumptions of the Muslim moral panic by imitating local terrorism so well. Their satirical stunts, whether ill-judged or not, constitute a post-modernist moment of 'simulacra' to amuse and entertain online peers who may well share both their experiences in the diaspora and their counter-view.

Positive celebrities

The charismatic Australian media personality Waleed Aly has been mentioned several times. Public figures like Waleed Aly, and new London mayor Sadiq Khan, provide highly significant role models for young Muslims in the diaspora. Another celebrated young public intellectual in Australia is feminist journalist and film-maker Ruby Hamad, born into an Arab Muslim family. She blogs regularly about Islamophobia, and actively challenges stereotyped ideas about Muslim women, with frequent television appearances. Ruby offers a viable role model for young Muslim women in Australia who want to speak out. Her life story of public achievement embodies a compelling counter-narrative to the Islamist hardline position.

Waleed Aly came up through the influential liberal study group YMA (Young Muslims Australia). He is now arguably Australia's most prominent young intellectual, Muslim or otherwise. He also makes his mark as a rock guitarist. His popular book *People Like Us* argues that arrogance on both sides divides Islam and the West. He has received an award for his contribution to Australian multiculturalism (Roose 2012: 157). He is currently the host of Australia's highest rating television current affairs show *The Project*, for which he was awarded a prestigious Golden Logie in 2016. This notable achievement was publicly condemned by radical Islamist group *Hizbut-Tahrir*. A spokesman warned that Waleed Aly would no longer find 'an adequate home in Islam', and that Muslims should not be celebrating this apparent victory for Islam in Australia. Waleed remains firm in his position. He is married to equally high profile Muslim convert Susan Carland, who wears the headscarf and donates a dollar to charity every time she receives racist comments on social media.

Waleed found YMA involvement in his teens to be not only valuable but 'fun'. He remembers them as a good group of people to hang out with. He feels that what YMA did best was to create 'an affection for Islam'. He found this contrasted greatly with other guiding approaches that create 'fear' (Roose 2012: 161–162). The YMA mentor Imam Kürkçü follows the Sunni Hanafi school and teaches a spiritual (non-political) form of Islam known as *Tasawwuf* (Sufism). He adopts a contextual approach to understanding the *sunna* rather than strict literalist interpretations. His guidance goes well beyond the fear-inducing '*haram, haram, haram, halal, halal, halal*' approach (Roose 2012: 161). Many of Australia's best known Muslims came up through YMA. Among them are founding members of The Brothahood and comedy team Salam Café, as well as Tasneem Chopra and Sherene Hassan.

Tasneem Chopra is currently chair of the Australian Muslim Women's Centre for Human Rights and Senior Curator of the Islamic Museum of Australia. Tasneem feels that through YMA she learned values based on respect, achievement and positivity (Roose 2012: 160). She now actively mentors young Muslim women, as does another early YMA member Sherene Hassan, the first female vice-president of the Islamic Council of Victoria. Sherene has written, 'I suppose the greatest challenge for me as a Muslim is trying to reclaim the *narrative* of Islam'[19] (my emphasis).

These examples of positive public role models demonstrate that success is possible for confident young Muslims in Australia. Most importantly, they can communicate and inspire the new generation of Muslim youth through bridging the apparent gap between Islam and being Australian. They significantly confound the strong 'victim' discourse of the radical Islamist meta-narrative.

Conclusion

In the spirit of the book, this chapter has given sustained attention to Australian Muslim youth. It demonstrates that young Australian Muslims not only react to the moral panic over Islam in Australia but creatively produce their own stories of where they stand. Their main concerns are getting a job and making a good life for themselves. They were shown to be re-asserting positive religious values – of peace and harmony through social media, and of civic responsibility through volunteering. They expressed their own counter-narratives to the radical Islamist meta-narrative in popular culture and through humour and satire. Finally, attention was drawn to the great significance of positive Muslim role models in public life, and inspirational guidance in pro-youth Islamic organisations. The next chapter concludes the book by looking at current configurations of Islam and youth in the diaspora, and future possibilities.

Notes

1 When British colonisation ended and the Australian constitution was passed in 1901, the constitution differed from the United States precedent in rejecting a bill of rights. Fear was expressed at the time that a bill of rights could undermine laws and practices, considered desirable at the time, which disadvantaged Aboriginal people and Chinese.
2 Most of the reported incidents occurred online (55 per cent), while in-person verbal abuse (33 per cent) and physical abuse (12 per cent) was primarily directed at women wearing a *hijab* or *niqab* or men with long beards.
3 Human Rights and Equal Opportunity Act 1986, Racial Discrimination Act 1975, Racial Hatred Act 1995.
4 Similar overestimations were made by Americans, Canadians, Belgians and French.
5 Australian Muslims are represented by a diverse range of organisations. They include: the Australian National Imam's Council; the Islamic Council of Victoria (ICV); the New South Wales Islamic Council (NSWIC); the Muslim Women's National Network Australia (MWNNA); The Muslim Women's Association (MWA); the Australian Muslim Women's Centre for Human Rights (AMWCHR); the Hume Islamic Youth Centre (HIYC); the Islamic Information and Support Centre of Australia (IISCA); the Islamic Information and Services Network of Australia (IISNA) in Melbourne; Affinity Intercultural Foundation; the Lebanese Muslim Association (LMA); Muslim student associations, refugee advocacy groups and many others. The *Ahlu Sunnah wal Jamm'ah* Association of Australia (ASWJAA) represents an ultraconservative Muslim group that defies moderate Islam. ASWJAA promotes gender segregation, discourages Muslims from socialising with non-Muslims, and recommends traditional clothing and growing a beard. *Hizb ut-Tahrir* Australia (HTA) encourages the Islamist goal of global caliphate (Sohrabi 2015).
6 Sherene Hassan is Secretary and Board member of the Islamic Council of Victoria.
7 In 2015, more than 60 Muslim community organisations and individuals signed a statement to the effect that counter-terrorism laws in Australia were unjust and unjustified because they target Muslims.
8 Monis had previously been diagnosed with mental health problems.
9 Anzac Day commemorates the first major military action fought by Australian and New Zealand forces in Turkey during World War I.
10 The published date is 1437.
11 Musa was originally Robert Cerantonio, a former internet security software worker. He is not yet 30.
12 A medium level of alert indicates a terrorist attack could occur.
13 A high level of alert indicates a terrorist attack is probable.
14 www.abc.net.au/radionational/programs/lifematters/the-face-of-young-muslim-aust ralia/6541622.
15 www.abc.net.au/radionational/programs/lifematters/the-face-of-young-muslim-aust ralia/6541622.
16 https://www.wsws.org/en/articles/2015/10/12/jaba-o12.html.

17 Department of Immigration and Citizenship Project Grant 'Muslim jobseekers in Australia', T. Lovat, W. Mitchell, P. Nilan, H. Hosseini, B. Cooke, I. Samarayi. See www.dss.gov.au/sites/default/files/documents/01_2014/muslim-jobseekers.pdf.
18 www.facebook.com/talkislam/videos/927607720663026/.
19 museumvictoria.com.au/immigrationmuseum/whatson/past-exhibitions/faith-fashio n-fusion/stories/sherene-hassan/.

Chapter 9

Conclusion

Neo-theo-tribalism of Muslim youth

Introduction

This book has described and explained a range of counter-narratives that Muslim youth collectively construct and disseminate in their distinctive popular culture. These counter-narratives challenge the radical Islamist meta-narrative, sometimes implicitly, sometimes directly. Muslim youth select from the popular culture resources on offer to generate appropriated and particularised meanings in their everyday practices of making a successful self. This concluding chapter spells out the contribution of the book to debates that rage in the West about Muslim youth as politically positioned subjects. It re-examines the starting proposition that young Muslims in the diaspora frame up their sense of self, their identity, in relation to the binary discourse of 'good' and 'bad' Muslims within contemporary Islam as a revitalised religion. It is proposed that ludic play by Muslim youth with the radical meta-narrative can disrupt the idea of the 'good' Muslim in the diaspora without ever involving militant action. The radical Islamist meta-narrative is revisited in terms of the many counter-narratives that Muslim youth appear to produce in their engagement with it. Possible future positionings of Muslim youth identity and popular culture in Western countries are considered.

The matter of belonging

One conclusion that emerges from this book is that counter-discursive reactions to the media dominance of the radical Islamist meta-narrative – and the war on terror – fuel forms of tribalism in the popular culture of Muslim youth in the diaspora. In these bounded collective spaces they feel they belong. Following Bennett's (1999a) work on neo-tribal youth cultures, I have argued that this can best be described as neo-theo-tribalism. It is within the Muslim youth groupings suggested by this term that distinctive counter-narratives to the Islamist meta-narrative were discerned throughout the chapters. The most salient constitution of piety here was faith as chosen and negotiated, rather than faith as enforced. It is perhaps this distinctive epistemological orientation that in principle distances the majority of young Muslims in the diaspora from the rigidity of the radical Islamist meta-narrative.

There are certainly local examples of success to inspire them. For although the moral panic about Muslims in the diaspora remains pervasive at the time of writing, there are signs that this might be breaking down in some countries. For example, the recent high profiles of moderate Muslim public figures in Australia (Waleed Aly, Ed Husic[1]) and the UK (Sadiq Khan) would seem to signal a certain shift in the public discourse of Islamophobia.[2] In Canada, an unprecedented number of Muslim Canadians ran in the 2015 federal elections, and eleven of them won office, including Canada's first Somali-Canadian MP Ahmed Hussen and Canada's first Afghan-Canadian MP Maryam Monsef. However, in the USA, France and Germany, the public position of Muslim people seems to be worse than ever before. For example, at the time of writing in 2016, US president-elect Donald Trump has promised on several occasions that he will ban altogether the entry of foreign Muslims to America and increase surveillance of Muslim Americans. In Germany, a recent poll found 60 per cent of those surveyed believe that Islam 'does not belong in Germany'. This was linked to a sense of cultural incompatibility, discontent over the refugee influx from conflict in the Middle East, and fear of a domestic terrorist attack.[3]

In politically troubled France, Muslim communities still live in the marked socio-economic ghettos of major cities. Plenel (2016) demonstrates how republican and secularist fundamentalism masks virulent Islamophobia, exacerbated at every turn by ongoing terrorist attacks. The civic and constitutional emphasis on secularity penalises devout followers of the faith across all life domains. For example, not only does France ban clothing symbols of Islam in public, but unlike the UK, US, Canada and Australia, France allows no Islamic banking institutions for financing *sharia*-secured loans. Fredette (2014) argues that French elite public discourse in and of itself frames Muslims as failed, incomplete citizens. This framing of cultural and moral deficit strengthens the very separations, exclusions, and anger that the French government routinely deplores. Domestic jihadist attacks in 2015 and 2016 have increased the intensity of problems that French Muslims face daily. Abo-Zena et al. (2009) claim such events produce Muslim subjectivities inflected by experiences of misunderstanding, fear and marginalisation. Contemporary anti-Muslim voices in France echo the sentiments of Donald Trump in calling for Muslims to be expelled from the country. It seems the most notable Muslims in the French public domain are either clerics or rappers, or soccer players, although French-speaking Swiss intellectual and modern Islamist Tariq Ramadan is also influential. Yet he attracts an extraordinary level of hatred for his views.

Finally, although Scandinavian countries have by and large taken a more tolerant view of Muslim people, the refugee influx since 2014 has resulted in a change in attitude, with Sweden and Finland deporting many thousands of

Muslim would-be migrants in early 2016. In summary, while some countries are moving towards inclusionary trends, other countries are enshrining exclusionary anti-Islam discourse. As many sources have pointed out, the latter is very much the desired goal of radical Islamists. Through domestic terrorism they work to bring about the increased marginalisation and persecution of Muslims in the diaspora because they see this as leading towards the end-of-days battle and/or the global caliphate.

Exclusionary anti-Islam discourse is also a worrying trend because the global Muslim population is set to increase to 30 per cent of the total world population by 2050 (Lipka 2015). Islam will be the fastest growing religion in the world over the next four decades because of religious conversion, high fertility rates and the size of the youth population (Lipka 2015). Thus by mid-century, Muslims in the world will nearly equal Christians – currently the largest religious group. Moreover, the global Christian population 'bulge' will be at late middle age, while the Muslim population 'bulge' will still be youthful (Lipka 2015). Most of the predicted youthful Muslim population 'bulge' will be located in Muslim-majority countries, where local conditions of unemployment and economic decline make life in the diaspora seem attractive to young people, encouraging both legal and illegal migration. It seems that in the future, some Western countries will likely have banned Muslims from entering, and some will have enacted forced assimilation measures for their existing Muslim citizens. Other Western countries will not purposefully limit Muslim migration and will continue to pursue multicultural policies that do not force integration. It will be interesting to see how these very different pathways lead to long-term outcomes in terms of local civil conflict and harmony. As Plenel (2016) points out, countries that develop a hardline position may significantly violate the very spirit of democracy they ostensibly seek to defend, and thereby go some way towards creating the defined conditions of crisis favoured by radical Islamists for provoking the 'final battle'.

In everyday life it seems clear that many youth in the diaspora embrace the category of Muslim above ethnic self-labelling. Possibly the *big story* of being a Muslim appears more exciting and affirming than stories about being Lebanese-Australian, for example. And the same might be said of being Algerian-French, or Pakistani-British, or Iranian-American. Against those generationally enshrined, fixed categories, the story of being Muslim may be the very thing that takes youth lives out of the ordinary; a global identity that breaks the borders of nation states. They can play with its meanings, they can reinvent personal piety. Excitement inheres in the generation of discourses from the raw materials of the story of Islam as represented online rather than locally in many cases. The many different stories offered in virtual reality nevertheless all represent 'doing' Muslim (see West and Zimmerman 1987) and thereby belonging in Islam. In their diverse neo-theo-tribalism they calibrate their discursive and narrative negotiations of a Muslim self in relation to age and gender peers. They engage in the reflexive co-production of salient identities relevant to a viable contemporary Muslim self. The claim that there is a neo-theo-tribalism evident in Muslim youth culture in the diaspora aligns with Paul Willis' (1990) proposal that critical moments of coherence, identity and even resistance for young people lie in their creative reclamation of common culture. The productive assembly of like-to-like Muslim peers partly takes place in digital spaces which offer a kind of 'intimate public' – 'a porous, affective scene of identification among strangers that promises a certain experience of belonging' (Berlant 2008: viii). Such spaces also constitute for young Muslims an 'affective public' (Papacharissi 2014) which has a mobilising effect on the development of collective identity (see Robards and Bennett 2011).

In contexts of local intolerance, young Muslims in the diaspora band together because they do not want to fail and be victims. They want to succeed. An important conclusion of the book is that young Muslims in the diaspora draw a strong sense of positive self-esteem from belonging to the global *ummah* as it is constituted for them through the interactive space of new media, social media and *halal* popular culture. Here they can express themselves openly to their age peers who share the faith, and to interested others. There are certainly theological disputes in this space, and some of it can be ugly, especially in regard to condemnation of women, GLBITQ people and other sects of Islam. Yet it is anything but a fixed space. It is a 'field of struggle' (Bourdieu 1998) in which conscious distinctions and choices are made. To illustrate, let's explore a hypothetical situation for Muslim youth.

The appeal of Islamism for Muslim youth in the diaspora

Let us imagine that the Islamist ideal has come to appear extremely attractive to a small group of young people (Muslim-born and/or converts) in a Western country. They embrace the idea that all aspects of their everyday lives ought to be ruled by Islamic law. They desire pan-Islamic solidarity and removal of non-Muslim elements from their surrounding environment. We can ask: What happens then? There are a number of possible trajectories suggested by the content and arguments of this book.

Perhaps the most common and straightforward journey from an Islamist trigger point is towards the achievement of greater piety, following the journey to higher moral purity as a personal jihad; one that anticipates the utopia of caliphate on earth and the garden of rewards in heaven. Devotion to piety may manifest in a range of visible orthopraxies, from ever more modest or traditional clothing, to very long periods of prayer each day,[4] to spending all leisure time in Koranic reading or recitation. Other public expressions of piety may include following a notable Islamist preacher, offline or online, joining prayer and Koranic discussion groups, saving for the *hajj* pilgrimage and giving a larger percentage of salary to Muslim charities (*zakat*). They might also avoid contact with non-Muslims and with Muslim people deemed less pious.

Yet so far there is no obvious link to jihad sympathies or civil unrest. It is perfectly possible for a young Islamist in the diaspora to remain just there – at that point of personal piety, studying the *sunna* and strictly observing the tenets of Islam. And that is where they may well stay, without taking up a militant position, because the research evidence assembled in this book suggests that *the more profound his or her knowledge of Islam, the less likelihood there is of a young person supporting violence.* In other words, the young person in question stops at an Islamist position and does not move beyond it to claim the gendered identity of jihadi militant, or jihadi 'bride'. They thus embrace the celebratory ideal of Islamism without buying into the radical Islamist meta-narrative that mandates militant action on behalf of a narrowly defined, oppressed *ummah*.

Let us look then at a perhaps even more common pathway from the point at which Islamism seems attractive to a young Muslim in the diaspora. He or she stays with rigorous personal practices of piety for a while, but finds them too hard to sustain over time and moves back into a less rigid lifestyle that better fits with family and friends. In the case of a young Islamist in the diaspora who still lives in the family home for example, parents and siblings may disapprove because strict piety diverges from their own more moderate beliefs and practices (Roy 2007). Moreover, the new affinity with Islamism does not promise the young person a successful future as a legitimate and prosperous neo-liberal citizen of the Western state in which they live. So the extended family might also be concerned. Finally, an uncompromising Islamist position may restrict a young person's marriage prospects. In this way there is pressure throughout the age period of the twenties to construct oneself as an accommodating Muslim who fits in with others, and this pressure is likely to have a moderating effect on their Islamism as they approach the age of 30. McGrath and McGarry (2014) point out the many tensions between an Islamist ideal of life and dominant discourses of Western secular-liberal society for young Muslims. In the view of Harris and Roose (2014: 808) the moral reference points of Islam 'intersect with the requirement of modern self-making' for Muslim youth. Their young informants positioned themselves as active choosers; 'self-consciously constructing an ethical self from self-sourced and often hotly contested religious guidelines'. They were synthesising viable ways of being Muslim in the diaspora. They were putting to use what Jakubowicz et al. (2014: 56) call 'Muslim cultural capital', resources that blend tradition and modernity, with the purpose of making a good life in the future.

In post-structuralist terms young Muslims in the diaspora access narratives at a macro level to tell themselves important stories about who they are: their national, ethnic, gendered and religious identities. They position themselves within each shaping narrative. In other words they constitute their subjectivities relevant to the viable and valued subject positions offered within big stories of selfhood. As young people, this positioning and negotiation of subjectivity, of identity, is intense. They are vitally engaged in the transition to adulthood, which is characterised in present times by fracture, precariousness and risk perception (see Woodman 2012). Their transition traces a journey towards successful labour force participation and marriage/partnership; a journey characterised by family and collective cultural pressure, as well as the demand to 'make' the successful self in neo-liberal times. Given that Western youth per se are supposed to have higher levels of reflexivity compared to previous generations (Threadgold and Nilan 2009), Muslim youth in the West must logically share this enhanced capacity to some extent. In fact, it can be argued that they must exercise *more* reflexivity in everyday choices to successfully achieve viable identity in both the religious and the secular sphere. They also experience pressure to locate themselves within a theocratic register of morality, especially girls and young women.

In short, *the embrace of Islamism seems to happen most often in the context of growing up, of trying out different discourses within the faith before a comfortable accommodation of faith and citizenship in the adult years.* For example, in Muslim majority Indonesia a shift away from Islamism usually happens because a young person finishes school or university and gets a job, or they meet a prospective boyfriend or girlfriend with different views (Parker and Nilan 2013). They go back to being ordinary Indonesian Muslims who just want to make prosperous and secure lives for themselves, while still following the faith. The same may well be true for young Muslims in the diaspora who take up Islamism for a while in their formative years and then move away from it.

Finally, the much, much less common journey is for the young Islamist in the diaspora (Muslim-born or convert) to move quickly to radical action. As Pantucci (2015) points out, the role that Islam itself actually plays in forming the identity of violent jihadis is controversial because the link is tenuous at best. *Radicalisation is not usually driven by a deep knowledge of the faith but by other kinds of motivations, and it is usually rapid rather than slow.* The prevailing wisdom used to be that Islamist radicalisation happened because the young person closely associated over time with local others who already held the radical position. However, the internet has changed that. Recruitment relies on support for a virtually disseminated ideology which seeks to impose a global caliphate by force and which generally holds that dissenters are deserving of death (Pantucci 2015). Therefore the common thread is a strong narrative that offers the young Islamist an attractive collective identity as a warrior for Islam, enacting an immediate resolution to any current life dilemmas. Their collective affinity (Anderson 1991) is enshrined in the radical Islamist meta-narrative, to be operationalised in 'acts of war' on either the domestic front or in the Middle East/North Africa.

This is actively constructed as a heroic position. 'Jihadists offer Muslim youth an internally cohesive and preferred identity based on an Islamic revival bound to militant revolutionary action' (Cheong and Halverson 2010: 1110). The radical Islamist meta-narrative constitutes them discursively in the greatly oppressed *ummah*, where they can self-narrate the story of themselves as a heroic band of brothers (and sisters) fighting a desperate battle for the victory of Islam. Online discourse with radical others is inclusive and constitutes a strong sense of belonging. Location as heroes and heroines within the radical Islamist meta-narrative elevates the co-membered interlocutors to the status of moral superiority. In this sacralised space the highly significant plot element of struggle against the odds – the quest for victory – offers them a place of personal redemption in the cause of something greater; nothing less than saving the world for God. The promised utopia of the caliphate derives its iconography from a key principle of Islamic art. As a vision of orderliness and moral purity, it draws the imagination and the intellect away from the three-dimensional, ambivalent chaos of everyday life to the order and harmony of pure form. It is thus a metaphor of transcendence and invulnerability. As young jihadi Jake Bilardi quoted from Ibn Taymiyyah: 'What can my enemies do to me? My paradise is in my heart' (Bachelard and Cordoba 2015). On the other hand, *martyrdom is literally a dead end in this world, whereas the vast majority of young Muslims want to make a good life for themselves. It is really no wonder that the jihadi path attracts so few.*

Muslim youth and popular culture

It is certainly much more fun to be pious *and* cool. Accordingly, young people throughout the Muslim world enthusiastically consume the many Islamic popular culture products and experiences on offer as an act of distinction (Bourdieu 1984) in theological terms. The extensive range promises youth culture consumption that is *halal* yet not embarrassing. In the praxis of Muslim youth culture in Western countries, Islam is not any kind of deficit discourse then, but represents a cultural repertoire of beliefs and practices enabling moral navigation and orientation within the social realities surrounding young people today. *Through the selective consumption of Muslim popular culture they experience the sense of being blessed; constituting a modern self empowered by intensity of religious affect.* Moreover, for young Muslims in the diaspora, popular culture not only provides important frameworks of social identity, but offers space to form transnational solidarities around human rights (Nasir 2015).

Studying the popular culture of Muslim youth in the diaspora is important for understanding the seemingly oppositional relationship between the suggested neo-liberal (primarily secular), successful, individualised self of Western late modernity, and the collectively constituted 'good' Muslim subject. These framings of self are not in fact antithetical, as I have shown, although there is a prevalent discourse on both sides that they are at odds. It is from this antagonistically imagined set of relations that different iterations of counter-narrative emerge. There are notably few significant means of expressing engagement with important narratives about Islam that do not involve the internet and social media. So we may assume that Muslim youth of all kinds in Western countries have online access and use it dialogically in this regard. Dialogic internet sites illustrate the polyvalence of cyber-Islamic discourses. The virtual *ummah* can be either a representation of oppression or an emotional and exuberant experience of stylish solidarity. Technological capacities for personalisation allow the virtually inspired young Muslim in the diaspora to make these imaginings highly personal, devolving the sense of a quest for pious practice. However, *this heroic quest only very infrequently takes the form of violent jihad because this means an extreme step on a separated life journey from all the significant others around you.*

I contend that the engagement of young Muslims in the diaspora with their religion is one characterised by strong *affect*. Not only do they feel deeply the pleasures and pains of their faith, and how it is constructed by others, as well as the relevant international crises, but they are engaged in a compelling relational process of becoming; subjectivity in motion, as they move towards adulthood. This transition is conducted in conditions which they often experience as a confining and restricting social space (Deleuze and Guattari 1987). Young Muslims feel pinned 'under the gaze' in the Western country where they live. They know themselves to be the subjects of surveillance by two different 'masters' who appear to hold morally opposed ideas of good and bad Muslims, and good and bad youth. In the play of varying authoritative voices that tell them who they should be, they come to desire clarity, an affective sensation of meaningful relationality. This favours the development of *neo-theo-tribalism: group formations of youthful cultural sociality and consumption that span the faith-based offline and online worlds.* This phenomenon can be glimpsed in their near-tribal patterns of popular culture consumption, in their communications about gaming, and in the fandom and celebrity of Muslim music cultures. Thus Muslim popular culture choices articulate a kind of 'distinction' (Bourdieu 1984), one that articulates the moral order of orthopraxy and a 'sense of one's place' in the *ummah*. However, this is a highly diverse positioning, reflected in the variety of neo-theo-tribal affiliations.

Conclusion

This book has examined the hotly debated issue of Muslim youth identity in the diaspora. It has illustrated how young Muslims frame up their identities in relation to the radical Islamist meta-narrative, as well as to the binary notion of 'good' and 'bad' Muslims; a dichotomous judgement that operates on both sides of the apparent boundary between Islam and the West. The chapters on Muslim youth consumerism, gaming and music demonstrate how the radical Islamist meta-narrative is contested, critiqued, ridiculed, transformed and transcended in the popular culture of Muslim youth even as they deal with the local intolerance they frequently encounter. The case study chapter on Australia allowed a detailed focus on what these processes look like in a new world democracy which ostensibly embraces multiculturalism and equal opportunity, but has no Bill of Rights to protect human rights, and no official log of hate crimes.

At many points throughout the book I have pointed out that there are high-pressure individualising processes we cannot ignore in the lives of Muslim youth in the diaspora – experiences they share with other young people in late modernity. These include the pressure of finding work in a precarious labour market, the upward credentialling of that same labour market even as higher education loses its income value, marriage 'choice', and the challenge of creating a prosperous family life in the future. The local Muslim community and families would like their youth to show themselves as good Muslims, manifested in pious, conservative behaviour directed towards prosperity. Yet being a Muslim can be a labour market disadvantage.

Into this picture we must insert the pressure and appeal of youth culture, both offline and online. There is a whole youth culture world of fashion, music, gaming, product consumption and socialising which is highly compelling. However, within the big story of Islam and the *ummah* of believers, this compelling world of youth culture should be negotiated piously. At the same time Muslim youth are expected by the nations in which they live to implicitly (and sometimes explicitly) declare how they stand on radical Islamist precepts and practices. This is a difficult balance to achieve, yet they manage it.

Regardless of the local circumstances though, like other young people, each young Muslim in the diaspora is under pressure to consciously tailor-make his or her own life trajectory towards successful adulthood. In such conditions, the 'self' becomes something to be consciously worked on by the young person to create a successful biography. This is best conducted from a position of 'ontological security' (Giddens 1991: 44) – a space of safety and certainty such as that provided by the 'intimate public' of faith-sharing peers offline and online. This approximates Hage's 'immune space' (2011) in which a racialised person can 'pick up the pieces'. Identification with Islam through Muslim youth culture provides this. It does not threaten the viable adult life of the young person, as might be imagined in the moral panic, but makes it possible.

Notes

1 Ed Husic has just become the first Australian Muslim to break into federal government ministerial level (2016). In 2013 he attracted some virulent abuse for swearing his oath of office on the Koran not the Bible.
2 Although 'Brexit' in 2016 could herald a new era of immigrant intolerance in the UK.
3 www.dw.com/en/almost-two-thirds-of-germans-believe-islam-does-not-belong-in-germany-poll-finds/a-19251169.
4 Spending long periods in prayer with the head pressed to the floor may produce a darker patch on the forehead. This is widely regarded as proof of piety among young Muslim men in Indonesia (Nilan 2013).

References

ABC (2015) 'How a young Australian couple came to die in Syria.' Australian Broadcasting Corporation. Online. Available from: www.abc.net.au/news/ 2014-09-09/amira-karroum-tyler-casey-syria/5729764 [accessed 9 March 2015].

Abdul Haleem, M.A.S. (2010) *'Qur'anic "jihād"*: A linguistic and contextual analysis'. *Journal of Qur'anic Studies*, 12(1–2): 147–166.

Abou El Fadl, K. (2007) *The Great Theft: Wrestling Islam from the extremists*. New York: Harper.

Abo-Zena, M., Sahli, B. and Tobias-Nahi, S. (2009) 'Testing the courage of their convictions: Muslim youth respond to stereotyping, hostility, and discrimination'. In O. Sensoy and C. Stonebanks (eds) *Muslim Voices in School*, Rotterdam: Sense Publishers, pp. 3–26.

ABS (2012) 'Reflecting a Nation: Stories from the 2011 census, 2012–2013 – cultural diversity in Australia'. 2071.0. Australian Bureau of Statistics. Available from: www. abs.gov.au/ausstats/abs@.nsf/Lookup/2071.0main+features902012-2013 [accessed 1 December 2015].

Abu El-Haj, T.R. (2010) '"The beauty of America"': Nationalism, education, and the war on terror'. *Harvard Educational Review*, 80(2): 242–274.

Ahmad, A. (2016) 'The ties that bind and blind: Embeddedness and radicalisation of youth in one Islamist Organisation in Pakistan'. *Journal of Development Studies*, 52 (1): 5–21.

Ahmadi, A. (2015) 'Iran'. In M. Wolf (ed.) *Video Games around the World*, Cambridge, MA: MIT Press, pp. 271–292.

Ahmed, H. (2010) 'The growing threat of female suicide attacks in western countries'. *CTC Sentinel*. Online. Available from: www.ctc.usma.edu/v2/wp-content/uploads/ 2010/08/CTCSentinel-Vol3Iss7-art6.pdf [accessed 5 May 2016].

Ahmed, S. (2003) 'The politics of fear in the making of worlds'. *International Journal of Qualitative Studies in Education*, 16(3): 377–398.

Ahmed, T. (2012) 'Punk drunk love'. In N. Musnavi and A. Mattu (eds) *Love, InshAllah: The secret love lives of American Muslim women*, Berkeley, CA: Soft Skull Press, pp. 58–74.

Aidi, H. (2004) '"Verily, there is only one hip-hop umma": Islam, cultural protest and urban marginality'. *Socialism and Democracy*, 18(2): 107–126.

Aidi, H. (2014) *Rebel Music: Race, empire, and the new Muslim youth culture*. New York: Pantheon Books.

Aidi, H. (2015) 'Rap and radicalism: Does hip hop create extremists? European rappers called on to explain the relationship between their music and youth alienation'. *Al Jazeera*. Online. 28 Jan 2015. Available from: www.aljazeera.com/indepth/opinion/ 2015/01/rap-radicalism-hip-hop-create-extremists-150128075110992.html [accessed 19 March 2015].

Akbarzadeh, S. (2013) 'Investing in mentoring and educational initiatives: The limits of deradicalisation programmes in Australia'. *Journal of Muslim Minority Affairs*, 33(4): 451–463.

Akhbarzadeh, S. (2015) 'Islamic State: A young rebel's guide to terror'. *The Australian*, 1 May 2015. Online. Available from: www.theaustralian.com.au/opinion/islamic-state-a -young-rebels-guide-to-terror/news-story/217045dad786837e0014809ba413d34c [accessed 13 April 2016].

Alagha, J. (2011) 'Pious entertainment: Hizbullah's Islamic cultural sphere'. In K. van Nieuwkerk (ed.) *Muslim Rap, Halal Soaps, and Revolutionary Theater: Artistic developments in the Muslim world*, Austin: University of Texas Press, pp. 149–177.

Alagha, J. (2013) 'Jihad through "music": The Taliban and Hizbullah'. *Performing Islam*, 1(2): 263–289.

Alexander, C. (2004) 'Imagining the Asian gang: Ethnicity, masculinity and youth after "The Riots"'. *Critical Social Policy*, 24(4): 526–549.

Alexander, D. C. and Ceresero, R. (2013) 'Is the woman next door a terrorist?'. *Security: Solutions for Enterprise Security Leaders*, 50(9): 52–56.

Ali, A.H. (2015) *Heretic: Why Islam needs a reformation now*. New York: HarperCollins.

Ali, R.M. and Moss, S. (2010) 'The Search for Meaning: Exploring the radical worldview of Islamist extremists in Victoria'. Paper presented to the conference on Understanding Terrorism from an Australian Perspective. Melbourne, Monash University Caulfield Campus, 2010. Online, pp. 1–21. Available from: http://artson line.monash.edu.au/radicalisation/files/2013/03/conference-2010-the-search-for-mean ing-ra.pdf [accessed 17 March 2015].

Alim, S. (2006) 'Re-inventing Islam with Unique Modern Tones: Muslim hip-hop artists as verbal mujahidin'. *Souls*, 8(4): 45–58.

Al Jazeera (2015a) 'Hip-hop hijabis'. Online. 5 March 2015. Available from: www.alja zeera.com/programmes/witness/2015/03/hip-hop-hijabis-150305091541022.html [accessed 23 March 2015].

Al Jazeera (2015b) 'Hundreds attend anti-Islam rallies across Australia'. Online. Available from: www.aljazeera.com/news/2015/04/hundreds-attend-anti-islam-ra llies-australia-150404174512135.html [accessed 4 April 2015].

Al Jazeera (2015c) 'Australia's jihadis'. Online. Available from: www.aljazeera.com/p rogrammes/101east/2015/01/australia-jihadis-150128191940883.html [accessed 9 February 2015].

Al Jazeera (2016) 'Backlash: France's new hard line on terror'. Online. Available from: www.aljazeera.com/programmes/peopleandpower/2016/03/backlash-frances-hard-lin e-terror-160310080855190.html [accessed 16 July 2016].

Allen, C. (2010) *Islamophobia*. Farnham: Ashgate.

Al-Natour, R.J. (2015) 'The constructions of Sydney's "Muslim ghettoes"'. *Contemporary Islam*, 9(2): 131–147.

Al Raffie, D. (2012) 'Whose hearts and minds? Narratives and counter-narratives of salafi jihadism', *Journal of Terrorism Research*, 3(2): 13–31.

Al-Saggaf, Y. (2013) 'Males' trust and mistrust of females in Muslim matrimonial sites'. *Journal of Information, Communication and Ethics in Society*, 11(3): 174–192.

Al-Tabaa, E. (2013) 'Targeting a female audience: American Muslim women's perceptions of Al-Qaida propaganda'. *Journal of Strategic Security*, 6(3): 10–21.

Aly, A. (2007) 'Australian Muslim responses to the discourse on terrorism in the Australian popular media'. *Australian Journal of Social Issues*, 42(1): 27–40.

Aly, A. (2012) 'Fear online: Seeking sanctuary in online forums'. In A. Hayes and R. Mason (eds) *Cultures in Refuge: Seeking sanctuary in modern Australia*, Farnham: Ashgate, pp. 163–179.

Anderson, B. (1991) *Imagined communities: Reflections on the origin and spread of nationalism*. London: Verso.

Andrews, M. (2004) 'Counter-narratives and the power to oppose'. In M.G.W. Bamberg and M. Andrews (eds) *Considering Counter Narratives: Narrating, resisting, making sense*, Philadelphia, PA: John Benjamins, pp. 1–7.

Amer, A., Howarth, C. and Sen, R. (2015) 'Diasporic virginities: Social representations of virginity and identity formation amongst British Arab Muslim women'. *Culture and Psychology*, 21(1): 3–19.

Amghar, S. (2003) Rap et islam: Quand le rappeur devient imam [Rap and Islam: When the rapper becomes a preacher]. *Revues hommes et migrations*, 1243: 78–86.

Anker, E. (2005) 'Villains, victims and heroes: Melodrama, media and September 11'. *Journal of Communication*, 55(1): 22–37.

Anooshe Mushtaq (2015) 'Radicalisation: The tone of Muslim community discussion must change'. *The Age*, 18 November. Online. Available from: www.theage.com.au/comment/price-of-acceptance-in-muslim-communities-in-australia-is-seclusion-from-broader-society-20151108-gktuym.html [accessed 13 April 2016].

Appadurai, A. (1996) *Modernity at Large: Cultural dimensions of globalization*. Minneapolis: University of Minnesota Press.

Arendt, H. (1951) *The Origins of Totalitarianism*. New York: Schocken Books.

Aronson, P. (2008) 'The markers and meanings of growing up: Contemporary young women's transition from adolescence to adulthood'. *Gender and Society*, 22(1): 56–82.

Asad, T. (1996) 'Comments on conversion'. In P. van der Veer (ed.) *Conversion to modernities: The globalization of Christianity*, New York and London: Routledge, pp. 263–273.

Aslam, M. (2012) *Gender-based Explosions: The nexus between Muslim masculinities, jihadist Islamism and terrorism*. New York: United Nations University Press.

Atie, R. and Dunn, K. (2013) 'The ordinariness of Australian Muslims: Attitudes and experiences of Muslims'. In N. Gopalkrishnan and H. Babacan (eds) *Third International Conference on Racisms in the New World Order: Realities of culture, colour and identity conference proceedings*, Cairns, QLD: The Cairns Institute, James Cook University, pp. 2–11.

Australian Stategic Policy Institute (2015) *Gen Y Jihadists: Preventing radicalisation in Australia*. Canberra, ACT: ASPI.

Bachelard, M. (2015) 'Muslim community still waiting for Abbott government's anti-terror funds'. *The Age*. Online. Available from: www.theage.com.au/federal-politics/political-news/muslim-community-still-waiting-for-abbott-governments-antiterror-funds-20150422-1mqzzx.html [accessed 22 April 2015].

Bachelard, M. and Cordoba, A. (2015) 'Media coverage of Israel's conflict with Palestine turned Jake Bilardi to Islamic State'. *The Age*. Online. Available from:

www.theage.com.au/victoria/media-coverage-of-israels-conflict-with-palestine-turned-jake-bilardi-to-islamic-state-20150310-140epo.html [accessed 11 March 2015].

Back, L., Keith, M., Khan, A., Shukra, K. and Solomos, J. (2009) 'Islam and the new political landscape: Faith communities, political participation and social change'. *Theory, Culture and Society*, 26(4): 1–23.

Badahdah, A.M. and Tiemann, K.A. (2009) 'Religion and mate selection through cyberspace: A case study of preferences among Muslims'. *Journal of Muslim Minority Affairs*, 29(1): 83–90.

Bainbridge, W. S. (2013) *eGods: Faith versus fantasy in computer gaming*. Oxford: Oxford University Press.

Bamberg, M. (2004) 'Considering counter-narratives'. In M. Bamberg and M. Andrews (eds) *Considering Counter-Narratives: Narrating, resisting, making sense*, Philadelphia, PA: John Benjamins, pp. 351–371.

Barber, B. (1996) *Jihad vs. McWorld: Terrorism's challenge to democracy*. New York: Ballantine Books.

Barendregt, B. (2006) 'Cyber-Nasyid: Transnational soundscapes in Muslim Southeast Asia'. In T. Holden and T. Scrase (eds) *Medi@asia: Communication, culture, context*, London: Routledge, pp. 171–187.

Barendregt, B. (2012) 'Sonic discourses on Muslim Malay modernity: The Arqam sound'. *Contemporary Islam*, 6(3): 315–340.

Bartlett, J. and Miller, C. (2011) *Truth, Lies and the Internet*. London: Demos.

Bartlett, J. and Miller, C. (2012) 'The edge of violence: Towards telling the difference between violent and non-violent radicalization'. *Terrorism and Political Violence*, 24 (1): 1–21.

Barton, G. (2004) *Indonesia's Struggle: Jamaah Islamiyah and the soul of Islam*. Sydney: University of New South Wales Press.

Battersby, L. (2015) 'Veil lifts on daily abuse faced by Australian Muslims'. *Sydney Morning Herald*. Online. Available from: www.smh.com.au/national/people/veil-lifts-on-daily-abuse-faced-by-australian-muslims-20151130-glc4yt.html [accessed 2 December 2015].

Baudrillard, J. (1991) *The Gulf War Did Not Take Place*. Bloomington: Indiana University Press.

Baudrillard, J. (1994) *Simulacra and Simulation*. Trans. F. Glaser. Ann Arbor: University of Michigan Press.

Bauman, Z. (1976) *Socialism: The active utopia*. New York: Holmes and Meier.

Bauman, Z. (2004) *Identity*. Cambridge: Polity.

Bayat, A. (2007) 'Islamism and the politics of fun'. *Public Culture*, 19(3): 433–459.

Bayat, A. and Herrera, L. (2010) 'Introduction: Being young and Muslim in neo-liberal times'. In L. Herrera and A. Bayat (eds) *Being Young and Muslim: New cultural politics in the global south and north*, New York: Oxford University Press, pp. 3–26.

Beck, U. (1992) *Risk Society: Towards a new modernity*. London: Sage.

Beck, U. (1994) 'Self-dissolution and self-endangerment of industrial society: What does this mean?' In U. Beck, A. Giddens and S. Lash (eds) *Reflexive Modernization*, Cambridge: Polity Press, pp. 174–183.

Beck, U. (2010) *A God of One's Own: Religion's capacity for peace and potential for violence*. Cambridge: Polity.

Beck, U. and Beck-Gernsheim, E. (2002) *Individualization: Institutionalised individualism and its social and political consequences*. London: Sage.

Becker, H. (1973) *Outsiders: Studies in the sociology of deviance*. New York: The Free Press.

Bendixsen, S. (2013) *The Religious Identity of Young Muslim Women in Berlin: An ethnographic study*. Leiden: Brill.

Bennett, A. (1999a) 'Subcultures or neo-tribes? Rethinking the relationship between youth, style and musical taste'. *Sociology*, 33(3): 599–617.

Bennett, A. (1999b) 'Hip hop am Main: The localization of rap music and hip hop culture'. *Media, Culture and Society*, 21(1): 77–91.

Bennett, A. (2000) *Popular Music and Youth Culture: Music, identity and place*. Basingstoke: Palgrave Macmillan.

Bennett, A. and Peterson, R. (2004) *Music Scenes: Local, translocal, and virtual*. Nashville, TN: Vanderbilt University Press.

Bennett, W.L. (2012) 'The personalization of politics: Political identity, social media and changing patterns of participation'. *Annals of the American Academy of Political and Social Science*, 644: 20–39.

Benoit, B. (2014) 'Hajj selfies: A new trend in da'wah? A Muslim woman's view'. *OnIslam*, 9 October 2014. Available from: www.onislam.net/english/culture-and-en tertainment/iblog/478355-hajj-selfies-a-new-trend-in-dawah.html [accessed 25 May 2015].

Berlant, L. (2008) *The Female Complaint*. Durham, NC: Duke University Press.

Bernardi, D.L., Cheong, P.H., Lundry, C. and Ruston, C.W. (2012) *Narrative Landmines: Rumours, Islamist extremism and the struggle for strategic influence*. New Brunswick, NJ: Rutgers University Press.

Beski-Chafiq, C., Birmant, J., Benmerzoug, H., Taibi, A. and Goignard, A. (2010) *Youth and Islamist Radicalisation*. Aarhus University, Denmark: Centre for Studies in Islamism and Radicalisation.

Beydoun, K. (2016) 'The myth of the "moderate Muslim": Deconstructing the mythic "good versus bad" Muslim paradigm'. *Al Jazeera English*. Online. Available from: www.aljazeera.com/indepth/opinion/2016/05/myth-moderate-muslim-160511085819521. html [accessed 21 May 2016].

Bhatti, G. (2011) 'Outsiders or insiders? Identity, educational success and Muslim young men in England'. *Ethnography and Education*, 6(1): 81–96.

Bhui, K. and Ibrahim, Y. (2013) 'Marketing the "radical": Symbolic communication and persuasive technologies in jihadist websites'. *Transcultural Psychiatry*, 50(2): 216–234.

Bianchi, R. (2004) *Guests of God: Pilgrimage and politics in the Islamic world*. Oxford: Oxford University Press.

Bigo, D., Bonelli, L., Guittet, E.P. and Ragazzi, F. (2014) *Preventing and Countering Youth Radicalisation in the EU*. Brussels: European Union. Available from: https://p ublicintelligence.net/eu-youth-radicalization/ [accessed 7 September 2015].

Billaud, J. (2015) 'Snapshots of British Islam: Exploring self, identity, and the good ethical life in the global megalopolis'. *Journal of Contemporary Ethnography*, 1–26. Online. Available from: http://jce.sagepub.com/content/early/2015/04/13/ 0891241615578904.full.pdf [accessed 4 June 2015].

Bloustien, G. (2007). '"Wigging people out": Youth music practice and mediated communities'. *Journal of Community Applied Social Psychology*, 17(6): 446–462.

Boellstorff, T. (2008) *Coming of Age in Second Life: An anthropologist explores the virtually human*. Princeton, NJ: Princeton University Press.

Bogost, I. (2007) *Persuasive Games: The expressive power of videogames*. Cambridge MA: MIT Press.

Booth, A., Leigh, A. and Varganova, E. (2012) 'Does ethnic discrimination vary across minority groups? Evidence from a field experiment'. *Oxford Bulletin of Economics and Statistics*, 74(4): 548–574.

Booth, R. (2016) 'Labour's Sadiq Khan elected mayor of London'. *Guardian*. Online. 7 May 2016. Available from: www.theguardian.com/politics/2016/may/07/sadiq-khan-elected-mayor-of-london-labour [accessed 17 May 2016].

Bornemark, H. (2013) 'Success factors for e-sport games'. In S. Bensch and F. Drewes (eds) *Proceedings of Umea's 16th Student Conference in Computing Science*, pp. 1–12. Available from: www8.cs.umu.se/research/uminf/reports/2013/001/part1.pdf [accessed 31 August 2015].

Borum, R. (2011) 'Radicalization into violent extremism II: A review of conceptual models and empirical research'. *Journal of Strategic Security*, 4(4): 37–62.

Boubekeur, A. (2005) 'Cool and competitive: Muslim culture in the West'. *ISIM Review*, 16: 12–13.

Bouma, G., Cahill, D., Dellal, H. and Zwartz, A. (2011) *Freedom of Religion and Belief in 21st Century Australia*. Canberra ACT: Australian Human Rights Commission.

Bouma, G. (2016) 'Quest for inclusion: Australia and Islamophobia'. In D. Pratt and R. Woodlock (eds) *Fear of Muslims? International perspectives on Islamophobia*, Dordrecht: Springer, pp. 67–78.

Bourdieu, P. (1984) *Distinction*. Trans. R. Nice. Cambridge, MA: Harvard University Press.

Bourdieu, P. (1998) *Outline of a Theory of Practice*. Trans. R. Nice. Cambridge: Cambridge University Press.

Bourdieu, P. (2001). *Masculine Domination*. Trans. R. Nice. Stanford, CA: Stanford University Press.

Bourke, L. (2016) 'Australian Liberty Alliance, the anti-Islam, Donald Trump-style party, claims major growth'. *Sydney Morning Herald*, 7 April. Online. Available from: www.smh.com.au/federal-politics/political-news/australian-liberty-alliance-the-antiislam-donald-trumpstyle-party-claims-major-growth-20160406-go08lq.html#ixzz455e0BBr0 [accessed 7 April 2016].

Bourke, L. and Calligeros, M. (2015) 'Australian Islamic State recruits in talks to return home'. *Sydney Morning Herald*, 19 May. Online. Available from: www.smh.com.au/federal-politics/political-news/australian-islamic-state-recruits-in-talks-to-return-home-20150518-gh4nda.html?rand=6461975 [accessed 19 May 2015].

boyd, d. (2009) 'Friendship'. In M. Ito, S. Baumer, M. Bittanti, d. boyd, R. Cody, B. Herr-Stephenson, H. Horst, P. Lange, D. Mahendran, K. Martinez, C.J. Pascoe, D. Perkel, L. Robinson, C. Sims and L. Tripp (eds) *Hanging Out, Messing Around, Geeking Out: Living and learning with new media*, Cambridge, MA: MIT Press, pp. 79–116.

boyd, d. (2010) 'Social network sites as networked publics: Affordances, dynamics, and implications'. In Z. Papacharissi (ed.) *Networked Self: Identity, community, and culture on social network sites*, London and New York: Routledge, pp. 39–58.

boyd, d. (2014) *It's Complicated: The social lives of networked teens*. New Haven, CT: Yale University Press.

Brachman, J. M. (2006) 'High-tech terror: Al-Qaeda's use of new technology'. *The Fletcher Forum of World Affairs*, 30(2): 149–164.

Braddock, K. (2012) 'Fighting words: The persuasive effect of online extremist narratives on the radicalization process'. Unpublished Ph.D. thesis, Pennsylvania State University.

Brandon, J. (2008) *Virtual Caliphate: Islamic extremists and their websites*. London: Centre for Social Cohesion.

Brannen, J. and Nilsen, A. (2007) 'Young people, time horizons and planning'. *Sociology*, 41(1): 153–160.

Broadbent, R. (2013) 'Using grass roots community programs as an anti-extremism strategy'. *Australian Journal of Adult Learning*, 53(2): 188–210.

Brown, M. (2014) 'Islamic State: Australian teenager Jake Bilardi believed to be involved in suicide bombing in Iraq'. *ABC Online*. Available from: www.abc.net.au/news/2015-03-12/australian-believed-involved-in-islamic-state-suicide-bombing/6305304 [accessed 12 March 2015].

Bruner, J. (1990) *Acts of Meaning*. Cambridge, MA: Harvard University Press.

Bryson, B. (1996) 'Anything but heavy metal: Symbolic exclusion and musical dislikes'. *American Sociological Review*, 61(5): 884–899.

Bucci, N. (2015) 'Prevention better than deradicalisation as number of teenage jihadis grows'. *Sydney Morning Herald*. Online. Available from: www.smh.com.au/national/prevention-better-than-deradicalisation-as-number-of-teenage-jihadis-grows-20150514-gh1q2l.html [accessed 15 December 2015].

Buchanan, R. (2014) 'Syria crisis: British rapper turned Isis fighter posts image of himself holding severed head'. *Independent*. Online. Available from: www.independent.co.uk/news/world/middle-east/syria-crisis-british-rapper-turned-isis-fighter-posts-image-of-himself-holding-severed-head-9669603.html [accessed 12 June 2016].

Buckingham, D. (2013) 'Is there a digital generation?' In D. Buckingham and R. Willett (eds) *Digital Generations: Children young people and new media*, London and New York: Routledge, pp. 1–18.

Bunt, G. R. (2009). *iMuslims: Rewiring the house of Islam*. Chapel Hill, NC: University of North Carolina Press.

Butler, J. (1990) *Gender Trouble*. New York and London: Routledge.

Butler, J. (2004) 'What is critique? An essay on Foucault's Virtue 2000'. In S. Salih (ed.) *The Judith Butler Reader*, Oxford: Blackwell, pp. 302–322.

Butler, J. (2008) 'Sexual politics, torture, and secular time'. *British Journal of Sociology*, 59(1): 1–23.

Butler, J. (2015) *Notes Toward a Performative Theory of Assembly*. Cambridge, MA: Harvard University Press.

Calligeros, M. (2015) 'Islamic State recruiter Neil Prakash calls for attacks in Australia in propaganda video'. *The Age*. Online. Available from: www.theage.com.au/victoria/islamic-state-recruiter-neil-prakash-calls-for-attacks-in-australia-in-propaganda-video-20150422-1mqkcl.html [accessed 22 April 2015].

Calvert, J. (2010) *Sayyid Qutb and the Origins of Radical Islamism*. New York: Columbia University Press.

Campbell, H. (2013) 'Islamogaming: Digital dignity via alternative storytelling'. In C. Detweiler (ed.) *Halos and Avatars: Playing (video) games with God*, Louisville, KY: Westminster Press, pp. 63–74.

Campbell, H. (2016) 'Surveying theoretical approaches within digital religion studies'. *New Media and Society.* Online, pp. 1–10. DOI: 10.1177/1461444816649912.

Canter, D.V., Sarangi, S. and Youngs, D.E. (2014) 'Terrorists' personal constructs and their roles: A comparison of the three Islamic terrorists'. *Legal and Criminological Psychology,* 19(1): 160–178.

Castells, M. (1996) *The Network Society: The information age: Economy, society and culture, vol. I.* Cambridge, MA: Blackwell.

Castells, M. (1997) *The Power of Identity: The information age: Economy, society and culture, vol. II.* Cambridge, MA: Blackwell.

Cevik, N. (2015) *Muslimism in Turkey and Beyond: Religion in the modern world.* Bansingstoke: Palgrave Macmillan.

Chalkley-Roden, S. (2014) 'One in four Australians has negative attitude towards Muslims: report'. *ABC News.* Online. Available from: www.abc.net.au/news/2014-10-29/ one-in-four-australians-had-a-negative-attitude-towards-muslims/5849744 [accessed 2 December 2015].

Chalmers, M. (2015) 'Muslim zombies and death metal jihad: The aussie band making Islamophobes' nightmares come true'. *New Matilda Online.* 23 October 2015. Available from: https://newmatilda.com/2015/10/23/muslim-zombies-and-death-meta l-jihad-the-aussie-band-making-islamophobes-nightmares-come-true/ [accessed 8 May 2016].

Cheong, P.C. and Halverson, J.R. (2010) 'Youths in violent extremist discourse: Mediated identifications and interventions'. *Studies in Conflict and Terrorism,* 33 (12): 1104–1123.

Cherney, A. and Murphy, K. (2015) 'Being a "suspect community" in a post 9/11 world: The impact of the war on terror on Muslim communities in Australia'. *Australian and New Zealand Journal of Criminology.* Online first: 1–17. DOI: 10.1177/ 0004865815585392.

Chien, I. (2010) 'Playing against the grain: Machinima and military gaming'. In N.B. Huntemann and M.T. Payne (eds) *Joystick Soldiers: The politics of play in military video games,* New York: Routledge, pp. 239–251.

Cieslik, M. and Pollock, G. (2002) 'Introduction'. In M. Cieslik and G. Pollock (eds) *Young People in Risk Society: The restructuring of youth identities and transitions in late modernity.* Farnham: Ashgate, pp. 1–21.

Clifford, J. (1994) 'Diasporas'. *Cultural Anthropology,* 9(3): 302–338.

Coates, C. (2001) *Utopia Britannica: British utopian Experiments 1325–1945.* London: Diggers and Dreamers Publications.

Cohen, S. (1972) *Folk Devils and Moral Panics: The creation of Mods and Rockers.* London: MacGibbon & Kee.

Connell, J. and Gibson, C. (2004) 'World music: Deterritorializing place and identity'. *Progress in Human Geography,* 28(3): 342–361.

Connell, R.W. (2005) *Masculinities.* 2nd edn. Sydney: Allen & Unwin.

Cook, D. (2008) *Contemporary Muslim Apocalyptic Literature.* New York: Syracuse University Press.

Corner, J. and Pels, D. (2003) 'Introduction: The re-styling of politics'. In J. Corner and D. Pels (eds) *Media and the Restyling of Politics: Consumerism, celebrity and cynicism,* London: Sage, pp. 1–18.

Cottee, S. and Hayward, K. (2011) 'Terrorist (e)motives: The existential attractions of terrorism'. *Studies in Conflict and Terrorism,* 34(12): 963–986.

Courmont, B. and Clément, P.-A. (2014) 'When geopolitics meets the game industry: A study of Arabic video games and what they teach us'. *Hemispheres*, 29(1): 31–46.

Cowie, T. and Butt, C. (2016) 'Melbourne brothers charged after staging hoax drive-by shooting with fake AK-47'. *The Age*. Online. Available from: www.theage.com.au/victoria/melbourne-brothers-charged-after-staging-hoax-drive-by-shooting-with-fake-ak-47-20160224-gn313g.html [accessed 25 February 2016].

Cragin, K. and Daly, S. (2009) *Women as Terrorists*. Oxford: ABC-CLIO.

Crawford, G., Gosling, V. and Light, B. (2011) 'The social and cultural significance of online gaming'. In G. Crawford, V. Gosling and B. Light (eds) *Online Gaming in Context: The social and cultural significance of online games*, London and New York: Routledge, pp. 3–22.

Crenshaw, M. (2015) 'There is no global jihadist movement'. *The Atlantic*. 11 March 2015. Online. Available from: www.theatlantic.com/international/archive/2015/03/there-is-no-global-jihadist-movement/387502/ [accessed 18 May 2015].

Dabiq (2015) 'Just Terror: Foreword'. *Dabiq*, issue 12. Available from; www.clarionproject.org/docs/islamic-state-isis-isil-dabiq-magazine-issue-12-just-terror.pdf [accessed 3 December 2015].

Dalgaard-Nielsen, A. (2010) 'Violent radicalization in Europe: What we know and what we do not know'. *Studies in Conflict and Terrorism*, 33(9): 797–814.

Davies, B. (1989) *Frogs and Snails and Feminist Tales: Preschool children and gender*. Sydney: Allen & Unwin.

Davies, B. and Harré, R. (1990) 'Positioning: The discursive production of selves'. *Journal for the Theory of Social Behaviour*, 20(1): 43–63.

Davies, G., Neudecker, C., Ouellet, M., Bouchard, M. and Ducol, B. (2016) 'Toward a framework understanding of online programs for countering violent extremism'. *Journal for Deradicalization*, 6: 51–86.

Dégh, L. (1995) *Narratives in Society: A performer-centered study of narration*. Helsinki: Suomalainen Tiedeakatemia.

Deleuze, G. and Guattari, F. (1980) *Anti-Oedipus: Capitalism and schizophrenia*. London: Athlone Press.

Deleuze, G. and Guattari, F. (1987) *A Thousand Plateaus*. London and New York: Continuum.

De Nawi, T. (2016) 'Why actor Tyler De Nawi changed his name from Mustafa, and why he wishes he hadn't needed to'. *The Age*. Online. Available from: www.theage.com.au/comment/why-actor-tyler-de-nawi-changed-his-name-from-mustafa-and-why-he-wishes-he-hadnt-needed-to-20160518-goxv7n.html [accessed 27 May 2016].

DeNora, T. (2000) *Music in Everyday Life*. Cambridge: Cambridge University Press.

Detweiler, C. (2010) 'Conclusion: Born to play'. In C. Detweiler (ed.) *Halos and Avatars: Playing video games with God*, Louisville, KY: Westminster John Knox Press, pp. 190–196.

Detweiler, C. and Taylor, B. (2003) *A Matrix of Meanings: Finding God in popular culture*. Grand Rapids, MI: Baker Academic.

DIAC (2009) *The Australian Journey: Muslim communities*. Canberra, ACT: Department of Immigration and Citizenship.

Donelly, B. (2016) 'Muslims on what it's like to live in Australia'. *Sydney Morning Herald*, 2 May. Online. Available from: www.smh.com.au/national/muslims-on-what-its-like-to-live-in-australia-20160429-goi953#ixzz47YYAYcpl [accessed 3 May 2016].

Doosje, B., Loseman, A. and Van den Bos, K. (2013) 'Determinants of radicalization of Islamic youth in the Netherlands: Personal uncertainty, perceived injustice, and perceived group threat'. *Journal of Social Issues*, 69(3): 586–604.

Driessens, O. (2015) 'On the epistemology and operationalisation of celebrity'. *Celebrity Studies*, 6(3): 370–373.

Driscoll, M. (2015) 'My ISIS boyfriend: A reporter's undercover life with a terrorist'. *New York Post*, 7 March 2015. Online. Available from: http://nypost.com/2015/03/07/my-isis-boyfriend-a-reporters-undercover-life-with-a-terrorist/ [accessed 20 September 2015].

Drissel, D. (2011) 'Pan-Islamist networks of the apocalypse: Mobilizing diasporic Muslim youth on Facebook'. In R.G. Howard (ed.) *Network Apocalypse: Visions of the end in an age of internet media*, Sheffield: Phoenix Press, pp. 145–182.

Dubnick, M.J., Olshfski, D.F. and Callahan, K. (2009) 'Aggressive Action: In search of a dominant narrative'. In M. Morgan (ed.) *The impact of 9/11 on the Media, Arts, and Entertainment*, New York: Palgrave Macmillan, pp. 9–24.

Ducol, B. (2012) 'Uncovering the French-speaking jihadisphere: An exploratory analysis'. *Media, War and Conflict*, 5(1): 51–70.

Dunn, K., Klocker, N. and Salabay, T. (2007) 'Contemporary racism and Islamaphobia in Australia: Racialising religion'. *Ethnicities*, 7(4): 564–589.

Eid, P. (2007) *Being Arab*. Montreal and Kingston: McGill-Queen's University Press.

Eidelson, R.J. and Eidelson, J.I. (2003) Dangerous ideas: Five beliefs that propel groups toward conflict'. *American Psychologist*, 58(3): 182–192.

Eisenstadt, S.N. (1995) 'Fundamentalism, phenomenology, and comparative dimensions'. In M.E. Marty and R.S. Appleby (eds) *Fundamentalisms Comprehended*, Chicago, IL: University of Chicago Press, pp. 259–276.

El-Affendi, A. (2009) 'A clash of xenophobic narratives: The symbiotic relationship between Islamaphobia and extremism'. In Southeast Asian Regional Center for Counter-Terrorism (ed.) *SEARCCT's Selection of Articles*, Kuala Lumpur, Malaysia: SEARCCT, pp. 30–56.

El-Saeed, Y. (2015) 'Hipster hijabi: Fashionable but modest dressing – exclusive interview with Summer Al Barcha'. *OnIslam*. Available from: www.facebook.com/pages/OnIslam-Culture-Entertainment/259148867589775 [accessed 25 May 2015].

ESA (2016) '2015: Essential facts about the computer and video game industry: Sales, demographic, and usage data'. Online. Available from www.theesa.com/wp-content/uploads/2016/04/Essential-Facts-2016.pdf [accessed 19 June 2016].

Esposito, J.L. (2002) *Unholy War: Terror in the name of Islam*. New York: Oxford University Press.

Esposito, J.L. (2007) 'A mainstream of modernists, Islamists, conservatives and traditionalists'. In M.A.M. Khan (ed.) *Debating Moderate Islam: The geopolitics of Islam and the West*. Salt Lake City: University of Utah Press, pp. 25–33.

Fasenfest, D. (2015) 'Western societies and Islam'. *Critical Sociology*, 41(1): 3–4.

Fekete, L. (ed.) (2009) *A Suitable Enemy: Racism, migration and Islamophobia in Europe*. London: Pluto Press.

Fife-Yeomans, J. (2013) 'Western Sydney Imam Afroz Ali says 100 extremists living in our suburbs'. *Daily Telegraph*, 27 June. Online. Available from: www.dailytelegraph.com.au/news/nsw/western-sydney-imam-afroz-ali-says-100-extremists-living-in-our-suburbs/story-fni0cx12-1226670491716 [accessed 3 December 2015].

Fiscella, A.T. (2012) 'From Muslim punks to taqwacore: An incomplete history of punk Islam. *Contemporary Islam*, 6(3): 255–281.

Flew, T. and Humphreys, S. (2005) 'Games: Technology, industry, culture'. In T. Flew (ed.) *New Media: An introduction*. 2nd edn. Oxford: Oxford University Press, pp. 101–114.

Flitton, D. (2015) 'Muslim youth speak on Islamophobia and questions of faith'. *The Age*. Online. Available from: www.theage.com.au/victoria/muslim-youth-speak-on-i slamophobia-and-questions-on-faith-20150605-ghha7q.html [accessed 6 June 2015].

Follorou, J., Piel, S. and Suc, M. (2015) 'Les frères Kouachi et Coulibaly, des pionniers du djihadisme français' [The Kouachi brothers and Coulibaly, pioneers of French jihadism]. *Le Monde*, 10 January. Online. Available from: www.lemonde.fr/societe/a rticle/2015/01/10/des-pionniers-du-djihadisme-francais_4553301_3224.html#Eipv3pV 3UbVBl1ZW.99 [accessed 21 September 2015].

Foucault, M. (1972) *The Archeology of Knowledge and the Discourse on Language*. New York: Pantheon Books.

Foucault, M. (2003) *Abnormal: Lectures at the Collège de France, 1974–1975*. New York: Picador.

Fouquet, H. (2016) 'Eight terror attacks in 19 months in France leaves nearly 230 people dead'. *Sydney Morning Herald*. Online. Available from: www.smh.com.au/world/eight-terror-attacks-in-19-months-in-france-leaves-nearly-230-people-dead-20160715-gq6hg7. html [accessed 16 July 2016].

Fozdar, F. (2011) 'Social cohesion and skilled Muslim refugees in Australia: Employment, social capital and discrimination'. *Journal of Sociology*, 48(2): 167–186.

Franceschelli, M. and O'Brien, M. (2015) '"Being modern and modest": South Asian young British Muslims negotiating multiple influences on their identity'. *Ethnicities*, 15(5): 696–714.

Fredette, J. (2014) *Constructing Muslims in France: Discourse, public identity, and the politics of citizenship*. Philadelphia, PA: Temple University Press.

Fry, D. (2016) 'Kāfir Pride: An examination of the recent apparent rise in Australian anti-Islamic activity and the challenges it presents for national security'. *Journal for Deradicalization*, 6: 105–131.

Furlong, A. and Cartmel, F. (2004) *Vulnerable Young Men in Fragile Labour Markets: Employment, unemployment and the search for long-term security*. York: York Publishing.

Furlong, A. and Cartmel, F. (2007) *Young People and Social Change: New perspectives*. 2nd edn. London: Oxford University Press.

Furlow, R.B., Fleischer, K. and Corman, S.R. (2014) *De-romanticizing the Islamic State's vision of the caliphate*. Report no. 1402. Tempe AZ: Center for Strategic Communication, Arizona State University. Available from: http://csc.asu.edu/2014/ 10/28/de-romanticizing-the-islamic-states-vision-of-the-caliphate-2/ [accessed 5 June 2015].

Furnish, T.R. (2002) 'Bin Ladin: The man who would be Mahdi'. *Middle East Quarterly*, (Spring): 53–59. Available from: www.meforum.org/159/bin-ladin-the-ma n-who-would-be-mahdi/ [accessed 20 September 2015].

Gazzah, M. (2010) 'Maroc-hop: Music and youth identities in the Netherlands'. In L. Herrera and A. Bayat (eds) *Being Young and Muslim: New cultural politics in the global south and north*, New York: Oxford University Press, pp. 309–324.

Gee, J.P. (2003) *What Video Games Have to Teach us about Learning and Literacy*. 2nd edn. New York: Palgrave.

Gerami, S. (2005) 'Islamist masculinities and Muslim masculinities'. In M. Kimmel, J. Hearn and R.W. Connell (eds) *Handbook of Studies on Men and Masculinities*, Thousand Oaks, CA: Sage, pp. 448–457.

Geser, H. (2007) 'A very real virtual society: Some macrosociological reflections on "Second Life"'. *Sociology in Switzerland: Towards cybersociety and vireal social relations*. Available from: http://socio.ch/intcom/t_hgeser18.htm [accessed 31 July 2015].

Ghaffar-Kucher, A. (2015) '"Narrow-minded and oppressive" or a "superior culture"? Implications of divergent representations of Islam for Pakistani-American youth'. *Race, Ethnicity and Education*, 18(2): 202–224.

Giddens, A. (1991) *Modernity and Self-Identity*. Stanford, CA: Stanford University Press.

Gilbert, J. (2014) *A Cycle of Outrage: America's reaction to the juvenile delinquent in the 1950s*. New York: Oxford University Press.

Göle, N. (2002) 'Islam in public: New visibilities and new imaginaries'. *Public Culture*, 14(1): 173–190.

Goodwin, I., Griffin, C., Lyons, A., McCreanor, T. and Barnes, H.M. (2016) 'Precarious popularity: Facebook drinking photos, the attention economy, and the regime of the branded self'. *Social Media and Society*. Online first. DOI: 10.1177/2056305116628889.

Goshert, L.A. (2007) 'Performing identities: The creation of a popular Muslim music culture in the United States'. Unpublished M.A. thesis, Indiana University.

Gosney, J.W. (2005) *Beyond Reality: A guide to alternate reality gaming*. Boston, MA: Thomson.

Green, S. (2015) 'The young faces of terror'. *The Age*. Online. Available from: www.theage.com.au/national/the-young-faces-of-terror-20140926-10mf9v.html [accessed 4 October 2015].

Greene, A. (2016) 'Islamic State: Two Australians killed in US air strikes, including terrorist recruiter Neil Prakash'. *ABC Online*. 5 May. Available from: www.abc.net.au/news/2016-05-05/islamic-state-recruiter-neil-prakash-killed-in-us-air-strike/7385078 [accessed 6 May 2016].

Grieve, G. and Campbell, H. (2014) 'Studying religion in digital gaming'. In S. Heidbrink and T. Knoll (eds) *Religion in Digital Games: Multiperspectival and interdisciplinary approaches*, Heidelberg, Germany: University of Heidelberg, pp. 51–67.

Gross, A. (2012) *Reaching Wa'y: Mobilization and recruitment in Hizb al-Tahrir al-Islami*. Berlin: Klaus Schwarz.

Habib, S. (2009) *Islam and Homosexuality*. Volume 1. Westport, CT: Praeger.

Hafez, M.M. (2007) 'Martyrdom mythology in Iraq: How jihadists frame suicide terrorism in videos and biographies'. *Terrorism and Political Violence*, 19(1): 95–115.

Hage, G. (2011) 'Multiculturalism and the ungovernable Muslim'. In R. Gaita (ed.) *Essays on Muslims and Multiculturalism*, Melbourne: Text, 155–186.

Hagedorn, J. (2003) 'Gang'. In M. Kimmel and A.M. Aronson (eds) *Encyclopedia of Masculinities*, New York: Sage, pp. 329–331.

Haider, H. (2015) *Radicalisation of Diaspora Communities*. Report for GSDRC. Online. Available from: www.gsdrc.org/docs/open/HDQ1187.pdf [accessed 8 September 2015].

Halafoff, A. and Wright-Neville, D. (2009) 'A missing peace? The role of religious actors in countering terrorism'. *Studies in Conflict and Terrorism*, 32(11): 921–932.

Hall, S. (1990) 'Cultural identity and diaspora'. In J. Rutherford (ed.) *Identity: Community, culture, difference*, London: Lawrence & Wishart, pp. 222–237.

Hall, S., Critcher, C., Jefferson, T., Clarke, J. and Roberts, B. (1978) *Policing the Crisis: Mugging, the state and law and order*. London: Macmillan.

Halverson, J.R., GoodallJr, H.L. and Corman, S.R. (2011) *Master Narratives of Islamist Extremism*. New York: Palgrave Macmillan.

Hamad, R. (2016) 'Why Christian and Muslim fundamentalists actually aren't enemies'. *The Age*. Online. Available from: www.dailylife.com.au/news-and-views/dl-opinion/why-christian-and-muslim-fundamentalists-actually-arent-enemies-20160525-gp3o4x.html [accessed 27 May 2016].

Hamzeh, M. (2011) 'Deveiling body stories: Muslim girls negotiate visual, spatial, and ethical hijabs'. *Race, Ethnicity and Education*, 14(4): 481–506.

Haq, F. (2007) 'Militarism and motherhood: The women of the Lashkar-i-Tayyabia in Pakistan'. *Signs*, 32(4): 1023–1046.

Harb, C. (2014) 'Arab youth values and identities: Impact of the Arab uprisings'. In IEM (ed.) *European Institute of the Mediterranean Yearbook 2014*, Barcelona: Instituto Europeo del Mediterraneo, pp. 72–77.

Harris, A. (2004) *Future Girl: Young women in the twenty-first century*. London and New York: Routledge.

Harris, A. (2008) 'Young women, late modern politics, and the participatory possibilities of online cultures'. *Journal of Youth Studies*, 11(5): 481–495.

Harris, A. (2013) *Young People and Everyday Multiculturalism*. London and New York: Routledge.

Harris, A. and Roose, J. (2014) 'DIY citizenship amongst young Muslims: Experiences of the "ordinary"'. *Journal of Youth Studies*, 17(6): 794–813.

Hasan, N. (2010) 'The drama of jihad: the emergence of Salafi youth in Indonesia'. In L. Herrera and A. Bayat (eds) *Being Young and Muslim: New cultural politics in the global south and north*, New York: Oxford University Press, pp. 44–62.

Hassan, R. (2010) 'Socio-economic marginalization of Muslims in contemporary Australia: Implications for social inclusion'. *Journal of Muslim Minority Affairs*, 30(4): 575–584.

Hatch, P. (2015) 'Australian women joining Islamic State not just "jihadi brides": Study'. *The Age*. Online. Available from: www.theage.com.au/national/australian-women-joining-islamic-state-not-just-jihadi-brides-study-20150530-ghd1k0.html [accessed 30 May 2015].

Hawreliak, J. (2013) '"To be shot at without result": Gaming and the rhetoric of immortality'. In R. Luppicini (ed.) *Handbook of Research on Technoself: Identity in a technological society*, Hershey, PA: ICI Global, pp. 531–553.

Hecker, P. (2012) *Turkish Metal: Music, meaning, and morality in a Muslim society*. Farnham: Ashgate.

Hefner, R.W. (2002) 'The struggle for the soul of Islam'. In C. Calhoun, P. Price and A. Timmer (eds) *Understanding September 11*, New York: The New Press, pp. 41–52.

Herding, M. (2013) *Inventing the Muslim Cool: Islamic youth culture in western Europe*. Bielefeld, Germany: Transcript Verlag.

Hervik, P. (2015) 'What is in the Scandinavian nexus of "Islamophobia", multiculturalism, and Muslim–western relations?' *Intersections: East European Journal of Society and Politics*, 1(1): 66–82.

Hett, A. and Groth, H. (2011) *Upcoming Demographic Changes in Islamic Countries.* Conference report 1–3 November 2010. Swiss Re Centre for Global Dialogue and World Demographic and Ageing Forum. Available from: www.demographic-cha llenge.com/files/downloads/37e2d7838111dfd6bb9d70d2b3c58b50/dc_upcoming_de mographic_changes_in_islamic_countries_wdaconferencereport_011110.pdf [accessed 14 April 2015].

Hine, C. (2000) *Virtual Ethnography.* London: Sage.

Hogg, M. and Adelman, J. (2013) 'Uncertainty–identity theory: Extreme groups, radical behavior, and authoritarian leadership'. *Journal of Social Issues,* 69(3): 436–454.

Hogg, M., Kruglanski, A. and van den Bos, K. (2013) 'Uncertainty and the roots of extremism'. *Journal of Social Issues,* 69(3): 407–418.

Holbrook, D. (2010) 'Using the Qur'an to justify terrorist violence: Analysing selective application of the Qur'an in English-language militant Islamist discourse'. *Perspectives on Terrorism,* 4(3): 15–28.

Holden, M. (2015) 'Over 700 Britons have travelled to Syria, half now home and pose threat: Police'. *Sydney Morning Herald,* 15 May. Online. Available from: www.smh. com.au/world/over-700-britons-have-travelled-to-syria-half-now-home-and-pose-threa t-police-20150514-gh239f.html [accessed 12 December 2015].

Honneth, A. (1996) *The Struggle for Recognition: The moral grammar for social conflicts.* Cambridge, MA: MIT Press.

Hopkins, P.E. (2006) 'Youthful Muslim masculinities: Gender and generational relations'. *Transactions of the Institute of British Geographers,* 31(3): 337–352.

Hosseini, S.A.H. and Chafic, W. (2016) 'Muslim youth identity: A review of Australian research since the 1980s'. SSRN Research Paper no. 2016–2011. Available from: http://ssrn.com/abstract=2711732 [accessed 5 June 2016].

Hoyle, C., Bradford, A. and Frenett, R. (2015) *Becoming Mulan? Female western migrants to ISIS.* London: Institute for Strategic Dialogue.

Huizinga, J. (1955) *Homo Ludens.* Boston, MA: Beacon Press.

Huntington, S.P. (1993) 'The clash of civilizations?' *Foreign Affairs,* 72(3): 22–24.

Huq, R. (2006) *Beyond Subculture: Pop, youth and identity in a post-colonial world.* London: Routledge.

Husain, E. (2007) *The Islamist: Why I joined radical Islam in Britain, what I saw inside and why I left.* Harmondsworth: Penguin.

Ibrahine, M. (2015) 'Video games as civilisational configurations: US–Arab encounters'. In A. Hamdar and L. Moore (eds) *Islamism and Cultural Expression in the Arab World,* London and New York: Routledge, pp. 206–221.

Jackson, R. (2009) 'The 9/11 attacks and the social construction of a national narrative'. In M. Morgan (ed.) *The Impact of 9/11 on the Media, Arts, and Entertainment,* New York: Palgrave Macmillan, pp. 25–36.

Jacobsen, C. (2010) *Islamic Traditions and Muslim Youth in Norway.* Leiden: Brill.

Jacques, K. and Taylor, P.J. (2013) 'Myths and realities of female-perpetrated terrorism'. *Law and Human Behavior,* 37(1): 35–44.

Jakubowicz, A., Collins, J., Reid, C. and Chafic, W. (2014) 'Minority youth and social transformation in Australia: Identities, belonging and cultural capital'. *Social Inclusion,* 2(2): 5–16.

Janmohammed, S.Z. (2010) 'Rebuilding Islam's brand'. *Emel Media.* Online. Available from: www.emel.com/article?id=73&a_id=2047 [accessed 17 March 2015].

Javed, H. (2013) 'How generation Y is energising the "Muslim" brand through novelty t-shirts'. *International Journal of Social Entrepreneurship and Innovation*, 2(1): 33–41.

Jenkins, H. (2003) 'Transmedia storytelling'. *MIT Technology Review*. Available from: www.technologyreview.com/news/401760/transmedia-storytelling/ [accessed 30 August 2015].

Jenkins, H. (2006) *Fans, Bloggers, and Gamers*. New York: New York University Press.

Jennings, P. (2015) *Gen Y Jihadists: Preventing radicalisation in Australia*. Canberra, ACT: Australian Strategic Policy Institute.

Johns, A. (2014) 'Muslim young people online: "Acts of citizenship" in socially networked spaces'. *Social Inclusion*, 2(2): 71–82.

Joosse, P., Bucerius, S.M. and Thompson, S.K. (2015) 'Narratives and counternarratives: Somali-Canadians on recruitment as foreign fighters to Al-Shabaab'. *British Journal of Criminology*, 1–22. DOI: 10.1093/bjc/azu103. First published online, 6 March.

Jouili, J.S. (2013) 'Rapping the republic: Utopia, critique, and Muslim role models in secular France'. *French Politics, Culture and Society*, 31(2): 58–80.

Juul, J. (2005) *Half-Real: Video games between real rules and fictional worlds*. Cambridge, MA: MIT Press.

Kabir, N. (2008) 'To be or not to be an Australian: Focus on Muslim youth'. *National Identities*, 10(4): 399–419.

Kabir, N.A. (2010) *Young British Muslims: Identity, culture, politics and the media*. Edinburgh: Edinburgh University Press.

Kabir, N.A. (2012) *Young American Muslims: Dynamics of identity*. Edinburgh: Edinburgh University Press.

Kashyap, R. and Lewis, V.A. (2013) 'British Muslim youth and religious fundamentalism: A quantitative investigation', *Ethnic and Racial Studies*, 36(12): 2117–2140.

Kearney, J. and Taha, M. (2015) 'Sydney Muslims experience discrimination at three times the rate of other Australians: Study'. *ABC News Online*. Available from: www.abc.net.au/news/2015-11-30/muslims-discrimination-three-times-more-than-other-australians/6985138 [accessed 1 December 2015].

Kelly, P. (2006) 'The entrepreneurial self and "youth at-risk": Exploring the horizons of identity in the twenty-first century'. *Journal of Youth Studies*, 9(1): 17–32.

Kenny, M. and Allard, T. (2015) 'Tony Abbott names Greg Moriarty as new counter-terror tsar'. *Sydney Morning Herald*. Online. Available from: www.smh.com.au/federal-politics/political-news/tony-abbott-names-greg-moriarty-as-new-counterterror-tsar-2015 0524 -gh8kj7.html [accessed 25 May 2015].

Kenny, M. and Wroe, D. (2015) 'Federal budget 2015: Abbott government commits $450m more to fight local jihadis'. *Sydney Morning Herald*. Online. Available from: www.smh.com.au/business/federal-budget/federal-budget-2015-abbott-government-commits-450m-more-to-fight-local-jihadis-20150511-ggz828.html [accessed 12 June 2015].

Kenway, J., Kraack, A. and Hickey-Moody, A. (2006) *Masculinity Beyond the Metropolis*. Basingstoke: Palgrave Macmillan.

Kepel, G. (2000) 'Islamism reconsidered: A running dialogue with modernity'. *Harvard International Review*, 22(2): 22–27.

Kepel, G. (2004) *Jihad: The trail of political Islam*. Cambridge, MA: Harvard University Press.

Khabeer, S.A. and Alhassen, M. (2013) 'Muslim youth cultures'. In J. Hammer and O. Safi (eds) *The Cambridge Companion to American Islam*, Cambridge: Cambridge University Press, pp. 299–311.

Khan, K. (2007) 'Islamic popular music and the discourses of social revolution'. *Muziki*, 4(2): 247–253.

Khan, K. (2011) 'Gendering Islam: Ms Undastood and the search for alternative models of black womanhood', *Muziki*, 8(2): 60–71.

Khan, K. (2013) 'Gangsta tales, culture, Christianity, American Islam and the re-formation of Muslim identities in black American hip-hop music: Scarface'. *Muziki*, 10(1): 94–106.

Khan-Harris, K. (2007) *Extreme Metal: Music culture on the edge*. New York: Berg.

Khosrokhavar, F. (1997) *L'islam des jeunes* [The Islam of Youth]. Paris: Flammarion.

Killian, C. (2007) 'From a community of believers to an Islam of the heart: "Conspicuous" symbols, Muslim practices, and the privatization of religion in France'. *Sociology of Religion*, 68(3): 305–320.

King, M. and Taylor, D.M. (2011) 'The radicalization of homegrown jihadists: A review of theoretical models and social psychological evidence'. *Terrorism and Political Violence*, 23(4): 602–622.

Kirby, A. (2007) 'The London bombers as "self-starters": A case study in indigenous radicalization and the emergence of autonomous cliques'. *Studies in Conflict and Terrorism*, 30(5): 415–428.

Kirkpatrick, G. (2013) *Computer Games and the Social Imaginary*. London: Polity.

Klopfenstein, B. (2006) 'Terrorism and the exploitation of new media'. In A. Kavoori and T. Fraley (eds) *Media, Terrorism, and Theory*, Boulder, CO: Rowman & Littlefield, pp. 107–120.

Knight, M.M. (2007) *The Taqwacores*. London: Telegram.

Kozinets, R.V. (2010) *Netnography: Doing ethnographic research online*. London: Sage.

Krinsky, C. (2008) 'Introduction'. In C. Krinsky (ed.) *Moral panics over Contemporary Children and Youth*, Farnham: Ashgate, pp. 1–8.

Kubala, P. (2005) 'The other face of the video clip. Sami Yusuf and the call for *al-fann al-hadif*'. In *Satellite Broadcasting in the Arab and Islamic Worlds. Culture Wars: The Arabic Music Video Controversy*, The American University Cairo: Transnational Broadcasting Studies, pp. 38–47.

Kugle, S.S.A. (2010) *Homosexuality in Islam: Critical reflection on gay, lesbian, and transgender Muslims*. Oxford: Oneworld.

Kugle, S.S.A. (2013) *Living Out Islam: Voices of gay, lesbian and transgender Muslims*. New York: New York University Press.

Kühle, L. and Lindekilde, L. (2010) *Radicalization among young Muslims in Aarhus*. Research report prepared for the Centre for Studies in Islamism and Radicalisation (CIR) Department of Political Science, Aarhus University, Denmark. Aarhus: CIR. Available from: http://cir.au.dk/fileadmin/site_files/filer_statskundskab/subsites/cir/radicalization_aarhus_FINAL.pdf [accessed 15 March 2015].

Kundnani, A. (2012) 'Radicalisation: The journey of a concept'. *Race and Class*, 54(2): 3–25.

Kundani, A. (2014) *The Muslims are Coming! Islamophobia, extremism and the domestic war on terror*. London: Verso.

Kuruvilla, C. (2014) 'Americans think the country's Muslim population is much bigger than it really is'. *Huffington Post*, 11 February. Available from: www.huffingtonpost.com/2014/11/02/american-muslim-population_n_6076872.html [accessed 15 April 2015].

Larsson, G. (2011a) *Muslims and the New Media: Historical and contemporary debates*. Farnham: Ashgate.

Larsson, G. (2011b) 'The return of Ziryab: Yusuf Islam on music'. In T. Bossius, A. Hager and K. Kahn-Harris (eds) *Religion and Popular Music in Europe*, London: I.B. Tauris, pp. 92–104.

Lawrence, B. (2002) 'Allah online: The practice of global Islam in the information age'. In S. Hoover and L. Clark (eds) *Practicing Religion in the Age of the Media*, New York: Columbia University Press, pp. 237–253.

Le Grand, C. (2015) 'Australia an estranged country to many Muslims including Sheik Omran'. *The Australian*. Online. Available from: www.theaustralian.com.au/in-dep th/community-under-siege/australia-an-estranged-country-to-many-muslims-includi ng-sheik-omran/story-fnubfp6c-1227365820475?sv=62a1286be147096fe35e5a2edd31 d94e [accessed 1 December 2015].

Letsch, C. (2015) 'Laughing at ISIS: Syrian video artists go beyond fear to ridicule jihadis'. *Guardian*. Available from: www.theguardian.com/world/2015/mar/12/laugh ing-at-isis-syrian-video-artists-jihadis-refugee-islamic-state [accessed 26 October 2015].

Leuprecht, C., Hataley, T., Moskalenko, S. and McCauley, C. (2010) 'Containing the narrative: Strategy and tactics in countering the storyline of global jihad'. *Journal of Policing, Intelligence and Counter Terrorism*, 5(1): 42–57.

LeVine, M. (2008) *Heavy Metal Islam: Rock, resistance and the struggle for the soul of Islam*. New York: Three Rivers Press/Random House.

LeVine, M. (2009) 'Doing the devil's work: Heavy metal and the threat to public order in the Muslim world'. *Social Compass*, 56(4): 564–576.

Levitas, R. (2010) *The Concept of Utopia*. Bern: Peter Lang.

Lim, M. (2012) 'Life is local in the imagined global community: Islam and politics in the Indonesian blogosphere'. *Journal of Media and Religion*, 11(3):127–140.

Lipka, M. (2015) 'Seven key changes in the global religious landscape'. Pew Research Center. 2 April. Available from: www.pewforum.org/2015/04/02/religious-projec tions-2010-2050/ [accessed 7 April 2016].

Lo, M. and Aziz, T. (2009) 'Muslim marriage goes online: The use of internet match-making by American Muslims'. *Journal of Religion and Popular Culture*, 21(3). Online. Available from: https://www.questia.com/library/journal/1G1-213033176/m uslim-marriage-goes-online-the-use-of-internet-matchmaking [accessed 11 October 2015].

Lofland, J. and Stark, R. (1965) 'Becoming a world-saver: A theory of conversion to a deviant perspective'. *American Sociological Review*, 30(6): 862–874.

Lovat, T., Nilan, P., Hosseini, H., Samarayi, I., Mansfield, M. and Alexander, W. (2013) 'Australian Muslim jobseekers: Equal Employment Opportunity and equity in the labor market'. *Journal of Muslim Minority Affairs*, 44(3): 435–450.

Lovat, T., Nilan, P., Hosseini, H., Samaryi, I., Mansfield, M. and Alexander, W. (2015) 'Australian Muslim jobseekers and social capital'. *Canadian Ethnic Studies*, 47(2): 165–185.

Lynch, O. (2015) 'Suspicion, exclusion and othering since 9/11: The victimisation of Muslim youth'. In J. Argomaniz and O. Lynch (eds) *International Perspectives on Terrorist Victimisation: An interdisciplinary approach*, London: Palgrave Macmillan, pp. 173–200.

Lyotard, J-F. (1993) *The Postmodern Condition: A report on knowledge*. Trans. G. Bennington and B. Massumi. Minneapolis: University of Minnesota Press.

Mac an Ghaill, M. and Haywood, C. (2014) 'British-born Pakistani and Bangladeshi young men: Exploring unstable concepts of Muslim, Islamophobia and racialization'. *Critical Sociology*, 41(1): 97–114.

Machin, D. and Suleiman, U. (2006) 'Arab and American computer wargames: The influence of a global technology on discourse'. *Critical Discourse Studies*, 3(1): 1–22.

Maffesoli, M. (1996) *The Time of the Tribes: The decline of individualism in mass society*. London: Sage.

Mahmood, S. (2005) *Politics of Piety: The Islamic revival and the feminist subject*. Princeton NJ: Princeton University Press.

Maikovich, A.J. (2005) 'A new understanding of terrorism using cognitive dissonance principles'. *Journal for the Theory of Social Behaviour*, 35(4): 373–397.

Malbon, B. (1998) 'Clubbing, consumption, identity and the spatial practices of everynight life'. In T. Skelton and G. Valentine (eds) *Cool Places: Geographies of youth culture*, London: Routledge, pp. 266–288.

Mamdani, M. (2002) 'Good Muslim, bad Muslim: A political perspective on culture and terrorism'. *American Anthropological Association*, 104(3): 766–775.

Mamouri, A. (2014) 'Why hundreds of westerners are taking up arms in global jihad'. *The Conversation*, 2 July. Available from: http://theconversation.com/why-hundreds-of-westerners-are-taking-up-arms-in-global-jihad-28302 [accessed 15 March 2015].

Mandaville, P. (2001) 'Reimagining Islam in diaspora: The politics of mediated community'. *Gazette*, 63(2–3): 169–186.

Mandaville, P. (2002) 'Muslim youth in Europe'. In S.T. Hunter (ed.) *Islam, Europe's Second Religion: The new social, cultural, and political landscape*. Westport, CT: Praeger, pp. 219–229.

Mandaville, P. (2007a) 'Globalization and the politics of religious knowledge: Pluralizing authority in the Muslim world'. *Theory, Culture and Society*, 24(2): 101–115.

Mandaville, P. (2007b) *Global Political Islam*. London: Routledge.

Mannheim, K. (1936) *Ideology and Utopia*. London: Routledge & Kegan Paul.

Mannheim, K. (1952) 'The sociological problem of generations'. In P. Kecskemeti (ed.) *Essays on the Sociology of Knowledge*, London: Routledge & Kegan Paul, pp. 286–320.

Mariani, E. (2011) 'Cyber-fatwas, sermons and media campaigns: Amr Khaled and Omar Bakri Muhammad in search of new audiences'. In M. Van Bruinessen and S. Allievi (eds) *Producing Islamic knowledge: Transmission and dissemination in Western Europe*, London: Routledge, pp. 142–168.

Marshall, A. (2015) *Republic or Death! Travels in search of a national anthem*. London: Random House.

Marshall, D. (1997) *Celebrity and Power: Fame and contemporary culture*. Minneapolis: University of Minnesota Press.

Martin Jones, D. and Smith, M.L.R. (2014) 'Western responsibility and response to the death cult of the Islamic State'. *Quadrant* (October): 10–18.

Marx, K. (1978/1852) 'The eighteenth brumaire of Louis Bonaparte'. In R.C. Tucker (ed.) *The Marx-Engels Reader*. 2nd edn. New York and London: W.W. Norton.

Marx, K. and Engels, F. (1985) *The Communist Manifesto*. Chicago, IL: Gateway Editions.

Mayer, A. and Timberlake, J.M. (2014) '"The fist in the face of God": Heavy metal music and decentralized cultural diffusion'. *Sociological Perspectives*, 57(1): 27–51.

McAlveen, F. (2011) *Islam Exposed: Islam 101 and what it means to America. Are we in danger? Are Muslims a real threat to our freedom?* Alabama: Big Mac Publishers.

McCauley, C. and Moskalenko, S. (2008) 'Mechanisms of political radicalization: Pathways toward terrorism'. *Terrorism and Political Violence*, 20(3): 415–433.

McCauley, C. and Moskalenko, S. (2011) *Friction: How radicalisation happens to them and us.* Oxford: Oxford University Press.

McCauley, C. and Moskalenko, S. (2014) 'Toward a profile of lone wolf terrorists: What moves an individual from radical opinion to radical action'. *Terrorism and Political Violence*, 26(1): 69–85.

McDowell, A. (2014) 'Warriors and terrorists: Antagonism as strategy in Christian hardcore and Muslim "Taqwacore" punk rock'. *Qualitative Sociology*, 37: 255–276.

McDowell, A. (2016) '"This for the brown kids!" Racialization and the formation of "Muslim" Punk Rock'. *Sociology of Race and Ethnicity*. Published online, 9 May. DOI: 10.1177/2332649216647747.

McGrath, B. and McGarry, O. (2014) 'The religio-cultural dimensions of life for young Muslim women in a small Irish town'. *Journal of Youth Studies*, 17(7): 948–964.

McRobbie, A. (2011) 'Unveiling France's border strategies'. *Feminist Media Studies*, 11(1): 101–106.

Meer, N. (2010) *Citizenship, Identity, and the Politics of Multiculturalism: The rise of Muslim consciousness.* Basingstoke: Palgrave Macmillan.

Meier, S. (2013) '"Truth, justice and the Islamic way": Conceiving the cosmopolitan Muslim superhero in The 99'. In S. Denson, C. Meyer and D. Stein (eds) *Transnational Perspectives on Graphic Narratives: Comics at the crossroads*, London: Bloomsbury, pp. 181–196.

Meijer, R. (2014) 'Islamist movements and the political after the Arab uprisings'. In M. Lynch (ed.) *Rethinking Islamist Politics.* Project on Middle East Political Science (POMEPS), George Washington University. Washington, DC: George Washington University, pp. 44–46.

Mendelsohn, B. (2012) 'God vs. Westphalia: Radical Islamist movements and the battle for organising the world'. *Review of International Studies*, 38(3): 589–613.

Messerschmidt, J. (1993) *Masculinities and Crime: Critique and reconceptualization of theory.* Lanham, MD: Rowman and Littlefield.

Mills, T. and Bucci, N. (2016) '"ISIS cheerleader" among five Melbourne men stopped from sailing to Indonesia'. *Sydney Morning Herald.* Online. Available from: www. smh.com.au/national/isis-cheerleader-among-five-melbourne-men-stopped-from-saili ng-to-indonesia-20160510-gos38b.html [accessed 16 July 2016].

Mirkin, B. (2013) *Arab Spring: Demographics in a region in transition.* Arab Human Development Report. Research Paper Series, United Nations Development Program (UNDP). Available from: www.arab-hdr.org/publications/other/ahdrps/AHDR%20ENG%20Arab%20Spring%20Mirkinv3.pdf [accessed 14 April 2014].

Mishra, S. and Shirazi, F. (2010) 'Hybrid identities: American Muslim women speak'. *Gender, Place and Culture*, 17(2): 191–209.

Miyakawa, F. (2015) 'Poetic Protest: Women, hip-hop, and Islam'. *The Avid Listener*, 28 September. Available from: www.theavidlistener.com/2015/09/poetic-protest-wom en-hip-hop-and-islam.html [accessed 12 April 2016].

Modood, T. (2005) 'Foreword'. In T. Abbas (ed.) *Muslim Britain: Communities under pressure*, London: Zed Books, pp. 1–17.

Modood, T. (2013) *Multiculturalism.* Cambridge: Polity Press.

Moghaddam, F.M. (2005) 'The staircase to terrorism: A psychological exploration'. *American Psychologist*, 60(2): 161–169.

Moje, E. (2002) 'But where are the youth? On the value of integrating youth culture into literacy theory'. *Educational Theory*, 52(1): 97–121.

Monson, M. (2012) 'Race-based fantasy realm: Essentialism in the World of Warcraft'. *Games and Culture*, 7(1): 48–71.

Moore, R. and Roberts, M. (2009) 'Do-It-yourself mobilization: Punk and social movements'. *Mobilization: An International Journal*, 14(3): 273–291.

Moosavi, L. (2015) 'Orientalism at home: Islamophobia in the representations of Islam and Muslims by the New Labour government'. *Ethnicities*, 15(5): 652–674.

Mosemghvdlishvili, L. and Jansz, J. (2013) 'Framing and praising Allah on YouTube: Exploring user-created videos about Islam and the motivations for producing them'. *New Media and Society*, 15(4): 482–500.

Mozaffari, M. (2007) 'What is Islamism? History and definition of a concept'. *Totalitarian Movements and Political Religions*, 8(1): 17–33.

Mullins, S. (2009) 'Parallels between crime and terrorism: A social psychological perspective'. *Studies in Conflict and Terrorism*, 32(9): 811–830.

Mullins, S. (2011) 'Islamist terrorism and Australia: An empirical examination of the "home-grown" threat'. *Terrorism and Political Violence*, 23(2): 254–285.

Mullins, S. (2013) '"Global jihad": The Canadian experience'. *Terrorism and Political Violence*, 25(5): 734–776.

Murthy, D. (2013) 'Muslim punk music online: Piety and protest in the digital age'. In K. Salhi (ed.) *Music, Culture and Identity in the Muslim World*, New York and London: Routledge, pp. 162–179.

Musgrove, F. (1964) *Youth and the Social Order*. London: Routledge & Kegan Paul.

Mushaben, J. (2008) 'Gender, hiphop and pop-Islam: The urban identities of Muslim youth in Germany'. *Citizenship Studies*, 12(5): 507–526.

Musso, S., Fanget, D. and Cherabi, K. (2002) 'An Arab-Muslim view'. *Prospect: Quarterly Review of Comparative Education*, 32(2): 85–92.

Naber, N. (2006) 'Arab American femininities: Beyond Arab virgin/American(ized) whore'. *Feminist Studies*, 32(1): 87–111.

Nacos, B.L. (2015) 'Young western women, fandom, and ISIS'. *E-International Relations*. Online. Available from: www.e-ir.info/2015/05/05/young-western-women-fandom-and-isis/ [accessed 20 September 2015].

Nasir, K.M. (2015) 'The September 11 generation, hip-hop and human rights'. *Journal of Sociology*, 51(4): 1039–1051.

Nasir, K.M. (2016) *Globalized Muslim Youth in the Asia Pacific*. Basingstoke: Palgrave Macmillan.

Nasr, V. (2010) *The Rise of Islamic Capitalism: Why the new Muslim middle class is the key to defeating extremism*. Washington, DC: Council on Foreign Relations.

Nayak, A. (2003) *Race, Place and Globalisation: Youth cultures in a changing world*. Oxford: Berg.

Nayak, A. and Kehily, M.J. (2008) *Gender, Youth and Culture: Young masculinities and femininities*. Basingstoke: Palgrave Macmillan.

Newgren, K. (2010) 'BioShock to system smart choices in video games'. In C. Detweiler (ed.) *Halos and Avatars: Playing video games with God*, Louisville, KY: Westminster John Knox Press, pp. 135–148.

Nilan, P. (2006) 'The reflexive youth culture of devout Muslim youth in Indonesia'. In P. Nilan and C. Feixa (eds) *Global Youth? Hybrid identities, plural worlds*, London and New York: Routledge, pp. 91–110.

Nilan, P. (2008) 'Youth transitions to urban, middle-class marriage in Indonesia: Faith, family and finances'. *Journal of Youth Studies*, 11(1): 65–82.

Nilan, P. (2011) 'The future of youth sociology must cross cultures'. *Youth Studies Australia*, 30(3): 20–26.

Nilan, P. (2012a) 'Young, Muslim and looking for work in Australia'. *Youth Studies Australia*, 31(1): 48–59.

Nilan, P. (2012b) 'Young women and everyday media engagement in Muslim Southeast Asia'. In Y. Kim (ed.) *The Precarious Self: Women and the media in Asia*, Basingstoke: Palgrave Macmillan, pp. 100–143.

Nilan, P. (2013) 'Une nouvelle identité chez les jeunes javanais?' In S. Ryan and J. Bonneville (eds) *Enjeux identitaires*, Paris: Les Indes Savantes, pp. 61–77.

Nilan, P. (2016a) 'Space, time and symbol in urban Indonesian schoolboy gangs'. In C. Feixa, C. Leccardi and P. Nilan (eds) *Youth, Space and Time: Agoras and chronotopes in the global city*, Leiden: Brill/KITLV Press, pp. 276–299.

Nilan, P. (2016b) 'Local modernities: Young women socializing together'. In K. Robinson (ed.) *Youth Identities and Social Transformations in Modern Indonesia*, Leiden: Brill/KITLV Press, pp. 156–177.

Nilan, P., Donaldson, M. and Howson, R. (2009) 'Indonesian Muslim masculinities in Australia'. In M. Donaldson, R. Hibbins, R. Howson and B. Pease (eds) *Migrant Men: Critical studies of masculinities and the migration experience*, London: Routledge, pp. 172–189.

Nilan, P. and FeixaC. (eds) (2006) *Global Youth? Hybrid identities, plural worlds*. London and New York: Routledge.

Noble, G. and Poynting, S. (2008) 'Neither relaxed nor comfortable: The uncivil regulation of the Muslim other'. In R. Pain and S. Smith (eds) *Fear: Critical geopolitics and everyday life*, Farnham: Ashgate, pp. 129–138.

Nordbruck, G. (2010) *Muslim Youth Cultures in Germany: Between fun, protest, and service to society*. Odense: Syddansk Universitet Center for Mellemøststudier.

Northcote, J. and Casimiro, S. (2010) 'Muslim citizens and belonging in Australia'. In S. Yasmeen (ed.) *Muslims in Australia: The dynamics of exclusion and inclusion*, Melbourne: Melbourne University Press, pp. 141–162.

O'Brien, J. (2013) 'Muslim American youth and secular hip hop: Manifesting "cool piety" through musical practices'. *Poetics*, 41(2): 99–121.

Olding, R. (2015) 'Religious radicalisation – it's sudden, secret and unexpected'. *Sydney Morning Herald*. Online. Available from: www.smh.com.au/nsw/religious-radicalisation–its-sudden-secret-and-unexpected-20150213-13dyan.html [accessed 15 February 2015].

Onega, S. and Landa, J.A.G. (1996) *Narratology*. New York: Longman.

O'Neill, S. and McGrory, D. (2006) *The Suicide Factory: Abu Hamza and the Finsbury Park Mosque*. London: Harper Perennial.

OnIslam (2014) 'Hajj "selfie fad" condemned by scholars'. *OnIslam*, 1 October. Available from: www.onislam.net/english/news/global/478125-selfies-fever-spoil-hajj-tranquility.html [accessed 25 May 2015].

Osman, M.N.M. (2014) 'ISIS's caliphate utopia'. RSIS Commentary no. 46, July 2014. Available from: http://hdl.handle.net/10220/24344 [accessed 15 March 2015].

Osumare, H. (2007) *The Africanist Aesthetic in Global Hip-Hop: Power moves*. New York: Palgrave.

Otterbeck, J. (2008) 'Battling over the public sphere: Islamic reactions to the music of today'. *Contemporary Islam*, 2: 211–228.

Otterbeck, J. (2014) 'What is Islamic Arts? And what makes art Islamic? The example of the Islamic discourse on music'. *The CILE Journal*, 1(1): 7–29.

Ouzgane, L. (2003) 'Islamic masculinities'. *Men and Masculinities*, 5(3): 231–235.

Pandith, F. and Havelicek, S. (2015) 'The female face of terror'. *The Telegraph*, 28 January. Available from: www.telegraph.co.uk/news/uknews/terrorism-in-the-uk/11374026/The-female-face-of-terror.html [accessed 6 March 2016].

Pankhurst, R. (2013) *The Inevitable Caliphate? A history of the struggle for global Islamic union, 1924 to the present*. Oxford: Oxford University Press.

Pantucci, R. (2015) *'We Love Death as you Love Life': Britain's suburban terrorists*. London: Hurst.

Papacharissi, Z. (2009) 'The virtual geographies of social networks: A comparative analysis of Facebook, Linkedin, and ASmallWorld'. *New Media and Society*, 11(1–2): 199–220.

Papacharissi, Z. (2014) *Affective Publics: Sentiment, technology and politics*. Oxford: Oxford University Press.

Pariser, E. (2011) *The Filter Bubble: What the internet is hiding from you*. London: Penguin Books.

Parker, L. and Nilan, P. (2013) *Adolescents in Contemporary Indonesia*. London and New York: Routledge.

Patil, T.V. (2015) '"You can't have the struggle without the ugly fringe" – Publicness in Australian national imagination: Media representations of the Muslim demonstrations in Sydney in 2012'. *Continuum: Journal of Media and Cultural Studies*, 29(1): 57–69.

Patterson, C. (2015) 'Role-playing the multiculturalist umpire: Loyalty and war in BioWare's *Mass Effect* series'. *Games and Culture*, 10(3): 207–228.

Payne, K. (2009) 'Winning the battle of ideas: Propaganda ideology and terror'. *Studies in Conflict and Terrorism*, 32(2): 109–128.

Payne, S. (2014) 'Sex shop El Asira targets 1.8bn Muslims through erotica chain Beate Uhse'. *International Business Times*, 5 June. Online. Available from: www.ibtimes.co.uk/halal-sex-shop-el-asira-targets-1-8bn-muslims-through-erotica-chain-beate-uhse-1451431 [accessed 25 May 2015].

Peek, L. (2011) *Behind the Backlash: Muslim Americans after 9/11*. Philadelphia PA: Temple University Press.

Peucker, M., Roose, J.M. and Akbarzadeh, S. (2014) 'Muslim active citizenship in Australia: Socioeconomic challenges and the emergence of a Muslim elite'. *Australian Journal of Political Science*, 49(2): 282–299.

Pew Research Center (2011) *The Future of the Global Muslim Population*. Pew Forum. Available from: www.pewforum.org/files/2011/01/FutureGlobalMuslimPopulation-WebPDF-Feb10.pdf [accessed 14 April 2015].

Pieslak, J. (2015) *Radicalism and Music*. Middletown CT: Wesleyan University Press.

Pisoiu, D. (2013) 'Coming to believe "truths" about Islamist radicalization in Europe'. *Terrorism and Political Violence*, 25(2): 246–263.

Plenel, E. (2016) *For the Muslims: Islamophobia in France*. Trans. D. Fernbach. London: Verso.

Pollard, R. (2015) 'Taking the mickey out of terrorism'. *Sydney Morning Herald.* Online. Available from: www.smh.com.au/world/mickey-mouse-rears-on-the-prez-ta king-on-terrorism-with-satire-20151022-gkfpol [accessed 10 May 2016].

Polletta, F. (2006) *It Was Like a Fever: Storytelling in protest and politics.* Chicago, IL: University of Chicago Press.

Poynting, S. and Mason, V. (2007) 'The resistible rise of Islamophobia: Anti-Muslim racism in the UK and Australia before 11 September 2001'. *Journal of Sociology,* 43 (1), 61–86.

PoyntingS. and MasonV. (2008) 'The new integrationism, the State and Islamophobia: Retreat from multiculturalism in Australia'. *International Journal of Law, Crime and Justice,* 36(4): 230–246.

Poynting, S. and Noble, G. (2006) 'Muslims and Arabs in the Australian media since 11 September 2001'. *Global Media Journal,* 2(2): 89–102.

Poynting, S., Noble, G., Tabar, P. and Collins, J. (2004) *Bin Laden in the Suburbs: Criminalising the Arab other.* Sydney: Federation Press/Institute of Criminology.

Pratt, D. and Woodlock, R. (2016) 'Introduction: Understanding Islamophobia'. In D. Pratt and R. Woodlock (eds) *Fear of Muslims? International perspectives on Islamophobia,* Dordrecht: Springer, pp. 1–18.

Rabasa, A. and Benard, C. (2014) *Eurojihad: Patterns of Islamist radicalization and terrorism in Europe.* Cambridge: Cambridge University Press.

Rahimullah, R.H., Lamar, S. and Abdalla, M. (2013) 'Understanding violent radicalization amongst Muslims: A review of the literature'. *Journal of Psychology and Behavioral Science,* 1(1): 19–35.

Ramakrishna, K. (2011) 'From virtual to violent: Preliminary conceptual explorations of religious radicalisation in youth'. In Southeast Asian Regional Center for Counter-Terrorism (ed.) *Youth and Terrorism: A selection of articles,* Kuala Lumpur, Malaysia: SEARCCT, pp. 1–14.

Rand Europe (2011) *Synthesis report on the results from work package 2: Inventory of the factors of radicalization and counterterrorism interventions.* Available from: www. safire-project-results.eu/documents/deliverables/2-inventory-of-the-factors-of-radicali zation-and-counterterrorism-interventions.pdf [accessed 5 May 2015].

Rane, H., Nathie, M., Isakhan, B. and Abdalla, M. (2010) 'Towards understanding what Australia's Muslims really think'. *Journal of Sociology,* 47(2): 123–143.

Rantakallio, I. (2011) 'Making music, making Muslims: A case study of Islamic hip hop and the discursive construction of Muslim identities on the internet'. Unpublished M.A. thesis, University of Helsinki.

Rashid, T. (2007) 'Configuration of national identity and citizenship in Australia: Migration, ethnicity and religious minorities'. *Alternatives: Turkish Journal of International Relations,* 6(3&4): 1–27.

Rauf, F.A. (2005) *What's Right with Islam Is What's Right with America.* New York: HarperCollins.

Read, J.G. (2004) *Culture, Class, and Work among Arab-American women.* New York: LFB Scholarly Publishing.

Read, J.G. (2015) 'Gender, religious identity, and civic engagement among Arab Muslims in the United States'. *Sociology of Religion,* 76(1): 30–48.

Reichmuth, P. and Werning, S. (2006) 'Pixel pashas, digital djinns'. *ISIM Review,* 18: 46–47.

Rettburg, J.W. (2013) *Blogging.* 2nd edn. London: Polity.

Ridley, Y. (2006) 'Post script to pop culture in the name of Islam'. *The Revival*. Wednesday 16 August. Available from: www.therevival.co.uk/forum/general/172 [accessed 5 October 2015].

Rieger, D., Frischlich, L. and Bente, G. (2013) *Propaganda 2.0: Psychological effects of right wing and Islamist extremist internet videos*. Cologne: Wolters Kluwer Deutschland GmbH.

Ritzer, G. (1993) *The McDonaldization of Society*. Thousand Oaks, CA: Sage.

Roach, K. (2011) *The 9/11 Effect: Comparative counter-terrorism*. Cambridge: Cambridge University Press.

Robards, B. and Bennett, A. (2011) 'MyTribe: Postsubcultural manifestations of belonging on social network sites'. *Sociology*, 45(2): 303–317.

Robins, K. (1995) 'Cyberspace and world we live in'. In M. Featherstone and R. Burrows (eds) *Cyberspace/Cyberbodies/Cyberpunk: Cultures of technological embodiment*, London: Sage, pp. 135–156.

Rodrigo, A. (2016) 'I follow Shari'ah. This is what it really means to me'. *Sydney Morning Herald*, 8 July. Online. Available from: www.dailylife.com.au/news-and-views/dl-culture/i-follow-shariah-this-is-what-it-really-means-to-me-20160707-gq143i.html [accessed 23 July 2016].

Rogan, H. (2006) *Jihadism Online: A study of how al-Qaida and radical Islamist groups use the internet for terrorist purposes*. Kjeller, Norway: Forsvarets Forsknings Institutt. Available from: www.ffi.no/no/rapporter/06-00915.pdf [accessed 2 June 2015].

Rogers, S. and Johnson, B. (2016) 'Saudi ELLs' digital gameplay habits and effects on SLA: A case study'. Paper presented to the Society for Information Technology and Teacher Education International Conference, 21 March 2016 in Savannah, GA. ISBN: 978-1-939797-13-1.

Rollings, A. and Adams, E. (2003) *Andrew Rollings and Ernest Adams on Game Design*. Indianapolis, IN: New Riders Publishing.

Roose, J. (2012) 'Young Muslims of Australia: Anatomy of a multicultural success story'. *The La Trobe Journal*, 89: 151–163.

Roose, J.M. and Harris, A. (2015) 'Muslim citizenship in everyday Australian civic spaces'. *Journal of Intercultural Studies*, 36(4): 468–486.

Rose, T. (1994a) 'A style nobody can deal with: Politics, style and the postindustrial city in hip hop'. In A. Ross and T. Rose (eds) *Microphone Fiends: Youth music and youth culture*, London: Routledge, pp. 71–88.

Rose, T. (1994b) *Black Noise: Rap music and black culture in contemporary America*. Hanover, NH: Wesleyan University Press.

Roy, O. (2004) *Globalized Islam: The search for a new ummah*. New York: Columbia University Press.

Roy, O. (2007) 'Islamic terrorist radicalisation in Europe'. In S. Amghar, A. Boubekeur and M. Emerson (eds) *European Islam: Challenges for public policy and society*, Brussels: Centre for European Policy Studies, pp. 52–61.

Roy, O. (2008) *Al Qaeda in the West as a Youth Movement: The power of a narrative*. CEPS Policy Brief no. 168. Available from: www.microconflict.eu/wp-content/uploads/2016/06/PWP2_OR.pdf [accessed 23 April 2015].

Rozario, S. (2012) 'Islamic marriage: A haven in an uncertain world'. *Culture and Religion*, 13(2): 159–175.

Rozario, S. and Samuel, G. (2012) 'Young Muslim women and the Islamic family: Reflections on conflicting ideals in British Bangladeshi life'. In T. Lovat (ed.)

Women in Islam: Reflections on historical and contemporary research, Dordrecht: Springer, pp. 25–42.

RT (2015) 'British jihadist brides on run from ISIS, trying to return to UK'. 14 May. Online. Available from: http://rt.com/uk/258497-british-jihadi-brides-escape/ [accessed 19 May 2015].

Rushdie, S. (1988) *The Satanic Verses*. London: Viking.

Rushkoff, D. (2013) *Present Shock: When everything happens now*. New York: Current/ Penguin.

Ryan, L. (2011) 'Muslim women negotiating collective stigmatisation: "We're just normal people"'. *Sociology*, 45(6): 1045–1060.

Ryan, L. (2014) '"Islam does not change": Young people narrating negotiations of religion and identity'. *Journal of Youth Studies*, 17(4): 446–460.

Saeed, A. (2014) 'Between hip-hop and Muhammad: European Muslim hip-hop and identity'. In G. Nash, K. Kerr-Koch and S.E. Hackett (eds) *Postcolonialism and Islam: Theory, literature, culture, society and film*, London and New York: Routledge, pp. 181–192.

Safran, J. (2015) 'Musa Cerantonio: Muslim convert and radical supporter of Islamic State'. *Sydney Morning Herald*, 17 January. Available from: www.smh.com.au/good-weekend/musa-cerantonio-muslim-convert-and-radical-supporter-of-islamic-st ate-20150115-121c8s.html [accessed 7 April 2016].

Sageman, M. (2004) *Understanding Terror Networks*. Philadelphia: Pennsylvania University Press.

Sageman, M. (2008) *Leaderless Jihad: Terror networks in the twenty-first century*. Philadelphia: University of Pennsylvania Press.

Sageman, M. (2014) 'The stagnation in terrorism research'. *Terrorism and Political Violence*, 26(4): 565–580.

SAIC (2007) *Games: A look at emerging trends, uses, threats and opportunities in influence activities*. Science Applications International Corporation. Available from: https://edwardsnowden.com/wp-content/uploads/2013/12/Third.pdf [accessed 5 September 2015].

Said, B. (2012) 'Hymns (nasheeds): A contribution to the study of the jihadist culture'. *Studies in Conflict and Terrorism*, 35(12): 863–879,

Said, E.W. (1978) *Orientalism*. New York: Vintage Books.

Said, E.W. (1997) *Covering Islam: How the media and the experts determine how we see the rest of the world*. London: Vintage Books.

Saltman, E.M. and Smith, M. (2015) *'Till Martyrdom Do Us Part': Gender and the ISIS phenomenon*. London: Institute for Strategic Dialogue.

Sametoğlu, S.U. (2015) 'Halalscapes: Leisure, fun and aesthestic spaces created by young Muslim women of the Gülen movement in France and Germany', In E. Toğuşlu (ed.) *Everyday Life Practices of Muslims in Europe*, Leuven, Belgium: Leuven University Press, pp. 143–164.

Samiezade'-Yazd, S. (2015) 'Zayn Malik and the pains of being a Muslim pop star'. *Guardian*, 8 April. Online. Available from: www.theguardian.com/music/musicblog/2015/apr/07/zayn-malik-muslim-pop-star [accessed 26 May 2015].

Samuel, T.K. (2012) *Reaching the Youth: Countering the terrorist narrative*. Kuala Lumpur, Malaysia: Southeast Asia Regional Centre for Counter-Terrorism (SEARCCT).

Sanchez, S.E. (2014) 'The internet and the radicalization of Muslim women'. Paper presented at the annual meeting of the Western Political Science Association, Seattle, April 2014. Available from: www.researchgate.net/publication/267568378_The_Internet_and_the_Radicalization_of_Muslim_Women [accessed 5 March 2015].

Sanghera, G.S. and Thapar-Björkert, S. (2012) '"Let's talk about? ... Men": Young British Pakistani Muslim women's narratives about co-ethnic men in "postcolonial" Bradford'. *International Journal of Postcolonial Studies*, 14(4): 591–612.

Savage, S. and Liht, J. (2009) 'Radical religious speech: The ingredients of a binary world view'. In Hare, I. and Weinstein, J. (eds) *Extreme Speech and Democracy*, Oxford: Oxford University Press, pp. 488–507.

SBS (2014) 'Computer games will increase in popularity'. SBS Broadcasting. 6 March. Online Available from: www.sbs.com.au/news/article/2014/03/06/computer-games-will-increase-popularity [accessed 31 July 2015].

SBS (2015) 'Western Jihadis: An Australian speaks out from Syria's frontline'. SBS Broadcasting. 24 March. Online. Available from: www.sbs.com.au/news/dateline/story/western-jihadis-australian-speaks-out-syrias-frontline [accessed 18 May 2015].

Schmid, A.P. (2011) 'The definition of terrorism'. In A.P. Schmid (ed.) *The Routledge Handbook of Terrorism Research*, London and New York: Routledge, pp. 39–98.

Schmidt, G. (2004) 'Islamic identity formation among young Muslims: The case of Denmark, Sweden and The United States'. *Journal of Muslim Affairs*, 1(1): 31–45.

Schulzke, M. (2013) 'The virtual war on terror: Counterterrorism narratives in video games'. *New Political Science*, 35(4): 586–603.

Scott, J.W. (2007) *The Politics of the Veil*. Princeton NJ: Princeton University Press.

Segall, L. (2016) 'Meet the hacker fighting ISIS with porn'. *CNN*. Available from: http://money.cnn.com/2016/06/16/technology/isis-hacker-porn-gay-pride/ [accessed 16 June 2016].

Shaw, I.G.R. (2010) 'Playing war'. *Social and Cultural Geography*, 11: 789–803.

Sheffield, H. (2015) 'Isis has built a global brand using Nutella, celebrity and social media'. *Independent*, 9 March. Online. Available from: www.independent.co.uk/news/business/news/isis-has-built-a-global-brand-using-nutella-celebrity-and-social-media-10095915.html [accessed 20 September 2015].

Sherifdeen, S.A.S. (2011) 'Youth, community and education: A study on Australian Muslim youth'. Unpublished Ph.D. thesis, Victoria University, Melbourne.

Shifman, L. (2013) *Memes in Digital Culture*. Cambridge, MA: MIT Press.

Silber, M.D. and Bhatt, A. (2007) *Radicalization in the West: The homegrown threat*. New York: New York Police Department.

Silber, M.D. (2012) *The Al Qaeda factor: Plots against the West*. Philadelphia: University of Pennsylvania Press.

Silke, A. (2008) 'Holy warriors: Exploring the psychological processes of jihadi radicalization'. *European Journal of Criminology*, 5(1): 99–123.

Silva, C. (2016) 'The end of ISIS? Islamic State leaders prepare for fall of caliphate in Iraq and Syria with plans for global terror network'. *International Business Times*. Available from: www.ibtimes.com/end-isis-islamic-state-leaders-prepare-fall-caliphate-iraq-syria-plans-global-terror-2391152 [accessed 15 July 2016].

Sirin, S.R. and Fine, M. (2007) 'Hyphenated selves: Muslim American youth negotiating identities on the fault lines of global conflict'. *Applied Developmental Science*, 11(3): 151–163.

Sirseloudi, M. (2012) 'The meaning of religion and identity for the violent radicalisation of the Turkish diaspora in Germany'. *Terrorism and Political Violence*, 24(5): 807–824.

Šisler, V. (2008) 'Digital Arabs: Representation in video games'. *European Journal of Cultural Studies*, 11(2): 203–220.

Šisler, V. (2013) 'Playing the Muslim hero: Construction of identity in video games'. In H. Campbell (ed.) *Digital Religion: Understanding religious practice in new media worlds*, London and New York: Routledge, pp. 136–146.

Šisler, V. (2014) 'From Kuma/War to Quraish: Representation of Islam in Arab and American video games'. In H. Campbell and G. Grieve (eds) *Playing with Religion in Digital Games*, Bloomington: Indiana University Press, pp. 109–133.

Šisler, V. (2016) 'Procedural religion: Methodological reflections on studying religion in video games'. *New Media and Society*. Online, pp. 1–16. DOI: 10.1177/1461444816649923.

Sobh, M. (2014) 'American Muslim consumer market worth billions'. *WBEZ*. 28 January. Online. Available from: www.wbez.org/news/culture/american-muslim-consumer-market-worth-billions-109587 [accessed 10 December 2015].

Sohrabi, H. (2015) 'Identity and Muslim leadership: The case of Australian Muslim leaders. *Contemporary Islam*. Online first: pp. 1–16. DOI: 10.1007/s11562–11015–0325–0323.

Sohrabi, H. and K. Farquharson (2012) 'Discursive integration and Muslims in Australia'. In F. Mansouri and V. Marotta (eds) *Muslims in the West and the Challenges of Belonging*. Melbourne: Melbourne University Press, pp. 134–156.

Sohrabi, H. and Farquharson, K. (2015) 'Social integration of Australian Muslims: A dramaturgical perspective'. *Journal of Sociology*. Online first: pp. 1–16. DOI: 10.1177/1440783314562415.

Soliman, A. (2016) 'European Muslims' engagement in the public sphere: Soft counterpublics'. *International Review of Sociology*. Online. DOI: 10.1080/03906701.2016.1148351.

Solomon, T. (2011) 'Hardcore Muslims: Islamic themes in Turkish rap between diaspora and homeland'. In K. Van Nieuwkerk (ed.) *Muslim Rap, Halal Soaps, and Revolutionary Theater: Artistic developments in the Muslim world*, Austin: University of Texas Press, pp. 27–53.

Somers, M.R. (1994) 'The narrative constitution of identity: A relational and network approach'. *Theory and Society*, 23(5): 605–649.

Song, M. (2012) 'Part of the mainstream? British Muslim students and Islamic student associations'. *Journal of Youth Studies*, 15(2): 143–160.

Spalek, B. and Lambert, R. (2008) 'Muslim communities, counter-terrorism and counter-radicalisation: A critically reflective approach to engagement'. *International Journal of Law, Crime and Justice*, 36(4): 257–270.

Speck, S. (2013) 'Ulrich Beck's "reflecting faith": Individualization, religion and the desecularization of reflexive modernity'. *Sociology*, 47(1): 157–172.

Speckhard, A. (2008) 'The emergence of female suicide terrorists'. *Studies in Conflict and Terrorism*, 3: 1–29.

Spivak, G.C. (1987) *In Other Worlds: Essays in cultural politics*. New York: Methuen.

Starrett, G. (2003) 'Muslim identities and the great chain of buying'. In D. Eickleman and J. Anderson (eds) *New Media in the Muslim World: The emerging public sphere*, Bloomington: Indiana University Press, pp. 80–101.

Stephenson, P. (2010) 'Home-growing Islam: The role of Australian Muslim youth in intra- and inter-cultural change'. *NCEIS Research Papers*, 3(6): 1–21.

Steuter, E. and Wills, D. (2010) '"The vermin have struck again": Dehumanizing the enemy in post 9/11 media representations'. *Media, War and Conflict*, 3(2): 152–167.

Suleiman, Y. (2009) *Contextualising Islam in Britain: Exploratory perspectives*. Cambridge: Centre of Islamic Studies.

Swedenburg, T. (2002) 'Hip hop music in the transglobal Islamic underground'. *The Black Arts Quarterly*, 6(3): 16–18.

Swedenburg, T. (2007) 'Imagined youths'. *Middle East Report*, 37(245): 1–4.

Swedenburg, T. (2010) 'Fun-da-mental's "jihad rap"'. In L. Herrera and A. Bayat (eds) *Being Young and Muslim: New cultural politics in the global south and north*, New York: Oxford University Press, pp. 291–308.

Sweetman, P. (2004) 'Tourists and travellers? "Subcultures", reflexive identities and neo-tribal sociality'. In A. Bennett and K. Kahn-Harris (eds) *After Subcultures: Critical studies in contemporary youth culture*, Basingstoke: Palgrave Macmillan, pp. 79–93.

Sylvan, R. (2002) *Traces of the Spirit: The religious dimensions of popular music*. New York: New York University Press.

Taha, M. (2015a) 'Young Australian Iraqis say self-styled preachers are radicalising youth, community calls for open debate'. *ABC News Online*. Available from: www.abc.net.au/news/2015-01-19/self-styled-preachers-blamed-for-radicalising-youth/6026102 [accessed 19 January 2015].

Taha, M. (2015b) 'Year 12 student Amar Hadid releases rap song paying tribute to Sydney siege victims'. *ABC News Online*. Available from: www.abc.net.au/news/2015-12-15/year-12-student-amar-hadid-releases-rap-song-paying-tribute-to-/7029648 [accessed 8 May 2016].

Tarlo, E. (2010) *Visibly Muslim: Fashion, politics, faith*. Oxford and New York: Berg.

Tawil Souri, H. (2007) 'The political battlefield of pro-Arab video games on Palestinian screens'. *Comparative Studies of South Asia, Africa and the Middle East*, 27(3): 536–551.

Taylor, B. (2008) *Entertainment Theology: New edge spirituality in a digital democracy*. Grand Rapids MI: Baker Academic.

Taylor, L. (2015) 'Muslim Tinder: Seeking love with a young Muslim hipster? There's an app for that'. *SBS News*. Available from: www.sbs.com.au/news/article/2015/02/10/muslim-tinder-seeking-love-young-muslim-hipster-theres-app [accessed 12 January 2016].

The Guardian (2014) 'Australians think Muslim population is nine times greater than it really is'. *Guardian*, 30 October. Online. Available from: www.theguardian.com/australia-news/datablog/2014/oct/30/australians-think-muslim-population-nine-times-greater[accessed 1 December 2015].

The Guardian (2015) 'Government steps up efforts to prevent young Muslims becoming jihadis'. *The Guardian*, 13 February. Online. Available from: www.theguardian.com/politics/2015/feb/13/prevent-counter-terrorism-support [accessed 18 May 2015].

Threadgold, S. and Nilan, P. (2009) 'Reflexivity of contemporary youth, risk and cultural capital'. *Current Sociology*, 57(1): 47–68.

Tilly, C. (2004) 'Terror, terrorism, terrorists'. *Sociological Theory*, 22: 5–13.

Tindongan, C.W. (2011) 'Negotiating Muslim youth identity in a post-9/11 world'. *High School Journal*, 95(1): 72–87.

Topsfield, J. (2016) 'Jihad Selfie: The story of how Indonesian teenagers are recruited to Islamic State'. *Sydney Morning Herald*, 24 July. Online. Available from: www.sm h.com.au/world/jihad-selfie-the-story-of-how-indonesian-teenagers-are-recruited-to-i slamic-state-20160721-gqb8gy.html [accessed 24 July 2016].

Toren, C. (1988) 'Making the present, revealing the past: The mutability and continuity of tradition as process'. *Man (NS)*, 23(4): 696–717.

Torres Soriano, M.R. (2012) 'Between the pen and the sword: The global Islamic media front in the West'. *Terrorism and Political Violence*, 24(5): 769–786.

Toscano, N. (2016) 'The Project host Waleed Aly attacks "irresponsible" Jalal brothers' terror stunt'. *Sydney Morning Herald*. Online. Available from: www.smh.com. au/entertainment/tv-and-radio/the-project-host-waleed-aly-attacks-irresponsible-jala l-brothers-terror-stunt-20160225-gn2v1o.html [accessed 7 March 2016].

Tufail, W. and Poynting, S. (2013) 'A common "outlawness": Criminalisation of Muslim minorities in the UK and Australia'. *International Journal for Crime, Justice and Social Democracy*, 2(3): 43–54.

Turner, B.S. (2007) 'Religious authority and the new media'. *Theory, Culture and Society*, 24(2): 117–134.

Turner, B.S. (2011) *Religion and Modern Social Theory: Citizenship, secularisation and the State*. Cambridge: Cambridge University Press.

Turner, G. (2014) *Understanding Celebrity*. 2nd edn. London: Sage.

Turner, M. (1998) *The Literary Mind*. New York: Oxford University Press.

Urdal, H. (2012) 'A clash of generations? Youth bulges and political violence'. United Nations Population Division, Expert Paper no. 2012/1. Available from: www.un.org/ esa/population/publications/expertpapers/Urdal_Expert%20Paper.pdf [accessed 14 April 2015].

Valentine, G. and Sporton, D. (2009) '"How other people see you it's like nothing that's inside": The impact of processes of dis-identification and disavowal on young people's subjectivities'. *Sociology*, 43(4): 735–751.

Van Dijck, J. (2013) *The Culture of Connectivity: A critical history of social media*. Oxford: Oxford University Press.

Van Nieuwkerk, K. (2011) 'Introduction'. In K. Van Nieuwkerk (ed.) *Muslim Rap, Halal Soaps, and Revolutionary Theater: Artistic developments in the Muslim world*, Austin: University of Texas Press, pp. 1–26.

Van Nieuwkerk, K. (2012) 'Popularizing Islam or Islamizing popular music: new developments in Egypt's wedding scene'. *Contemporary Islam*, 6(3): 235–254.

Van Zoonen, L. (2005) *Entertaining the Citizen: When politics and popular culture converge*. Lanham MD: Rowman and Littlefield.

Varzi, R. (2006) *Warring Souls: Youth, media and martyrdom in Post-Revolution Iran*. Durham NC: Duke University Press.

Veldhuis, T. and Staun, J. (2009) *Islamist Radicalisation: A root cause model*. Clingendael: Netherlands Institute of International Relations.

Vergani, M. (2014) 'Neo-jihadist prosumers and Al Qaeda single narrative: The case study of Giuliano Delnevo'. *Studies in Conflict and Terrorism*, 37(7): 604–617.

Wagner, R. (2012) 'First-person shooter religion: Algorithmic culture and inter-religious encounter'. *Cross Currents*, 62(2): 181–203.

Wagner, R. (2014) 'This is not a game: Violent video games, sacred space, and ritual'. *Iowa Journal of Cultural Studies*, 15(1–3): 12–35.

Ward, K.J. (1999) 'Cyber-ethnography and the emergence of the virtually new communities'. *Journal of Information Technology*, 14(1): 95–105.

Watt, D. (2011) 'From the streets of Peshawar to the cover of Maclean's Magazine: Reading images of Muslim women as currere to interrupt gendered Islamophobia'. *Journal of Curriculum Theorizing*, 27(1): 64–86.

Weedon, C. (1987) *Feminist Practice and Poststructuralist Theory.* Oxford: Blackwell.

Weimann, G. (2006) 'Virtual disputes: The use of the internet for terrorist debates'. *Studies in Conflict and Terrorism*, 29(7): 623–639.

Weinstein, D. (2011) 'The globalization of metal'. In J. Wallach, H. Berger and P. Greene (eds) *Metal Rules the Globe: Heavy metal music around the world*, Durham, NC: Duke University Press, pp. 34–62.

Werbner, P. (2004) 'The predicament of diaspora and millennial Islam: Reflections on September 11, 2001'. *Ethnicities*, 4(4): 451–476.

West, C. and Zimmerman, D. (1987) 'Doing gender'. *Gender and Society*, 1(2): 125–151.

Wetherell, M. (2012) *Affect and Emotion: A new social science understanding.* London: Sage.

Wiktorowicz, Q. (2003) *Islamic Activism: A social movement theory approach.* Bloomington: Indiana University Press.

Wiktorowicz, Q. (2005a) *Radical Islam Rising: Muslim extremism in the West.* Boulder, CO: Rowman and Littlefield.

Wiktorowicz, Q. (2005b) 'A genealogy of radical Islam'. *Studies in Conflict and Terrorism*, 28(2): 75–97.

Williams, R. and Vashi, G. (2007) 'Hijab and American Muslim women: Creating the space for autonomous selves'. *Sociology of Religion*, 68(2): 269–287.

Williams, G. (2011) 'A decade of Australian anti-terror laws'. *Melbourne University Law Review*, 35(3): 1136–1176.

Willis, P. (1990) *Common Culture: Symbolic work at play in the everyday cultures of the young.* Milton Keynes: Oxford University Press.

Wise, A. and Ali, J. (2008) *Muslim-Australians and Local Governments: Grassroots strategies to improve relations between Muslim and non-Muslim-Australians.* Sydney: Department of Immigration and Citizenship and Centre for Research on Social Inclusion, Macquarie University.

Wodak, R. and De Cillia, R. (2007) 'Commemorating the past: The discursive construction of official narratives about the "rebirth of the Second Austrian Republic"'. *Discourse and Communication*, 1(3): 315–341.

WojtowiczA. (2013) 'The emergence of female terrorism'. *Sécurité globale*, 3(25–26): 123–140.

Woodman, D. (2012) 'Life out of synch: How new patterns of further education and the rise of precarious employment are reshaping young people's relationships'. *Sociology*, 46(6): 1074–1090.

Woodward, M., Rohmaniyah, I., Amin, A. and Coleman, D. (2010) 'Muslim education, celebrating Islam and having fun as counter-radicalization strategies in Indonesia'. *Perspectives on Terrorism*, 4(4): 28–50.

Wright, R. (2012) *Rock the Casbah: Rage and rebellion across the Islamic world.* New York: Simon & Schuster.

Wright, S. (2015) 'Moral panics as enacted melodramas'. *British Journal of Criminology*. Online advance. DOI: 10.1093/bjc/azv025.

Wroe, D. (2015) 'ASIO issues "call to arms" for families to spot radicalisation of teenagers'. *Sydney Morning Herald*. Online. Available from: www.smh.com.au/federal-politics/political-news/asio-issues-call-to-arms-for-families-to-spot-radicalisa tion-of-teenagers-20150514-gh1hnk.html [accessed 15 May 2015].

Zackie, M.W. (2013) 'An analysis of Abu Mus'ab al-Suri's "Call to global Islamic resistance"'. *Journal of Strategic Security*, 6(1): 1–18.

Zakaria, R. (2015) 'Women and Islamic militancy'. *Dissent*, 62(1): 118–125.

Zaman, S. (2008) 'From imam to cyber-mufti: Consuming identity in Muslim America'. *The Muslim World*, 98(4): 465–474.

Zammit, A. (2010) 'Who becomes a jihadist in Australia? A comparative analysis'. Paper presented to the Conference on Understanding Terrorism from an Australian Perspective. Monash University Caulfield Campus, Melbourne, 2010, pp. 1–21. Available from: http://artsonline.monash.edu.au/radicalisation/files/2013/03/con ference-2010-who-jihadist-australia-az.pdf [accessed 17 March 2015].

Zammit, A. (2013) 'Explaining a turning point in Australian jihadism'. *Studies in Conflict and Terrorism*, 36(9): 739–755.

Zempi, I. and Chakraborti, N. (2014) *Islamophobia, Victimisation and the Veil*. Basingstoke: Palgrave Macmillan.

Zimmerman, E. (2014) 'Manifesto for a ludic century'. In S.P. Walz and S. Deterding (eds) *The Gameful World*, Cambridge MA: MIT Press, pp. 19–22.

Zine, J. (2007) 'Safe havens or religious "ghettos"? Narratives of Islamic schooling in Canada'. *Race, Ethnicity and Education*, 10(1): 71–92.

Žižek, S. (2002) *Welcome to the Desert of the Real: Five essays on September 11 and related dates*. New York: Verso.

Zulfikar, T. (2016) '"I feel different though": Narratives of young Indonesian Muslims in Australian public schools'. *Cogent Education*. Online. DOI: doi.org/10.1080/2331186X.2016.1139767.

Index